INTERRELIGIOUS EXPLORATIONS SERIES

Immortality and Human Destiny

Immortality and Human Destiny

A Variety of Views

EDITED BY
GEDDES MacGREGOR

A NEW ERA BOOK

PARAGON HOUSE
New York

Published in the United States by
Paragon House Publishers
2 Hammarskjöld Plaza
New York, NY 10017

A New Ecumenical Research
    Association Book

Library of Congress Cataloging in Publication Data
Main entry under title:

Immortality and Human Destiny.

   (Interreligious explorations series)
   "A New ERA book."
   Bibliography:
   Includes index.
   1. Future life—Comparative studies—Congresses.
I. MacGregor, Geddes. II. Series.
BL535.I43   1985   291.2'.3   85-12436
ISBN 0-913757-50-8 (hardbound)
ISBN 0-913757-61-6 (softbound)

Contents

Editor's Introduction

Whatever the merit of the essays presented in this symposium, no one can deny the width of the spectrum of opinion that they represent.

This is largely due to the fact that they emerge as a result of a conference held in Puerto Rico, February 8–12, 1984, one of a series hosted by the New Ecumenical Research Association (New ERA) as a project of the International Religious Foundation.

For such is the refreshing spirit of openmindedness that has permeated theological dialogue in these New ERA conferences that participants feel disposed to argue, in a disciplined way, for opinions, however unpopular and unconventional, knowing that they will evoke others' respect. In such an environment (far from the acrimony and *odium theologicum* of so many ecclesiastical assemblies, "liberal" and "conservative") both original thought and constructive critique prosper together, while personal conviction grows in strength as it deepens in authenticity. Our Unificationist hosts, who have strong convictions of their own, graciously set this irenic stage for all of us by their own willingness to accept and to study the critique, often copious, proffered by their guests, so encouraging us all to follow the spirit of the injunction given in the letter to the Ephesians, speaking the truth (as each one sees it) in love. It is what one would expect of an ideal academe.

The nature and degree of our belief in a personal afterlife generally reflects the nature and degree of our belief in God; for any belief in God can be authentically developed only out of a life of faith and has as its corollary a belief in afterlife. Thoughtful inquirers, when their reaction to questions of immortality, resurrection, or transmigration is sought, ask: "How can anyone know?" The response is natural, not least since, notoriously, many people who profess a religious faith have little awareness of the spiritual realities around them and tend to claim far more than their faith warrants. Yet belief in an afterlife can be abundantly warranted *to the extent* that it springs from a quality of life that issues in direct awareness of God's presence and action within it. Belief in God and belief in the afterlife that is a corollary of that belief are inseparable. By the same token, when you hear a person who claims to be a Christian insist on a disbelief in any life beyond the grave you may feel confident in concluding that such a person can have no awareness of the kind of God that the documents of the Christian Way proclaim, no matter how forcefully he or she may sing the Nicene Creed in church.

Even those who are not at all interested in theological speculations may claim to see beyond the present. They often believe, for example, that "from the way things are going" we must expect a nuclear holocaust and the collapse of civilization if not the demise of humankind, to say nothing of the rest of life on this planet. So it is that those of us who see life as a pilgrimage conducted under the guidance of God or within the ambit of a divine Providence or as the arena of a process of salvation through faith in Christ, or else as the working out of the karmic principle, are proclaiming, in effect, that from their stance they can see the future as fundamentally implied in the present and past. That does not mean that they can tell all the details any more than one who thought a nuclear holocaust inevitable would claim to know precisely at what day and hour and at what latitude and longitude it would begin. It does mean that as the present is to some extent a development of the past, so the future is to some extent a development of the present.

Past, present, and future are not separated as are three eggs in a basket; they form a continuum. From the way the universe has behaved in the past, astronomers, while they would not be so rash as to say exactly how it will behave in the future in every detail, can tell with considerable confidence the general lines it will follow. Nor is there any fatalism here. One is not saying that anyone's behavior is predictable, only that the principles governing the spiritual dimension of Being are as ineluctable and *to that extent* as predictable as are the principles that physicists and biologists see to be governing the evolution of matter and life. By the same token, if you believe in, say, the kind of God we read about in the Bible, you cannot say you know nothing at all about what is going to happen to you in the future, although with the American Quaker John Greenleaf Whittier you may be content to say only: "I know not where His islands lift / Their fronded palms in air; / I only know I cannot drift / Beyond His love and care." If, instead, you believe in Allah or in the Upanishadic view of divine Being or if you vehemently renounce all religious belief of every kind, your vision of the future will conform no less to your understanding of the present.

The essays in the present symposium are arranged under two distinct groups.

The first category is derived from papers presented at the New ERA conference in Puerto Rico. They are arranged in alphabetical order and are followed by a trilogy of papers expressing three Unificationists' views on a variety of aspects of Unificationist teaching.

The second category contains papers, which were not presented at the conference, written by distinguished scholars and thinkers who have been invited to participate in the published symposium.

In both, the approaches taken by the authors are so variegated, and their individual stances so fundamentally diverse, that any pretense of making them seem to conform to a structure would have been dishonest (if not impossible). I can but rejoice that this is so, since it helps to exhibit the openness of the climate of our discussions.

Professor Gier's paper bears a humanist label and, since "humanism" is a singularly ambiguous term, some notice should be taken of what he means by it. The term "humanism," much bandied about today, is a relative newcomer to the English language, having been invented by Coleridge (who loved neologisms) in or about 1834, specifically to designate a theological position: that of one who denied "the divinity of Christ" as understood in a period that was still comparatively unaware of modern biblical criticism. The term "humanist," however, had been long established, having been used, for instance, by Francis Bacon. It referred to the *umanisti,* the men who, in the *Quattrocento,* whose influence spread from Italy northwards, sought to go back to and revive the sources of classical learning. Many, if not most, of these humanists were deeply religious men. Nor is their religious spirit surprising, since they drew so much of their inspiration from the works of Plato, who accepted the reincarnational teachings of his Pythagorean heritage as part of his intellectual scenario, and from the Stoics, whose influence on early Christian thought, not least that of Augustine, is well-known.

In those days long before the Darwinian revolution, man could still seem so detached from "the lower creation" as to be unique. What gave the Renaissance the immense impetus it exercised over every field of literary, artistic, and philosophical development and inquiry was precisely this exaltation of man. Not only was man godlike, he was peerless. The notion had come in another and even more extreme form in Islam: A passage in the Qurān recounts that Allah, having created the angels, then created man, calling upon the angels to bow down before this culmination of the divine work. It was because Lucifer and his cohorts declined to do so that they were expelled from their high estate.

Very different is the humanism (sometimes called "scientific" or "secular" humanism and, perhaps more felicitously, hominism) of modern thinkers such as Dewey, Freud, and Marx, who focus on man from a post-Darwinian climate of thought.

The humanism that Professor Gier espouses seems to have features from a variety of positions historically bearing that label. The view that immortality is a needless notion and that belief in it is a mere symptom of human arrogance has had many advocates, ancient and modern. Santayana, for instance, in one of his essays, invites us to liken life to a dance to which the participants go in the evening, full of energy. As the festivities proceed and the excitement mounts, they may wish it could go on forever, but as the night wears on they weary and eventually, in the early hours of the morning, they recognize that all good things must come to an end. Tired of the frenzy, they are glad to go to sleep.

Dr. Gier, however, although he repudiates the customary "religious" alternatives, is not content with any "die-like-a-dog" view. Using the "image world" of H. H. Price, the distinguished Oxford philosopher and past-president of the Society for Psychical Research, he proposes a modernized form of *hades* or *sheol*—a temporary form of existence after death, emphasizing the notion (widespread in much ancient religious literature) of self-judgment.

Dr. Gordon-McCutchan, following Emerson and the Transcendentalists, whom he accounts forerunners of the "Aquarian Gospel," espouses a very different genre of humanism. He proposes that the human soul, as it increasingly recognizes its own divine nature and destiny, accepts its lonely but lofty moral consequences. Moreover, seeing divinity in itself, the soul is better able to perceive divinity in the world and so live life in harmony with Nature. He sees Emerson's theory of Compensation as a perception of the karmic principle and, like the later Emerson, he accepts its corollary: we are in the midst of an evolutionary process which, in its spiritual dimension, is attained through a long series of re-embodiments, eventually reaching complete divinization. He too sees judgment as self-judgment, following a widespread vision shared by many of the great religious thinkers of every age and tradition. None of this would add up to humanism in any of the commonly accepted senses of the term, but for his insistence on an extreme contrast between his position and the Christian one, which he sees as a cult of dependence on Christ in which grace takes the place of moral development and growth. In his view Christianity belongs to the Piscean Age, which is gradually giving way to the Age of Aquarius in which human beings will more and more appropriate their own divinity.

In Professor Hartley's paper we move to a radically different scene in which he takes us back to the nineteenth century and to a particular theological school that flourished in that period in which eschatological hopes ran high in several interesting sects such as the Millerites and Irvingites. The Mercersburg theology that is the focus of Dr. Hartley's interest in this essay is first described and then compared with other eschatologies and finally evaluated in terms of its worth today, now that contemporary theology can draw from or renounce the bequests of Barth and Bultmann, of Tillich and Rahner, to say nothing of modern forms of Christian socialism and liberation theology. The teachings of the Mercersburg theologians included a doctrine of the Real Presence and a sacramental emphasis rare in American Protestantism at that time and expounded by John Williamson Nevin (1803–1866), a leading exponent of the Mercersburg theology along with Philip Schaff (1819–93), a gigantic figure in his time. Nevin's *The Mystical Presence,* published in 1845, the year of John Henry Newman's reception into the Roman Catholic Church, reflects concerns such as were giving rise in England to the Tractarian movement. Although the principal focus of Mercersburg theology was on eschatological questions, it was linked with sacramental and liturgical concerns in such a way as to show a marked spiritual affinity with the spirit of the Scottish-born Edward Irving (1792–1834), founder of the "Catholic Apostolic Church" whose teachings became notably millenarian and whose form of worship sacramental and liturgical. Dr. Hartley shows the relevance of Mercersburg to our own time.

Gerald Jones, representing the Mormon stance, tells us how the early Mormons interpreted biblical writings about "the Last

Days," and how *The Doctrine and Covenants* and other scriptures, revered as divine revelation by the Church he represents, expanded and developed these early beliefs. Finally, he reports on commentary by more recent presidents of the Church on that corpus of revealed doctrine, noting a tendency toward belief that the righteousness of the people is what is to bring about the Millennium. This interpretation will hardly surprise those who have any personal acquaintance with members of the Church of Jesus Christ of Latter-day Saints, for however we view their theology, all who know them well respect their high moral principles.

Concern about "the End of the Age" is not all confined to what mainstream churchfolk like to call "cults." Ecologists and anti-nuclear groups, for example, are increasingly apprehensive about the fate of humankind on our planet. In his paper on Frank Kermode and Jacques Derrida, Professor Kort calls attention to the interest in eschatological questions that appears in forms of contemporary literature that would not be accounted religious in any customary sense of the word. Both Kermode and Derrida, each in his own way, have deeply influenced not only those who share their interest in the primacy of the spoken over the written word but also theologians and others concerned with "Last Things." Kermode, a Manxman (he was born on the Isle of Man in 1919), was educated at Liverpool University and taught at several universities before his appointment to his present position as King Edward VII Professor of English Literature, Cambridge, where he is also a Fellow of King's. His numerous writings include *The Classic* (Viking Press, 1975) and *The Genesis of Secrecy* (Harvard University Press, 1979). Derrida, born in Algiers in 1937, became professor at the Ecole Normale Supérieure. Influenced by Hegel, Nietzsche, Freud, Heidegger, and, not least, Husserl, he pioneered work on questions about the primacy of spoken over written language, a concern that has some affinity with that of Eric Havelock in his *Preface to Plato*. He has influenced French literary critics such as Michel Foucault, Claude Lévi-Strauss, and Jacques Lacan. His works include *La Voix et le phénomène (Speech and Phenomena,* Northwestern University Press, 1973) and *L'Ecriture et la différence (Writing and Difference,* University of Chicago Press, 1978). In his examination of these two thinkers, Dr. Kort notes that the mainstream of Christian thought has identified itself much too often with the "eternal present," in

Moltmann's phrase. One may indeed ask whether some of the religious groups that are emerging today are more in line with what has always nourished the life of the Church.

The aim of my own paper is to explore the maze of confusion about the afterlife that Christian theology has inherited, and, in so doing, to clear the ground for openminded discussion of alternatives in Christian thought about the afterlife among those who account themselves intelligently conservative. The confusion already present in the New Testament itself and reflecting an expectation of the imminence of the Parousia, proliferated in patristic and medieval writings as well as in conciliar decisions, and was certainly by no means mitigated by the heirs of the Reformation. I call for serious, scholarly consideration of some form of reincarnational solution, such as that to which the Christian Platonists of the Alexandrian school were inclined to consider in the second and third centuries. As an option for thoughtful Christians today, I suggest a form of reincarnation as a re-interpretation of the Tractarian understanding of the intermediate state (purgatory) with its implications of spiritual development and growth, as already proposed in my *Reincarnation in Christianity* (Quest Books, 1978), *Reincarnation as a Christian Hope* (Macmillan, 1982), and *The Christening of Karma* (Quest Books, 1984).

Professor Meadow, writing from a psychological stance, discusses features characteristic of certain stages in the development of many societies in their outlook on death and their expectations of afterlife. Drawing on three sources (proto-Indo-European eschatology, shamanism, and the near-death out-of-the-body experiences) she develops what she believes to be a common, underlying psychological motif: the universal human need for psychological assurance that, however dark the scene may look, all things will turn out well in the end. Reflecting much Freudian influence, she understands religion to have a predominantly "comforting" function, where "comforting" is understood in the contemporary sense rather than in the liturgical and etymologically stricter sense of "strengthening" as used by Cranmer in traditional Prayer Book language: "Take this holy Sacrament to your comfort," which means, of course, "take it to your spiritual invigoration." Seeing a parallel between Unificationist thought about afterlife and what she takes to be a widespread belief in primitivistic societies, she concludes that some may be "attracted by Unificationist arguments simply because of their comfort value."

Dr. Ogutu's paper, written with a deep personal understanding of the beliefs and customs of his own African background, is of singular interest to those of us who recognize that Christianity was usually exported to Africa packaged in a bundle of Western European prejudice and theological confusion. The Luo tradition he describes, for example, had a far more developed awareness of the meaning of the Communion of Saints than the vast majority of British Protestant missionaries were capable of attaining. These could have had little or nothing to say about what Dr. Ogutu calls "the gap" between death and the Second Coming of Christ. The christened Luo, having been forced to abandon their own perceptions of the veil between the living and the dead must have been indeed disappointed, to say the least, to have been offered nothing positive in exchange. They were also generally expected to abandon polygamy, which was writ deep into their societal heritage for reasons similar to those that had made it so central to the life of the biblical peoples in the time of the patriarchs. Indeed, although polygamy had gone out of fashion in Judaism around the time of Christ so that those of the Christian Way set out with a monogamous ideal, polygamy was not officially repudiated in Judaism until the tenth century C.E. Yet the missionaries commonly took polygamy to be one of the customs that stood as an obstacle to the acceptance of the Christian faith, when in fact it may well be of secondary relevance or perhaps no relevance at all in an African setting such as that of the Luo, while a greater sensitivity to questions about the afterlife should have had far greater priority. Dr. Ogutu, from his refreshing perspective, provides a salutary warning of the danger of burying the light of religious truth under a bushel of moribund local conventions.

Neither the doctrine nor the practice of the Unification Church can be easily understood without an understanding of its ethical and cultural roots. On the one hand, it has historical roots that go even further back into Chinese history than does Confucius himself, for that great sage (in many ways a counterpart to Socrates in the West) was as much a conservator of ancient Chinese tradition as he was an innovator. Westerners should remember that in, say, the sixth century C.E., China, with its great inheritance from Confucius more than a thousand years earlier, was probably the greatest and most cultured civilization in the world at a time when Europe, after the fall of the Roman Empire, was a cultural backwater. The Unification Church is much enriched by that ancient Confucian tradition of respect for family and elders, its practicality, and its high regard for intellectual life and artistic activity. On the other hand, the Unification Church also inherits a special form of Christian theology in the Reformation heritage. With an historic background in South Korea, traditionally Confucian and Buddhist and now one of the most Christian countries in Asia, its members wish to be accounted Christian and are certainly no less entitled to the designation than are many to whom the name is commonly and unquestioningly accorded.

In the present symposium Unificationist teaching on eschatological matters is interpreted in a trilogy by Andrew Wilson, James Fleming, and Thomas Azar.

Andrew Wilson begins with an affirmation that the belief that the world is approaching "the moment when God is to enter decisively into human affairs and bring history to its consummation" is central to Unificationist teaching. After discussing the biblical background from a Unificationist stance, he goes on to expound the eschatology of *Divine Principle,* the Church's most authoritative presentation of its beliefs and vision. Unificationist eschatology, like that of the New Testament itself, has grown out of apocalypticism. The Unification Church takes a pragmatic view of the situation, however, in the sense that in face of the reality of an interdependent world "there is no assurance of a power that can override the laws of the cosmos and separate the righteous from the wicked." The Unificationist believes, following the teaching of *Divine Principle,* that at the eschaton "the destiny of the world hangs in precarious balance." Decisive action is needed, and it can make the difference between catastrophe and spiritual triumph. Unificationism distinctively teaches that "there is no divine guarantee that the Messiah at the Second Advent will succeed"; on the contrary, "tragedy might befall him, as befell Jesus." So faith and action are the order of the day. There is definite opposition in Unificationist teaching to attitudes of resignation, of putting everything back into the lap of an omnipotent God. On the contrary, Unificationism is nothing if not a specific call to action arising out of a total commitment to the overthrow of the forces of evil.

James Fleming treats a very different and certainly no less important aspect of Unificationist doctrine: the notion of resurrection, based on awareness of a spiritual world populated by spiritual beings who are—at least to some extent—in communication with people on earth. Resurrection, then, is both a "realized" process going on in the believer's life and also a future event to be expected yet to be worked for with the greatest diligence. The aim is nothing short of a universal union with the Heart of God. *Divine Principle* teaches that resurrection means return to a "heavenly" lineage through Christ, leaving behind the "satanic" lineage of Adam's fall. Resurrection is seen in Pauline terms—a gift rather than a "birthright immortality." Yet Unificationism reflects both biblical elements and elements from a Confucian and Chinese inheritance. Paramount is an acute awareness of the presence of a spiritual world around us coupled with a recognition of the importance of "right-time-and-right-place." Yet one would grievously misunderstand the Unification Church if one were to think of it as doctrinaire, for on the contrary it stresses *praxis* over *theoria*. To what extent this concern for spiritual awareness may be an atittude characteristic of those churches that purport to stress practice over doctrine might be an interesting inquiry, which, however, Mr. Fleming wisely avoids, for it is beyond the scope of his present undertaking.

One of the most distinctive features of Unificationist practice is the Church's very special approach to the institution of marriage. Thomas Azar addresses himself to this and, as befits one whose life is focused on the pastoral ministry, he does so on the whole from a practical and pastoral standpoint rather than from a theological one. Nevertheless he sees the values in the Unificationist view of marriage to have been adumbrated in the teaching of Martin Luther on this subject. To establish a God-centered family is a divine vocation. Yet Unificationism goes further: salvation and the building of the Kingdom of God begin when the individuals are married by the Lord of the Second Advent. Unificationist marriage entails a lengthy period of separation and abstinence before the consummation of the marriage. Only then can it be blessed by God. Eschatology is rooted in the holy institution that is marriage and the family. In Unificationism the family is by no means merely a good, it is, as Thomas Azar suggests, "the institution of reform for humanity and even for the Unification Church itself." Marriage is therefore more than one of a series of holy sacraments; it becomes the supreme instrument for the salvation of the individual and the sanctification of the Church. In Unificationist eyes it transcends the romanticism and deeply personal choice that have become so much associated with marriage in the minds of many Christians (although such an emphasis on a romantic approach to it is a comparatively modern phenomenon in Christian society). Hence the acceptance in the Unification Church of the concept of marriages that are normally arranged by the Church for the couple who propose to engage in marriage. The Church takes very seriously its claim to constitute the Family of God. Since a tradition widespread not only in the Orient but in other cultures has for long provided that earthly families arrange marriages, the notion that the Family of God should arrange marriages that call for the holiest manifestation of the marital state seems an inevitable consequence of so taking seriously the reality of the Church as the Family of God.

Sylvia Cranston is a woman of unusual spiritual insight and perspicacity. A convinced reincarnationist who has written and edited well-known and valuable works on the subject, she has provided for the present collection an important dimension of thought that would otherwise have gone unrepresented. As she clearly recognizes, reincarnationism, although prominent in the outlook of India and rightly associated with that subcontinent, has had a much greater place in the history of religious thought in the Judeo-Christian tradition than is widely recognized even in academic circles today. The statistics she provides show how widespread belief in reincarnation is in the West at the present time, despite widespread ignorance, not to say fear, of it in church circles. This intrepid author, who has pioneered work in the field, has removed from the minds of many young seekers some of the vulgar and ignorant prejudices about reincarnation that thrive in mainstream churches. She ought to be read with diligence by all who are interested in the afterlife.

Preoccupation with concepts of immortality is as ancient as it is universal in the history of religions. Professor Kerkhoff, in his well-documented study of the eschatological implications of the Mesoamerican ball games, takes us to Central America and to an unusual ritual aspect of these ancient and universal concerns. His study sheds light on the concept of time that lies behind a worldview in which a ball game could acquire such eschatological significance. In an age in which the concept of right-time-and-right-place could permeate the entire outlook, the ball game could become, as it did, a sort of initiation into an eschatological destiny. One may even be tempted to wonder quite seriously whether, even in our more enlightened culture and more technologically advanced society, one may not hear, in the ritual of the ball games of today that play so large a part in the life of so many, some distant echoes of the outlook of a past that some tend to see as almost too primitive for them to understand!

In the minds of many, the battle between "science" and "religion" seems interminable. So it must have seemed to many in the thirteenth and once again in the nineteenth century. Yet in both of these lively periods of intellectual development perspicacious thinkers arose who showed that, since truth must be one, such a conflict is at best misguided and at worst fatuous. St. Thomas demonstrated its folly to his medieval contemporaries and the Christian evolutionists exhibited it to theirs in late Victorian times, each group speaking, of course, in the intellectual idiom of its own age. In our twentieth century, although the tension remains, the scenario has dramatically changed.

Dr. Polkinghorne, a distinguished British theoretical physicist who also happens to be an Anglican priest, succinctly presents the compatibility of Christian faith with what scientists know about the universe in the vastly changed intellectual climate of today. Some might wish that he had written more, but scientists, not least mathematicians, are often felicitously laconic (and who among us others might not sometimes wish that the virtue were more widespread?). Be that as it may, we have here a refreshing testimony to the fact that, while astronomy can no more "prove" religious faith than biology can provide a basis for ethical judgment, nothing in modern science stands as an obstacle to the kind of belief that Christians and others hold in the depths of their being. On the contrary, in the awesomely complex universe unfolded by the sciences of today, men and women of religious faith have less reason than ever before to fear the sciences but should look to them more and more as allies in the discovery of fundamental religious truths.

In a symposium such as this we ought to hear not only from academe but from the pulpit of a mainstream American church. Fortunate, therefore, are we to have a contribution from the distinguished occupant of one of New York's most famous pulpits: David Read of Madison Avenue Presbyterian Church. Dr. Read reviews the changes of attitude in the mainstream Churches since the outbreak in 1914 of World War I and shows how their reticence in dealing with the age-old questions about Last Things has had to give way in face of the challenges of a "secular apocalyp-ticism" arising from the threat of nuclear holocaust.

Dr. Read, in his youth, was much influenced by the theol-ogy of Karl Barth and in the present paper we have predictable echoes of the emphasis of that doughty champion of Protestant orthodoxy on the sovereignty of God; but we also have salutary reminders of the nature of the perennial problem of Last Things, whether it appears in ecclesiastical trappings or in secular dress. He speaks to our hearts, ably and in a scholarly way, out of his youth in his native Scotland, out of his experiences as a prisoner of war in Germany, out of his contact with the British royal court as well as with his experience in missions to students in many parts of the world, and not least of course out of his ministry for more than thirty years in New York City. Always he speaks from the stance from which he "first saw the Lord" yet with an unusually sensitive awareness to the nature of the ominous events of our time that so deeply distress us all. Once many years ago he expressed to me his wish to die "with his boots on" and prefera-bly in the pulpit, and I am glad to have captured him "on the wing" for the present symposium.

Those of us who have long ago learned to expect from Professor Scharlemann, whenever he tackles a difficult philo-sophical or theological problem, that combination of cool analy-sis and creative thought that makes for worthwhile intellectual enterprise will not be disappointed in the essay he has contributed to this symposium. Nailing to his masthead the alarmingly chal-lenging problem of time and eternity, he leads us to an example of its working out in the thought of Paul Tillich, on which he is a leading expert. In the "religious socialism" that Tillich proposed in opposition to Marxism, difficulties obviously arise, since so-cialism posits that the world can be radically changed through technical and human action, while Christianity and other re-ligions perceive the situation as one that can be changed only by God.

Tillich's religious socialism sought to provide a means of showing how the incompatibility might be overcome. Since the Kingdom of God, a fundamental symbol in Christian eschatol-ogy, is essentially bound to a kairos, it is meaningless apart from a political and social reality. It cannot be ahistorical. Scharlemann proposes an interpretation: "The Kingdom of God is always in the coming but is never present as such."

Among papers by invited contributors, the last is by a most distinguished biblical scholar long associated with Harvard, who has recently returned to his native Sweden as Bishop of Stockholm. It represents a particular view, defensible indeed in much of Scripture, yet one that evokes strong opposition, as Dr. Stendahl well knows, both within Christian circles and outside them. That the present symposium concludes with Dr. Stendahl's paper is due, of course, merely to alphabetical circumstance, for despite its learned and eminently plausible interpretation of Scripture its conclusion happens not to coincide at all with the opinion of many, including that of the Editor. It is, however, an important view that ought to be represented in a symposium such as this, which is at least partly designed to exhibit the variety of views to be found in the spectrum of scholarly opinion on the subject.

Dr. Stendahl finds the quest for individual immortality narrow and selfish and prefers to say: "The issue is not what happens to me but what happens to God's fight for his creation." The end of life, he contends, is not "my identity" but the coming of the kingdom. All this is easily defended in the Bible, which belongs to an age in which people did think much more readily in terms of community and covenant than in terms of the individual, for the notion of individuality came into its own much later, adumbrated by Scotus and others and coming into full bloom at the Renaissance with the rediscovery of Plato and the tradition of Christian Platonism that had its roots in Greco-Jewish thought and its beginnings in the Christian apologists of the first century and, most notably, of course, in the Christian school of theology at Alexandria founded in the later part of the second century. Dr. Stendahl, however, does not like the tradition of Christian Platonism, apart from which Christianity takes on a very different and, to some of us, a much drearier aspect. Yet the view Dr. Stendahl expounds does represent the outlook of many who lack the kind of self-awareness that demands concern about individual destiny, whether conceived in terms of resurrection, of reincarnation, or otherwise. Such self-awareness has its roots in a belief that God is of such a nature as not to allow his creatures to evolve as mere guinea pigs for the development of his Kingdom but, rather, to give them the capacity for citizenship within it.

The notion that the human soul has an intrinsic individual immortality in what seems to be Plato's sense would indeed be difficult to defend from Scripture. It certainly is not to be found in Paul, that great apostle of the Christian Way to the Gentile world. Paul's mode of thought was thoroughly Jewish as was his training rabbinic. Yet whatever Paul understands by the resurrection of Christ, he makes clear that because of it we who are entitled to nothing but death can *attain* immortality in a "glorious" body. If we go on to see our Christian faith illumined by our knowledge of the evolutionary process of all things, the notion that humanity is a turning point in that process in which individual immortality becomes *attainable* is surely, to say the least, a highly plausible view for a Christian to take, even apart from anything Paul says or does not say and even apart, too, from what we find attested in our personal experience of the grace of God in our lives.

Geddes MacGregor

PART ONE

The Spectrum of Conference Opinion

Humanistic Self-Judgment and After-Death Experience
NICHOLAS F. GIER

O my soul, do not aspire to immortal life, but exhaust the limits of the possible.
    PINDAR, *Pythian Odes*

Humanists are often described as those who attempt to move God aside and take God's place. Such a narrow view does an injustice to our humanist tradition, which, since Plato and Aristotle, has been dominated by theists. Indeed it was Christian thinkers such as Justin Martyr, Thomas Aquinas, and Desiderius Erasmus who attempted to synthesize biblical revelation and Greek humanism. *Secular* humanism has its origins in Protagoras's belief that human beings are the measure of all things. This was definitely a minority belief until the Enlightenment, but even then the tradition of the theistic humanists still prevailed as expounded, for example, by our Founding Fathers. Only during the last two centuries has secular humanism made any progress, culminating in our time with atheistic existentialism and other secular philosophies.

Humanism can best be defined as the view that all human beings have instrinsic value and dignity. Humanists believe that human beings are autonomous centers of value with free will and moral responsibility. Humanists trust reason as a guide to truth, but many of them recognize that even their own principles cannot be strictly demonstrated as true. The limited scope of human reason does allow theistic humanists to appeal to revelation, but only if these revealed truths do not undermine basic humanistic principles. For example, Calvin and Luther's belief in total human depravity and divine predestination absolutely remove

3

them from the humanist camp. Humanism, as I have defined it, cannot support a theology in which human autonomy is compromised by divine totalitarianism.

The perspective of this paper is theistic humanism as it relates to the issues of Last Judgment and the afterlife. My definition of humanism, drawn primarily from Kant, does not follow Protagoras's *homo mensura* thesis; rather, I assume a natural law basis for moral principles. If properly conceived, humanism does not involve the displacement of God in favor of humankind. True theistic humanism lets God be God and human beings be human beings. I call this the "Hebraic principle," based on the greatest discovery of the ancient Hebrews: the transcendence of God.[1] The priestly writers of the sixth century B.C.E. not only overcame the primitive anthropomorphisms of earlier Hebrew writers, but also made a clean break with other Near Eastern views in which, for example, gods battled with sea dragons or mated with humans. This of course blurred the distinction between the divine and the non-divine.

In the Judeo-Christian tradition only the Sadducees remained true to the Hebraic principle. Along with the Pharisees, the Sadducees rejected the Christian idea of the Incarnation (to them a pagan mixing of human and divine), but the Sadducees, unlike the Pharisees, also eschewed the concept of resurrection of the body and eternal life. A principal contention of this paper is that the concept of eternal life is just as much a violation of the Hebraic principle as is that of the Incarnation.

I am in agreement with Austin Duncan-Jones and John Hick who opine that it would be impossible to maintain a coherent and consistent personal identity over an infinite time. As Hick concludes his argument: "When we try to contemplate the contradictory notion of immortalized mortals, our thoughts turn away from what we know as human existence to something for which we are more inclined to invoke the notion of angels."[2] Hick's last point was confirmed long ago by Jesus himself: "For when they rise from the dead, they neither marry nor are given in marriage, but are like angels in heaven" (Mark 12:25).

While many humanists have been content to eliminate all notions of Last Judgment and an afterlife, some Christian humanists, such as the process theologians, have accepted Whitehead's view that all individuals are "objectively immortalized" in the mind of God. In fact, this theory is generally compatible with Old Testament ideas that the final end is the grave and that human "immortality" lies in a collective memory, both divine and human. If it is in fact true that traditional Judeo-Christian eschatology was essentially borrowed from Zoroastrianism, then Whitehead's view might be the best contemporary expression of the original Hebrew eschatology. The main difference, however, between a process and Hebrew eschatology is the fact that in the latter Yahweh is omnipotent and a moral judge in this life.

From a humanist standpoint, the process theologians are correct in rejecting God as "Cosmic Moralist"[3] and their denial of divine omnipotence and omniprescience offers the best protection for human autonomy. At the same time their organic view of reality and their relational view of the self allow humanists to avoid the alienation caused by the absolute autonomy of some forms of existentialism. Furthermore, the process theologians propose an intelligible theory of divine immanence which tempers the *via negativa* and its overemphasis on divine transcendence. Finally, the process theologians seem to be right about eliminating an individual afterlife.

The intent of this paper is to show that given certain assumptions, individual after-death experiences are not necessarily incompatible with humanist principles; and that humanist ethics may even require some sort of moral reckoning during such experiences. Recent empirical studies of "near-death" experiences not only strengthen the possibility of some sort of life after death, but also indicate the absence of any divine judgment. I then turn to Zoroastrianism and the *Tibetan Book of the Dead* for working models of self-judgment. But first I choose to use Kant to set the ethical framework for my scenario of Last Judgment as self-judgment.

I

Kant rejected all arguments for the existence of God except the "moral" argument: The only indubitable evidence of God's presence is the existence of human conscience. Kant essentially reduces religion to "the recognition of all duties as divine commands."[4] He abides by the assumptions of ethical objectivism: moral rules are eternal and uncreated and we must follow them to the goal of moral perfection. God himself is bound to the moral law: "Even the Holy One of the Gospels must first be compared with our ideal of moral perfection before we can recognize him as such. . . . "5 Even though he sometimes mentions the possibility of God's grace, Kant's moral objectivism cannot allow a suspension of the penalty for sin and exempt those who cannot conform to universal norms.

Kant recognized, of course, that a single lifetime is not enough for this great ethical project. He was also well aware that good people's virtue is not always rewarded and the wicked are not always punished. He therefore agreed that complete justice required the existence of an immortal soul and an infinite after-life. Kant then concluded that only a divine being could create these conditions for the reward of the righteous and the punishment of the wicked.

Kant, however, is far from traditional Christian orthodoxy in the details of his eschatology. Insofar as he has re-defined religion as the moral perfection of autonomous beings, he has eliminated most of the activities associated with religion: sacrifice, ritual, worship, and prayer. He says: "There are no special duties to God in a universal religion, for God can receive nothing from us; we cannot act for Him, nor yet upon Him."6 Our only duty is to follow our consciences (the divine commands within) and fulfill these among our fellow men and women. Divine obedience, which has been mistakenly externalized by traditional religion as "courtly obliga-tions" to God the king, has been completely internalized by Kant as obedience to conscience—being true to our rational selves. Kant's insight is crucial to a humanist rejection of God as a cosmic moralist and final judge.

Kant's philosophy contains some of the principal axioms of the humanist ethic which will be our framework. Kant is thor-oughly humanist in his insistence on complete moral autonomy and in his famous maxim that persons are to be treated always as ends and never as only means to ends. Although he is not clear or consistent on this point (indeed, Kant maintains that one of God's attributes is "just judge"7) I agree with Jeffery Reiman's argument that the exercise of moral authority is impossible if we are truly autonomous beings.8 Every humanist ethic, including Kant's, must accept this basic conclusion.

Aspects of Kant's ethics fall away, however, in the develop-ment of my own humanist eschatology. First, following Hick's critique of eternal life given above, we must reject Kant's notion of personal moral development in an unending afterlife. If Hick is correct, then the eternal moral life proves to be a significant exception to Kant's argument that "ought" implies "can." Given the arguments above, a person could not integrate an eternal life's worth of personal continuity, or even a million years. Kant does make a radical separation between the noumenal and the phenomenal, and one might respond that a purely rational being, unhindered by a body, could maintain personal continuity over an unending life span. But such a life could not possibly be a human life, if being in a sensible body is a necessary condition for such a life. Kant is not even clear about the resurrection of the body, but one would think that a noumenal "body" would be even more ethereal than Christianity's spiritual one.

Another problem involves an internal inconsistency in Kant himself. According to Kant, rewards in the future life will be based on "man's very natural expectation of an allotment of happiness proportional to man's moral conduct. . . ."9 Responding to this claim, critics have been able to reveal one of the major inconsistencies in all of Kant's philosophy. Kant believes that happiness is connected to a person's sensible nature, which is, by Kant's own admission, phenomenal and temporal. The afterlife is noumenal and atemporal. Therefore, Kant cannot impute any of his type of happiness to the noumenal, atemporal self of heaven.

Even if we assumed some sort of non-sensuous happiness, one could still ask why there must be a necessary connection between happiness and moral virtue. According to the Book of Proverbs, virtue is its own reward: "The righteousness of the upright delivers them, but the treacherous are taken by their lust" (11:6). Kant's view might be interpreted as a sophisticated version of the primitive barter system of religion and ethics, a rather self-centered *quid pro quo*: "OK God, I'll be virtuous, but you must guarantee my eternal happiness." The religion of the *Vedas* also contains this sort of barter system, one which most Hindus themselves, at least in theory, have left behind.

The Book of Job contains the biblical answer to this position. At first Job complains bitterly that it is not fair that a righteous man should suffer, but he finally recognizes that a *quid pro quo* would be the greatest offense against God's sovereign will and majesty. This point is crucial for an understanding of faith in the Bible and the rejection of works in the Protestant Reformation. Biblical faith, eminently expressed in the humbled Job, is based on "fear of the Lord," and such a position is compromised by any thought that we have "a handle on" God or any type of assurance of rewards exactly proportionate to deeds.[10]

My humanist eschatology is certainly not based on the fear of the Lord. Although theistic humanists support the Hebraic principle, they must reject the claim that God has absolute sovereignty over human beings. But I do agree with the authors of Job and Proverbs that virtue is its own reward. Therefore, the afterlife I am proposing will not be eternal and its focus will not be the reward of happiness and blissful fellowship with God. Indeed, my view, if correct, will encompass humanists who are atheists as well as theists. The sole reason for my positing an afterlife is moral, not religious. Ethical objectivism could be true without the existence of God, and if it is, then in this system even the atheist must be persuaded that the requirements of the moral law must be satisfied. The Stoics taught us long ago that one can have natural law theory without a transcendent God. Even Kant admitted that "this faith needs merely the idea of God . . . it need not presume that it can certify the objective reality of this idea."[11] As Rem Edwards says: "This would seem to require that Kant modify his definition of religion to the recognition of all duties as possibly divine commands. We may wonder to what extent Kant effects the complete reduction of the idea of God to the idea of morality."[12]

Although I am obviously indebted to Kant, I must diverge from him on yet another point. I see no reason why the requirements of the moral law dictate moral perfection. We have already seen that an eternal life is appropriate only for angels or gods, not human beings. So it is also with the concept of moral perfection, which I believe to be an impossible goal. My humanist ethic and eschatology would require only that we acknowledge our thoughts and deeds and take full responsibility for them. Heidegger's terms of "authentic" (*eigentlich*) and "inauthentic" (*uneigentlich*) existence are helpful at this point. In the German adjective *eigentlich* is the root *eigen,* which means "own" as in "my own." The most authentic expression of a Heideggerian *Dasein* is for one to face up to death as one's "own-most" possibility. I am assuming, contrary to Heidegger, that death is not the end, but the ethical imperative still remains: in the after-death experience persons will be obliged to "own up" to what they have done and thought. A humanist ethic would not require us to become gods, only authentic human beings.

II

My task now will be to establish the intelligibility of a limited after-death experience in which the "last things" of a humanist ethic could be fulfilled. I will talk not about an afterlife, but about an after-death experience. In response to John Hick's concept of eschatological verification, critics have attacked the notion of "being alive while not alive." The accepted meaning of the word "life" demands that we use it only with reference to life in the biological body. We should give credit to the ancient Hebrews and Homeric Greeks for recognizing this important point. In their mythical accounts of Hades, the Homeric Greeks gave vivid expression to the shadowy existence between life and death. For the Hebrews the soul in sheol was not alive, for life required the breath of God, but it was not dead either. Therefore, both the Greeks and the Hebrews knew intuitively that "life after death" is a misnomer but that this does not preclude the possibility of some sort of after-death experiences.

H. H. Price has been most successful in making intelligible the notion of after-death experiences. They would be fully human and they would support my eschatological proposals. Price argues that we could conceive of such experiences on the basis of an analogy with dream experiences. He contends that dream worlds and the hypothetical "next" world would be realms of real mental images. As Price states: "Mental images are not . . . imaginary at all. We do actually experience them, and they are no more imaginary than sensations."[13] Mental images do indeed resemble percepts. This similarity gives credibility to those accounts of mediumistic communication in which the dead find it difficult to believe that they are dead. "This is just what we should expect," says Price, "if the next world is an image-world."[14] Price goes on to observe that such a world is no less substantial than the world of modern phenomenalists, put together by custom and habit out of possible and actual sense data.

Price's after-world is built by the same phenomenalist rules: "Such a family of interrelated images would make a pretty good object. It would be quite a satisfactory substitute for the material objects which we perceive in this present life. And a whole world composed of such families of mental images would make a perfectly good world."[15] Such a world would be spatial-temporal as well as being filled with qualities. We would, for example, be able to tell the head from the tail of a dream tiger; we would be able to see color and spatial arrangement of its stripes; and we would experience the exciting temporal sequence of the tiger chasing us through an Indian forest. Therefore, the dream world has definite spatial-temporal relations and contains extended, bounded entities. Concluding that "there is no *a priori* reason why all extended entities must be in physical space,"[16] Price suggests the possibility of some non-physical body.

III

Price has given us a coherent and meaningful conceptual framework for after-death experiences. In contrast to other scenarios, Price's hypothesis is both compatible and continuous with earthly human existence. Recent scientific work with persons who have had close encounters with death offers some tentative, yet tantalizing, evidence that Price's ideas may be more than just hypothetical. Definite patterns have emerged in 3,000 cases studied and I shall extract the points relevant to Price's hypothesis and to my humanist eschatology.

Almost without exception, the patients reported that they found themselves outside their physical bodies. Although most of them did not speak of a "spiritual" body, they all described their experiences in terms of definite spatial-temporal relations. According to the accounts, the subjects claimed to have had super-normal powers, for example, the ability to see into other rooms. Kenneth Ring's patients also reported a "state of heightened mental clarity dominated by a (subjective) sense of logic, detachment, and rationality."[17] Except for one study done by Maurice Rawlings, there were virtually no accounts of "hellish" experiences and no signs of external judgment. Contrary to widespread opinion, even those who survived suicide attempts told of feelings of bliss and contentment. Maurice Rawlings claims that up to half of his cases contained "hellish" elements. Rawlings contends that most researchers interview their subjects too late, and that the negative dimensions of their near-death encounter have all been suppressed. As a cardiologist involved in many resuscitations, Rawlings has had the opportunity to speak to these people soon after their traumas.

Ring does not deny the possibility of some negative elements in the near-death experience, but he suspects that Rawlings has exaggerated their frequency. First, Rawlings, like Raymond Moody, has no statistical control over his data. Second, the suppression hypothesis does not seem to be borne out by data drawn from other areas, such as bad drug trips. Third, Michael Sabom, another cardiologist involved in resuscitation, does not report any hellish accounts. Fourth, Rawlings does not hide the fact that he is writing from a conservative Christian standpoint and that he is intent on demonstrating that the negative experiences are the result of not turning to Christ. Ring points out that Osis and Haraldsson's cross-cultural study, containing many non-Christians, did not show signs of judgment or damnation.[18]

Most of the subjects interviewed said they went through a dark tunnel into a realm of light. Moody's patients said that they met a great "being of light," identified by many as Jesus or God. Sabom's and Ring's subjects did not report so much an individual being as a "presence," which was usually not described in religious terms. Moody's being of light is reported in terms of total compassion—gentle and persuasive, never judgmental—and this being instigates a total review of the subject's life. Only 25 percent of Ring's subjects reported life-reviews, with the highest frequency—55 percent—among accident victims. Ring's patients generally described the life-review in terms of a crucial decision about whether to go back to the body or to continue on to "final" death. One subject reported that the "presence" "gave me a choice," and another said: "I had a decision to make and . . . it was totally up to me."[19] One suicide survivor gave the following account:

The only thing I felt judged by would be myself. Like in the very beginning, when I thought about these things, all these terrible things, then I thought about the good things, then it felt like I'd just run through my life and I'd think of all the stupid things . . . all the mistakes I've made. I think the judging was mainly myself judging myself.[20]

On the basis of this report and others like it, Ring suggests that the "presence" is actually the "higher" self encouraging the ordinary self on to full self-actualization. Ring himself has been profoundly influenced by Paul Brunton, an English mystic who explains the preceding point this way: "Through [the Overself's] eyes he will gaze afresh at the total impression rather than the episodal detail of his early life. Through its revelatory eyes he becomes his own incorruptible judge."[21]

Critics say that there must be "natural" explanations for these experiences. Some have proposed that some of the details—a long, dark tunnel, loud ringing noises, a brilliant light—might simply be a mental replay of the process of birth. Others claim that these experiences constitute some type of hallucination. In their books Ring and Sabom give plausible counter-arguments to these and other naturalistic explanations of near-death encounters. In contrast to most of the reports, Ring's and Sabom's investigation of 220 subjects was done under rigorous empirical controls. Sabom was able to demonstrate to his satisfaction that his clinically dead subjects were able to give accurate descriptions of medical attempts to revive them.

IV

Ring and Sabom stress the tentativeness of their conclusions. Much more careful research has to be done in this area before we can even begin to understand these intriguing accounts. It must be stressed, though, that my hypothesis does not stand or fall on the basis of these empirical studies. Speculation about eschatological matters has gone for millennia without the aid of science at all. Contemporary accounts of near-death experiences compare favorably with two ancient religious traditions—Zoroastrianism and Tibetan Buddhism. Zoroastrian scriptures describe the soul hovering close by the corpse for three days and three nights. More significant, however, for a humanist eschatology are implicit elements of self-judgment and, at least in Pahlavi scriptures, a limited period of trial and tribulation after death.

The Zoroastrian first meets his good deeds in the form of a beautiful maiden. At first the eschatological pilgrim does not realize that the maiden is his good deeds, so the maiden corrects him: "I am no girl but thy own good deeds, O young man whose thoughts and words, deeds and religion were good."[22] The maiden then goes on to describe the details of the man's virtuous life. In contrast the wicked are dragged off by demons, and they are met by an ugly hag who symbolizes their evil deeds. Zoroaster describes their demise: "Long-lasting darkness, ill food, and wailing—to such an existence shall your conscience lead you by your own deeds, O wicked ones" (*Yasna* 31:20).

These ideas of self-judgment go all the way back to Zoroaster's *Gathas*: "They shall be tortured by their own souls and their own consciences" (*Yasna* 46:11); "May all of their actions turn against them with hostility" (46:8); "Their sorrows shall be self-

induced, if they persevere in their hostility. Their own consciences would not only bring on their ruin, but would form part
of their punishment" (31:20). R. P. Masani, a modern Zoroastrian
from the Bombay Community, believes that the greatest contribution of Zoroastrianism is a clear doctrine that virtue is its own
reward and vice its own punishment. In contrast to earlier
Zoroastrians, Masani and his contemporaries reject the notion of
afterlife altogether: "Heaven is simply the best life or the region
of best mental state, and Hell is the worst life or the region of the
worst thought."[23]

This concept of self-judgment probably stems from the
Zoroastrian insistence that God is perfect goodness and that such
a God could not inflict the pain of punishment. As R. C. Zaehner
has said: "According to the Zoroastrian the Moslem God is not
good, neither does he pretend to be, while the Christian God
advertizes himself as good, and plainly is not."[24] (See Isa. 45:7) As
Ahura Mazda can create no evil, the pain of any hell must come
from demons independent of God's power or, as the *Gathas*
indicate, must be self-inflicted. Ahura Mazda does instigate the
final ordeal of molten metal, but it is clear that the suffering
depends on the person's nature, for the righteous swim in this
fluid as if it were warm milk.

The *Tibetan Book of the Dead* (*Bardo Thödol*) sheds interesting
light on contemporary accounts and offers the most consistent
support for my humanist eschatology. As in Zoroastrianism, the
soul remains in the vicinity of the dead body for some unspec-
ified time. It is imperative that a priest be present for the death
rites to read the *Bardo Thödol*. This scripture comes from the
eighth century C.E. and is designed as a guide for the soul during
the forty-nine-day "intermediate state"—the period between incarnations. At the beginning of the first *bardo,* the soul meets a clear
radiant light, which, in Mahayanist Tibet, is a symbol of the
Dharmakaya, the Body of Law, the Buddhist Godhead itself. If the
soul is advanced enough and recognizes the light as the Buddha,
then the soul can immediately reach Nirvana. Most souls, however, pass through the experience of the light without realizing
that it is their own true essence. This seems to be the Buddhist
equivalent of Ring's hypothesis that the being of light is one's
true self.

On the sixth day of the first *bardo,* the soul is met by "forty-
two perfectly endowed deities, issuing from within thy heart,

being the product of thine own pure love."[25] The priest emphasizes that "these realms are not come from somewhere outside
(thyself). . . . They issue from within [thee], and shine upon
thee. . . . They exist from eternity within the faculties of thine
own intellect. Know them to be of that nature."[26] By the eighth
day, blissful interaction with one's good deeds is completed and it
is time to confront one's evil deeds. They will come as "fifty-
eight flame-enhaloed, wrathful, blood-drinking deities. . .who
are only the former Peaceful Deities in changed aspect—according to the place (or psychic-centre of the *bardo*-body of the
deceased whence they proceed). . . ."[27] Here, even though it is
still possible to be liberated, most souls, even well-trained yogis,
react hysterically and attempt to seek refuge from the symbolic
projections of their own evil deeds. In Tibetan Buddhism the
hellish experiences come late, and this might be the reason for
their virtual absence in the contemporary reports.

The *Tibetan Book of the Dead* provides an excellent working
model of Last Judgment as self-judgment. The focus of the after-
death experience is exclusively moral. We are forced to acknowledge our thoughts and deeds and to accept them as our own. This
process may take, as it does in Buddhism, the form of a dialogue
with peaceful and wrathful deities, but we are continually reminded that these external forms are nothing but the past pro-
ductions of our own hearts.

V

There are obviously problems with the model I have constructed.
First, careful readers will have noticed the phrase "forced to acknowledge" in the last paragraph. A fundamental axiom of humanist ethics is that authentic people will not allow themselves to be
coerced. Kant's idea of a kingdom of ends is one in which the
sovereign rules by the dictates of reason such that any of its laws
would be completely compatible with laws made by self-legislating
citizens.

Although no ethical objectivist, except perhaps a Jain, would
conceive of the moral law acting in the same way as the law of
gravity, it is not at all impossible that the moral law, especially in the
after-world, would impress itself upon us in a particularly compelling way, one that would not necessarily undermine moral autonomy. Many of us, usually in times of death-threatening situations,

have had the experience of seeing our entire life in the mind's eye. Such experiences must initially be connected with the brain's memory function, but how these images could be generated in an out-of-body experience has yet to be explained. In any case, the life-review arises independently of the will. If the life-review is some sort of natural reflex, then it would not compromise moral autonomy.

This argument, however, does not take care of the problem. Even if the life-review is not initiated by a will, either human or divine, people could still refuse to "own up" to the acts of their lives. They could pat themselves on the back for their good deeds, but then refuse to acknowledge their immoral acts. At one time I thought I could argue that we are always harsher judges of ourselves than others ever could be, but the widespread practice of self-deception appears to be an insurmountable barrier to a successful defense of such an optimistic view of self-judgment. Even apart from the debilitating effects of self-deception, human beings are always much more adept at directing moral judgment outwards rather than inwards.

Buddhism and other religions of reincarnation have a solution to this problem: Persons who are reluctant to take responsibility for their acts must continue the cycle of death and rebirth until they do so. But reincarnation is incompatible with humanist eschatology for several reasons. First, the law of karma represents the strictest expression of moral objectivism and requires that moral perfection, sometimes through thousands of lifetimes, be reached. I have already argued that moral objectivism does not necessarily require that we become suprahumans. Second, reincarnation through thousands of lifetimes raises the problem of personal continuity and identity, a problem discussed thoroughly by John Hick in his *Death and Eternal Life*. It is not clear that reincarnationists can defend themselves successfully on this point.

With regard to a humanist ethic, Buddhism does have the fewest liabilities among the Indian alternatives. One of the basic problems of reincarnation arises from the belief in an eternal soul substance, which is the locus of an eternal personal identity. In the famous *Questions of Milinda,* the Buddhist monk-dialectician Nagasena argues brilliantly that personal continuity and moral responsibility can be grounded in a simple phenomenalist view of the self. Human selves are nothing but bundles of *skandhas* which acquire karma, and the karmic debt is passed along even though one bundle dissolves and is rearranged for rebirth as another person.

Buddhism also differs from other Indian philosophies on the question of moral perfection. The key to the Buddha's middle way is not some heroic, and ultimately self-indulgent, attempt to become a pure soul like the god Isvara of Sankhya-Yoga dualism. Liberation from the cycle of death and rebirth requires only that we stop craving. Ordinary desire—aiming only at those goals which can be attained—is acceptable, but craving must be stopped completely. The Buddhist solution to the problem of personal continuity is not without its problems, and the goal of not-craving could be interpreted as inimical to Western humanist ideas. First, the ability to stop craving may require the same suprahuman efforts as the Yogi's emulation of Isvara. (Instructive here is the Buddha's declaration that he was not actually a man.)[28] Second, humanists should be allowed to participate in the full range of human experience—most certainly craving—as long as they are willing to take responsibility for their acts. Therefore, humanists must reject the idea of reincarnation and uphold, rather, the concept of a limited afterlife and a simple, perhaps Nirvana-like, end after one has been reconciled with all of one's thoughts and deeds.

Humanists might object that I have added an unacceptable burden by insisting that thoughts as well as deeds must be a part of the judgment process. This could be interpreted as an un-welcome intrusion of Eastern philosophy into Western human-ism. Legally no one can be held accountable for inward "sins." Indeed, libertarians believe that we should be free to sin in private acts involving only ourselves and consenting adults. The notion that we are *morally* responsible for our thoughts as for our deeds is not, of course, exclusively Eastern; Jesus admonishes us that lust in the heart is just as reprehensible as lechery in deed. St. Au-gustine was the first Christian philosopher to reflect at length on this problem, and his arguments in the *Confessions* regarding sinning while dreaming have been taken seriously by at least one contemporary philosopher.[29]

The argument is especially strong if we assume that dreams are *bona fide* human experiences. I agree with Price that the after-world is best conceived as a type of dream world. It is true that in our dreams, thoughts and deeds do merge. This phenomenon may be similar to what the Arab Aristotelians meant when they

proposed that God's knowledge is "productive." Things are created directly from thought itself. Furthermore, there is no division between the conscious and the unconscious. Price believes
that if "repression is a biological phenomenon, [then] the 'thresh-
old' between conscious and unconscious no longer operates in
the disembodied state."[30]

This is perhaps a clue to the solution to a problem discussed
earlier: Self-deception and averting one's eye from one's own
deeds would no longer be possible. Price says that "the secrets of
[the] heart will be revealed"[31] and there will be no refuge from
the ultimate moral imperative of full self-judgment. He specu-
lates that disembodied souls could communicate telepathically, so
thoughts and deeds would indeed merge. And, if self-deception is
due to the biological body and its passions, as Plato and others
have held, then this time-honored psychological tactic would
simply not operate. Near-death patients also speak of telepathic
communication, and Kenneth Ring's subjects report that reasoning and objectivity dominated their experiences.

East and West are agreed that the type of after-death experiences will depend on how we have lived our lives. There is no
question that many people lead similar lives and have similar
desires and actions. If there is an afterlife, it is conceivable that
these people would then find themselves in the same "place," one
essentially of their own making. Dante's nine circles of hell are
designed according to a person's principal sins, and in Hindu
eschatology the notion of a great number of realms (loka) is based
on the same principle. Price finds these traditional views compatible with his own speculations about the after-world: "If this is
right, an image-world such as I am describing would not be the
product of one single mind only, nor would it be purely private.
It would be the joint product of a group of telepathically interacting minds and public to all of them. Nevertheless, one would not
expect it to have unrestricted publicity. It is likely that there
would still be many next worlds, a different one for each group
of like-minded personalities."[32]

VI

Earlier I noted some basic similarities between process theology and
early Hebrew thought. Although they are worlds apart philosophi-
cally, both views reject the concept of an afterlife and interpret

human immortality in terms of a living memory in human and divine minds. I agree with the basic assumption that appears to stand behind both views: There is a fundamental difference between human beings and divine beings. This is what I have called the Hebraic principle. This means that divine characteristics, like immortality, are incompatible with human attributes. Therefore, the desire for eternal life must be considered as the ultimate expression of the Greek *hubris*. While I agree that immortality is not and should not be a human predicate, I diverge from process theology and the early Hebrews on the question of an afterlife. Using various sources and my own devices, I have proposed a limited afterlife whose focus is exclusively moral and not religious. In addition to rejecting the immortality of the soul, I rejected the notions of heavenly happiness or fellowship with God. Drawing out the full implications of ethical objectivism, I have argued that persons in the after-death experience must reconcile themselves with all their thoughts and deeds.

Earlier I made the point that a humanist eschatology of self-judgment need not include a belief in God. It may not even require the moral objectivism of Kant or the Stoics. If there are after-death experiences with some sort of life-review, all of this could be possible without divine agency or a natural moral law. If behaviorists are correct about moral intuitions having their origins in socio-psychological conditioning, then it is possible that all aspects of this ingrained moral behavior would continue after death, even intensified, as I have speculated. Therefore, surprising though it be to some, an atheist worldview would not necessarily preclude eschatological considerations.

While strictly biblical Christians could never accept a humanist ethic of self-judgment, Christian humanists ought to consider the views I have proposed. My humanist eschatology has something to offer to Christians who are concerned about human autonomy and dignity. Many of these Christians have already rejected what John Hick calls the "Myth of God Incarnate," and they should also repudiate the idea of divine judgment and recognize that human immortality is yet another pagan myth which alienates us from our basic humanity. My ethical objectivism ought to please even some conservative Christians, who have always been concerned, and rightly so, about the fulfillment of justice. (In fact, my view is more just than Christian views that hold that great sinners, by means of death-bed conversions, escape the full brunt of their transgressions.) In my view, however, this justice is self-administered by morally autonomous individuals rather than being brought down from a divine judge. As we have found political totalitarianism abhorrent, we should likewise reject religious totalitarianism.

Notes

1   One must concede the possibility that Zoroaster may have pre-empted the priestly writers in this discovery. This would be even more likely if, as some recent scholars contend, Zoroaster is to be dated as early as about 1,000 B.C.E. See, for example, Gherardo Gnoli, *Zoroaster's Time and Homeland* (Naples: Istituto Universitario Orientale, 1980).

2   John Hick, *Death and Eternal Life* (New York: Harper & Row, 1976), 410.

3   John B. Cobb, Jr. and David Ray Griffin, *Process Theology: An Introductory Exposition* (Philadelphia: Westminster Press, 1976), 8.

4   Immanuel Kant, *Religion Within the Limits of Reason Alone,* trans. T. M. Greene and H. H. Hudson (New York: Harper Torchbook, 1960), 142.

5   Kant, *Foundations of the Metaphysics of Morals,* trans. L. W. Beck (Indianapolis: Bobbs-Merrill, 1959), 25.

6   Kant, *Religion Within the Limits of Reason Alone,* 142f.

7   Kant, *The Critique of Practical Reason,* trans. T. K. Abbott (London: Longmans, Green, and Co., 1898), 228 n.

8   Jeffery Reiman, *In Defense of Political Philosophy* (New York: Harper Torchbooks, 1972), xxiiff.

9   Kant, *Religion Within the Limits of Reason Alone,* 149.

10   George F. Thomas, *Religious Philosophers of the West* (New York: Scribner's, 1965), 252.

11   Kant, *Religion Within the Limits of Reason Alone,* 142n.

12   Rem B. Edwards, *Reason and Religion* (New York: Harcourt Brace Jovanovich, 1972), 48.

13   H. H. Price, "Survival and the Idea of 'Another World,'" *Proceedings of the Society for Psychical Research* 50 (January 1953), quoted in Edwards, 352.

14   Ibid.

15   Ibid. 353.

16   Ibid. 356.

17   Kenneth Ring, *Life at Death: A Scientific Investigation of the Near-Death Experience* (New York: Coward, McCann & Geoghegan, 1980), 92; see also Michael B. Sabom, *Recollections of Death* (New York: Harper & Row, 1981); and Raymond A. Moody, *Life after Life* (New York: Bantam Books, 1976).

18   Ibid., 193–94, 249; see Maurice Rawlings, *Beyond Death's Door* (Nashville: Thomas Nelson, 1978).

19   Ibid., 67, 73.

20   Ibid., 169.

21   Paul Brunton, *The Wisdom of the Overself* (New York: E. P. Dutton, 1943), 155.

22   Quoted in R. C. Zaehner, *The Teachings of the Magi* (New York: Oxford University Press, 1976), 134.

23   R. P. Masani, *Zoroastrianism: The Religion of the Good Life* (New York: Macmillan, 1968), 74.

24   Zaehner, 55.

25   *The Tibetan Book of the Dead,* trans. W. Y. Evans-Wentz (New York: Oxford University Press, 1960), 121.

26   Ibid., 121–22.

27   Ibid., 131.

28   Quoted in David J. Kalupahana, *Buddhist Philosophy: A Historical Analysis* (Honolulu: University of Hawaii Press, 1976), 112.

29   William Mann, "Dreams of Immortality" (paper presented at the American Philosophical Association meeting, Pacific Division, March, 1982).

30   Price, 357.

31   Ibid.

32   Ibid., 355.

2 | Transmigration in the Transcendentalists: The Aquarian Gospel
ROBERT C. GORDON-McCUTCHAN

God dwells in thee.
EMERSON, *Gnōthi Seauton*

Do not confuse the Son of Man with the Son of God, for the Son of Man is the higher spiritual realization which is born of man's inner experience; a newfound understanding, joy and at-one-ment. The Christ is born in Capricorn, but as He grows and His influence in humanity spreads, the Son of Man is brought forth in His image in Aquarius and reigns, first as an essence in heaven, then in its embodiment in man on Earth.[1]

According to astrologers, there is both a lesser and a greater zodiac. The lesser zodiac refers to the twelve months that it takes for the earth to revolve around the sun. Each of these periods is represented by one of the signs of the zodiac. In addition to the annual revolution of the earth around the sun, the sun and its whole system of planets makes a vastly greater orbit around the universe. While the lesser zodiac requires only twelve months for a complete revolution, the greater zodiac requires 25,920 years. This means that each of the signs in the greater zodiac lasts 2,160 years ($25,920 \div 12 = 2160$).

Our solar system has been under the Piscean dispensation for the last 2,000 years or so. Now it is moving into the next Age in the greater zodiac—the Age of Aquarius. When the universe enters a new Age, it encounters new conditions—physical, mental and spiritual. These conditions are made explicit through the teaching of the spiritual master for the Age. In the case of the Piscean dispensation now ending, Christ's message summed up the conditions for the Age. With the dawning of the Age of Aquarius, a new message is needed to guide souls living under the new dispensation.

For Americans, the philosophy of Transcendentalism perhaps best expresses the precepts of the Aquarian Age. Developed principally by Ralph Waldo Emerson (1803–1882), Transcendentalism is the gospel of the spirit for democratic nations. Marilyn Ferguson, author of *The Aquarian Conspiracy*, recognizes the connection between Transcendentalism and contemporary Aquarian thought:

Like that of the founding fathers and of the American Transcendentalists of the mid-1800s, the dream of the Aquarian Conspiracy in America is a framework for nonmaterialist expansion: autonomy, awakening, creativity—and reconciliation.[2]

For Emerson, Margaret Fuller, Henry David Thoreau, and Walt Whitman, Transcendentalism offered a liberating alternative to Christianity. Promising a new kind of spiritual freedom unrestricted by the tyranny of Christian dogma, it was the individual's declaration of spiritual independence. And it was the spiritual teaching necessary to complement the political freedom that had been won in the American Revolution. As Ferguson says, their new faith seemed a "logical extension of the American Revolution—spiritual liberation as a counterpart to the freedoms guaranteed by the United States Constitution."[3]

How this cry for spiritual liberation emerged, what it meant to its nineteenth-century proponents, and its significance for the Aquarians of today, will be the subjects of this paper.

The Rise of Transcendentalism: Panentheism and Process

The inception of Transcendentalism can be dated from 1832. It was during that year that Emerson broke formally with his Christian background. Ordained a Unitarian minister in 1826, he was beginning by 1829 to have doubts about his calling. Three years later his reservations became compelling, so he resigned his pastorate at Boston's prestigious Second Church.

At issue was the celebration of the Lord's Supper. Emerson's initial reason for declining to perform this sacred rite was simply that it made the religious focus an outward instead of an inward one. Ironically, it made religion formal and external when Christ himself had come "to redeem us from a formal religion, and teach us to seek our well-being in the formation of the soul"(W 11: 22).

A more powerful demurral turned upon the observation "that the use of this ordinance tends to produce confusion in our views of the relation of the soul to God" (W 11: 17). By emphasizing Christ's mediatorial role, the rite implies a separation of the soul from God. Since Christ alone of all humanity is fully divine, only he can intercede with the Father. Only through Christ can the soul know the divine presence. The rite is itself a celebration of this dogma.

Transcendentalism arose from Emerson's rejection of the Lord's Supper along with the separation of the soul from God that it presupposes. His grounds for that rejection are obvious. The soul needs no mediator with God since the soul is itself essentially divine. Emerson makes this point most eloquently in his poem *Gnōthi Seauton*, written just before leaving his parish:

If thou canst bear
Strong meat of simple truth . . .
Then take this fact unto thy soul
God dwells in thee. (JMN 3: 290)

As the soul does not require a mediator between itself and God, neither does it require external sacraments. Instead, it should turn within: "*there* is the celestial host" (YES 200).

According to Emerson, Jesus did not come to mediate between humanity and the divine. He came as "an instructor of man. He teaches us how to become like God" (W 11:18). It then follows that the soul should abandon the worship of Christ in favor of realizing its own divinity. Once Emerson realized this, he found the critical leverage that enabled him to break with his congregation. He achieved the spiritual insight that freed him from his religious perplexity. "I find," he said just after leaving Second Church, "that this amazing revelation of my immediate relation to God, is a solution to all the doubts that oppressed me" (YES 200). On the divinity of every sentient being Emerson took his stand. The Aquarian Gospel was then fully in the making.

In 1836, Emerson published *Nature*, the manifesto of Transcendentalism. In it he revealed that the relationship between nature and divinity parallels that between divinity and the individual soul. Both the soul and nature are ultimately divine. *Nature* affirms the panentheistic belief that Spirit underlies all manifest phenomena: "behind nature, throughout nature, spirit is present" (W I 64). With this step, Emerson renounced all dualistic conceptions of reality. All of the particulars of experience are reducible finally to Absolute Spirit. By rejecting Christianity's separation of God from the world, Emerson found a new faith conceived of nature as organic and living, suffused by an immanent divinity whose immediate energy sustained the world's existence.

In *Nature*, two axioms followed from its non-dualistic postulate. The first was repudiation of bondage to historical texts. If the divine suffuses nature, then the age of prophecy is not over. The divine is as present to us today as it was to the prophets in the biblical era. Unfortunately, as Emerson recognized, his own age was still "retrospective. It builds sepulchres of the fathers" (W 1:3). "Why," Emerson asked, "should not we have a poetry and philosophy of insight and not of tradition, and a religion by revelation to us, and not the history of theirs?" (W I 3).

Divine truth cannot be found in a book. It must come either through the insights of contemporary revelation or from the observation of nature. Emerson went so far as to insist that spiritual truths are learned from scientific theories. He maintained, "The axioms of physics translate the laws of ethics" (W 1:33), and that, "every natural process is a version of a moral sentence" (W I 41). Truth is not learned from ancient scripture, but from intuition and naturalistic observation.

The second great message of *Nature* centers on Emerson's philosophy of spiritual process which stated that spiritual growth derives from our immersion in daily experience: "every object rightly seen unlocks a new faculty of the soul" (W 1:35). The key to spiritual process is Emerson's conception of nature as a school. Pondering the reasons for man's earthly existence, Emerson concluded "that the world is for his education is the only sane solution of the enigma" (W 8:334). Emerson rejected the Christian view of the world as a place of trial, but instead thought of it as a vast process of spiritual instruction. Through experience in nature the soul's spiritual potential unfolds. Thus all of experience is providentially arranged to call forth the soul's spiritual resources. For this reason, "external nature is but the candle to illuminate in turn the innumerable and profound obscurities of the soul" (LC 2:200).

The development of his process philosophy brought Emerson to an explanation of nature's teleology quite different from

that of traditional Christianity. The purpose of nature, he proposed, is to lead individual souls to the knowledge of their
essential divinity:

The noblest ministry of nature is to stand as the apparition of God. It is the
organ through which the universal spirit speaks to the individual, and
strives to lead back the individual to it (W1:62).

Through experience in the world, the soul receives instruction
from the Absolute Spirit. Through this process of enlightenment,
the soul finally comes to the realization that the apparition of nature
is ultimately nothing but Spirit. Thus the whole of human life is an
organic progression. "As a plant in the earth so I grow in God"
(JMN 5:336). It progresses through worldly experience to spiritual
truth: the truth of non–duality. For the soul that reaches this mystical insight, "the act of seeing and the thing seen, the seer and the
spectacle, the subject and the object, are one" (W 2:269). It follows
then that the purpose of nature is to be ever "faithful to the cause
whence it had its origin. It always speaks of Spirit. It suggests the
absolute. It is a perpetual effect. It is a great shadow pointing always
to the sun behind us" (W 1:61).

Transcendentalism's Middle Years: From Christ to Compensation

In 1838 Emerson widened the gap between the Christian and the
Transcendentalist gospels. The occasion was the delivery of his
famous "Address" to Harvard's senior divinity class which Emerson opened by asserting that the Christian Church had falsified
Christ's message. While Christ had come to awaken all to the reality
of "the indwelling Supreme Spirit" (W 1:127) at the core of their
being, his followers deified him and insisted that he alone was
divine. They obscured his mystical teaching with a cult of personality. "The first defect of historical Christianity," Emerson asserted,
is its "exaggeration of the personal, the positive, the ritual. It has
dwelt, it dwells, with noxious exaggeration about the *person* of
Jesus" (W 1:130). By focusing on the exclusive divinity of Christ,
the church forgot his message–all are equally divine. The result of
this faulty teaching has been the spiritual enervation of the individual. As Emerson affirms, "The doctrine of the divine nature
being forgotten, a sickness infects and dwarfs the constitution"
(W 1:127).

The second defect of Christianity follows directly from the first. By dwelling on the person of Jesus, Christianity made salvation a matter of faith in him. Belief in Christ was thought to appropriate the power of his crucifixion. For those who had faith, his death on the cross atoned vicariously for their sins.

Emerson took exception to all of this "intermediary" theorizing. He insisted that we could neither be damned by Adam nor saved by Christ. Rather, the soul's spiritual state depended upon the moral quality of the life with which it was associated. The most damaging effect of the cult of Jesus was simply that it obscured the importance of morality. In stressing atonement, "Christianity destroys the power of preaching, by withdrawing it from the exploration of the moral nature of man" (W 1:141).

Clearly Emerson wished to articulate a spiritual vision rooted in the moral nature of humanity rather than in the person of Jesus. Throughout the "Address" Emerson gives trenchant expression to the new moral theory he believed would prevail— his theory of Compensation.

The theory of Compensation proves Emerson a truly original thinker, for the theory took a conceptually unique approach for New England in the 1830s. And although Emerson did not use the term karma, it is remarkably similar to the Oriental theory of karma. Compensation is plainly his equivalent term. The theory stresses deeds, not creeds, as the ground for spiritual salvation.

Emerson reveals the heart of his thinking on Compensation at the outset of the "Address": "In the soul of man there is a justice whose retributions are instant and entire. He who does a good deed is instantly ennobled. He who does a mean deed is by the action itself contracted" (W 1:122). Here Emerson suggests that the ontological level of the soul is affected positively or negatively by the moral quality of actions performed: Virtuous actions increase participation in Being; evil actions decrease it.

To explain his new approach to spiritual growth, Emerson kept faith with panentheism. The divinity that underlies the soul becomes manifest through the practice of virtue: A virtuous deed actualizes in the soul some degree of its divine potential. Performing a virtuous act allows an influx of divinity into the soul. Such influxes gradually reveal the soul's immanent divinity. To be virtuous is to be a channel for pure Spirit. By "channeling" Spirit, the agent directly contacts universal Mind, and it is this contact that increases the agent's ontological status. In contrast, when an agent performs evil acts "he bereaves himself of power, of auxiliaries; his being shrinks out of all remote channels and he disuniversalizes and he individualizes himself and becomes all the time less and less" (JMN 5:266). Hence to be virtuous is to be spiritually enhanced; to sin is to be spiritually diminished.

In addition to the effects they have immediately upon the soul, moral acts condition and influence the nature of subsequent experience. We are all familiar with this idea in the biblical form "as ye sow, so shall ye reap." The performance of virtuous acts redounds to the agent as subsequent positive experience. Conversely, evil deeds result in negative experience. Emerson expounded this point poetically when he said that the consequence of wrong action not only is "the greater hiding of the God within," but also involves

. . . next the consequence
More faintly as more distant wrought
Upon our outward fortunes
Which decay with vice
With virtue rise. (JMN 3:293)

This theme is reinforced, too, in "Fate": "Nature magically suits the man to his fortunes, by making these the fruit of his character" (W 6:40). Present actions do, he felt, have causal repercussions which return to the agent in the form of subsequent experience. "The evils we suffer are the just measure of those we have done" (JMN 14:161). In this way nature "replies to the purpose of the actor, beneficently to the good, penally to the bad" (W 6:215).

That the theory of Compensation judges and rewards every act at performance made the Christian conception of an ultimate Day of Judgment unnecessary. "Instead of denouncing a future contingent vengeance," Emerson insists, "I see that vengeance to be contemporary with the crime" (JMN 3:62). The vengeance contemporary with the crime is, of course, the soul's ontological reduction. And we have just seen that there will be subsequent vengeance in the form of negative experience as well. Since these short and long term consequences are inevitable, there is no need for an ultimate Day of Judgment. Rather, "The world is full of Judgment Days" (JMN 5:214) that take the form of karmic or compensatory retribution.

Not only did Emerson's new moral theory repudiate the idea

of Judgment Day, it also freed him to reject the doctrine of salvation through faith in the atonement of Christ. Compensation replaced atonement with the theory of ontological growth through moral effort as explained above. Emerson's new moral theory better explained how the soul reaches the teleology described in *Nature*. Earlier we saw that the goal of the spiritual process of life is the realization of non-duality. A signal value of the "Address" lies in its systematic explanation of this process. The influxional theory clarified the soul's inward process of divinization. The telling point behind Emerson's thinking is his assertion that this inner ontological change leads directly to outer epistemological transformation. Virtue and experience nurture the soul's divinity allowing it better to perceive divinity in the world:

A life in harmony with Nature, the love of truth and virtue, will purge the eyes to understand her text. By degrees we may come to know the primitive sense of the permanent objects of nature, so that the world shall be to us an open book, and every form significant of its hidden life and final cause. (W 1:35)

On completion of the soul's inner unfolding, it undergoes both an ontological and an epistemological metamorphosis. Ontologically the soul stands revealed as perfectly identical with God, enabling it then to perceive the divinity of the world. These simultaneous transformations bring the soul's mystical journey to fulfillment. Clearly, the religious core of Transcendentalism is its emphasis upon achieving this transformation here and now, not in an otherworldly heaven. The goal of Transcendentalism was knowledge of the divine while living. "Heaven is the name we give to the True State. . . . It is, as Coleridge said, another world but not to come" (JMN 5:48).

The Maturing of Transcendentalism: Evolution and Transmigration

The delivery of his "Address" marks the close of Emerson's early philosophical career. By this time he had registered his criticisms of Christianity and had laid the basis for his new spiritual vision. The year 1838 was not the end, however, of Emerson's philosophical growth. Over the next ten years his thinking underwent further maturation, bringing to completion, by 1850, the philosophy of American Transcendentalism.

One of the most important facets of Emerson's later growth concerned his fundamental ontology. From his first encounter with Berkeley's work, Emerson had been a philosophical idealist. He agreed with Berkeley's conclusion that the world is not irreducibly material, but is rather a thought or a projection. The question was simply: Whose? Was it the thought of God, as objective idealism teaches? Or was it the projection of the individual mind, as subjective idealism contends?

From the publication of *Nature* (1836) through 1845, Emerson's ontological thinking remained inconclusive as he considered both subjective and objective idealism. It was his extensive reading of Indian philosophy in 1845 that finally resolved his ontological perplexity. In his study of Indian thought, Emerson re-encountered the concept of *maya*, which confirmed his belief in objective idealism. *Maya* then became the single most important factor in the development of his mature ontology.

From Indian philosophy Emerson learned that the world is but an illusory manifestation of Vishnu, a transient painting ultimately identical with the Divine Energy causing its apparent existence. In technical terms, his position would be described as "acosmic panentheism." An acosmic panentheist believes that the absolute God (the Over-Soul or the One) makes up or pervades the total reality of manifest existence. The universe is ultimately reducible to Absolute Spirit. But Absolute Spirit is more than simply the manifest universe. While the Spirit includes the universe, it is at the same time more than the universe.

Physical reality, then, is conditional. It is unreal in the sense that all of the particulars of experience are really nothing but Absolute Spirit (acosmic), but it is real to the extent that its basis lies in Absolute Spirit (panentheism). In sum, while forms appear to exist, they are in reality Absolute Spirit. Emerson makes this point in "Plato": "As one diffusive air, passing through the perforations of a flute, is distinguished as the notes of a scale, so the nature of the Great Spirit is single, though its forms be manifold" (W 4:50).

By combining the concept of *maya* with his theory of spiritual process, Emerson developed a more complete philosophy of experience. In rejecting subjective idealism he concluded that the world is an objectively existent projection of the "Great Spirit." Its function is the moral and spiritual cultivation of souls. Thus the "appearances" in nature with which we interact reveal the soul's true essence and lead it to the intuitive knowledge of non-duality. Through experience in the world, the soul eventually penetrates the mask of nature "and the pupil is permitted to see that all is one stuff, cooked and painted under many counterfeit appearances" (W 7:173). Thus "Youth, age, property, condition, events, persons,—self, even,—are successive *maias* (deceptions) through which Vishnu mocks and instructs the soul" (W 8:14-15).

The second significant change in Emerson's philosophy grew out of his interest in science. Throughout the 1830s and 1840s Emerson avidly read works on geology, astronomy, botany, and zoology. These treatises convinced Emerson that the human race was not fallen, as traditional religion taught. Rather, man along with all other species, was rapidly evolving. Liberating as this conclusion was, Emerson reached it only after a long period of philosophical struggle. Emerson initially had trouble accepting the theory of evolution because of its implicit materialism. He was able to overcome this resistance through the aid of the St. Louis Hegelian Johann Bernard Stallo, whose influence proved crucial. He demonstrated to Emerson the reconcilability of philosophical idealism and emergent evolution. Stallo pointed out that all one need do is to assume that Spirit underlies the forward progress of material (or apparently material) evolution. As Stallo affirmed: "Matter is not a hearth, upon which afterwards the flame of the Spiritual is kindled; the Spiritual is at once the hearth, the process of combustion, and the appearing flame."[4] Starting from this postulate, Emerson was able to explain the entire evolutionary process as the progressively higher manifestation of the Spirit: "Every glance at society . . . suggests at once the German thought of the Progressive God, who has got thus far with his experiment, but will get out yet a triumphant, . . . faultless race" (JMN 11:263). In this manner, he reconciled his philosophical idealism with emergent evolution. For Emerson, the Great Spirit became progressively more manifest through the upward march of evolution. Evolution itself became God's *modus operandi*.

The third major shift in Emerson's philosophy stemmed from his unfulfilled hope for mystical transformation. In the early stages of his spiritual development, Emerson believed that adopting, and living in accordance with, his new religious vision would quickly bring him to full realization of the God within. But by 1841 this spiritual aspiration remained unfulfilled. This led, quite naturally, to his belief that at-oneness evolved from gradual organic growth rather than sudden transformation. Emerson's acceptance of evolution further intensified this "gradualist" reckoning. By radically expanding his concept of time, the acceptance of evolution made Emerson even more of a gradualist with respect to the spiritual life.

Although Emerson became more of a gradualist, that in no way caused him to abjure his hope for mystical at-oneness. He preserved this hope by postulating a fourth metaphysical construct: He rejected the Christian belief in one lifetime in favor of the theory of transmigration. In 1844 he asserted, "It was then I discovered the secret of the world that all things subsist, and do not die, but only retire a little from sight and afterwards return again" (JMN 9:73).

The 1840s were, for Emerson, a period of extension of boundaries, both historical and personal. While evolution expanded Emerson's temporal framework, transmigration extended human life so that it might more appropriately fit the larger frame. It is important to remember that the acceptance of evolution and the theory of transmigration developed concurrently in Emerson's thinking. The convergence of these themes enabled Emerson to accept the data of experience. He had not made the flight of the "alone to the Alone."

Another factor that made the theory of transmigration attractive to Emerson was its coincidence with his moral theory. We have already seen that his theory of Compensation is similar to the Hindu theory of karma, so we can see that when Emerson studied the Indian concept of karma in terms of transmigration, and when he recognized the close relationship between karma and Compensation, he could accept transmigration as the metatheory necessary for a satisfactory explanation of his moral theory. This explains how he came to believe that our present fate is the result of actions carried out in former lifetimes. Emerson, echoing the *Veshnoo Sarma*, wrote: "Fate is nothing but the deeds committed in a former state of existence" (JMN 7:489).

The final change Emerson underwent in his progress towards philosophical maturity was in more clearly defining the goal of human life. Even in his early philosophy he had broken with the Christian theory about the *telos* of human existence. Earlier we noted the distinction between the Christian goal of heaven and the Transcendental "True State." The Transcendentalists sought inner transformation in the here and now (the experi- ence of non–duality), not heavenly felicity after death. What Emerson failed to consider in his early thinking was the soteriological effect that experiencing the "True State" would have upon the individual. His mature philosophical thinking took this into account after further study of Indian metaphysics.

The Indian classics taught that the goal of human existence is mystical identification of the soul as Brahman. When such *gnosis* dawns, the soul is freed from the cycle of rebirth. Emerson came to agree: "That which the soul seeks is resolution into being above form, out of Tartarus and out of heaven,—liberation from nature" (W 4:51). Emerson acceded to the view of Advaita Ve- danta that the end and aim of the ecstatic game of life is realiza- tion of divinity (by cutting through the delusion of *maya*) and termination of the transmigratory cycle. The similarities between Emerson's mature view and Indian philosophy are no accident. In a journal entry from 1866, he looks back upon a life devoted to the widest philosophical study and concludes:

In the history of intellect no more important fact than the Hindoo theol- ogy, teaching that the beatitude or supreme good is to be attained through science: namely, by the perception of the real and the unreal, setting aside matter, and qualities, and affections or emotions and persons, and actions, as Maias or illusions, and thus arriving at the contemplation of the one eternal Life and Cause, and a perpetual approach and assimilation to Him, thus escaping new births or transmigration. (J 10:162)

Aquarian Gospel: The New Dispensation

Now that we understand how Transcendentalism developed, we are ready to compare and contrast the gospel of the Piscean Age (Christianity) with the gospel for the Age of Aquarius (Transcen- dentalism).

The most important difference between these gospels concerns their conception of the relationship between God and nature. Chris- tianity has traditionally thought about God in terms of transcen- dence. God is believed to have created the universe from nothing, and to have remained separate from, over, and beyond it. There is thus a strict dualism between Creator and created. This dualism pervades human nature as well—the mind is radically distinct from the body. Transcendentalism, on the other hand, stresses the immanence or indwelling presence of God throughout the universe. The divine is not separate from creation, but quite the opposite: The creation is in its ultimate essence perfect unchanging Being. Transcendentalism is non-dualistic—the universe, the soul, the body are all various manifestations of the One Mind or Over-Soul.

Emerson delineated the second difference between the Piscean and Aquarian gospels by his refusal to celebrate the Lord's Supper. Transcendentalism rejects outer ritual conformity in favor of inner spiritual piety. It fosters a strong sense of direct individual participation in divine life without the necessity for ritual intervention between the divine and the human.

The third break with the Piscean tradition came with Emerson's renunciation of the Bible. Transcendentalism insists that we learn religious truth from observation of and experience in nature. Proper understanding of nature's laws teaches us spiritual truths. And the very process of living itself reveals the potential of the soul and nurtures it in the knowledge of its essential divinity. Thus we grow in God through experience, not through reading the Bible.

The fourth dichotomy between Pisces and Aquarius arose when Emerson rejected the "cult of Jesus." He found its emphasis on Christ's exclusive divinity especially harmful. In a radical departure from Christianity, Transcendentalism stresses the essential divinity of all living beings. Although the knowledge of that divinity may be obscured, it is nonetheless real, and is the individual's most important aspect. Since human beings are ultimately divine, they do not need a mediator between them and God. Rather, they need a teacher to instruct them in how to reach divinity.

The fifth distinction between these gospels turns upon the issue of salvation. According to Christianity, we are *saved* from our fallen and evil human nature, and therefore from hell, by a miraculous act of grace or through supernatural sacraments. The divine elements the soul lacks are added to it by superhuman agency. Transcendentalism assumes the essential divinity of the soul, repudiating recourse to miraculous intervention. Instead, we *grow* in the knowledge of our immanent divinity by performing virtuous acts. Simply put, virtue itself increases our participation in Being. We are not saved by faith in Christ. We grow in God by performing Christ-like actions.

A sixth issue dividing Christianity and Transcendentalism centers upon differences in their basic conception of the nature of life. The Piscean gospel views life as a trial leading to Judgment

Day: the soul is tried in the court of earthly experience in order to determine its fate at death. The Christian metaphor for life is a court; the Transcendental metaphor is that of a school. Life is a process of education that leads finally to complete knowledge.

The seventh difference between Pisces and Aquarius grows naturally out of the sixth. According to a view characteristic of the Piscean dispensation, at Judgment Day the unredeemed face the ultimate punishment—the eternal fires of hell. The Aquarian gospel turns away from this all-or-nothing formula. The punishment for evil deeds and faithlessness is not eternal hell, rather it comes in the form of negative experience. If the soul does wrong, wrong will surely befall it. Through this repercussion, the soul expiates its past sins, thereby settling the cosmic account. The soul never faces an ultimate Judgment Day. Every action is judged immediately.

Divergent ideas about the goal of human life point up the eighth difference between the two traditions. For Christianity, the goal is favorable Judgment and entrance into heaven. For Transcendentalism, the aspiration of the soul is to experience the truth of non-duality in *this* life. It is to grow in knowledge of one's immanent divinity until achievement of complete mystical *gnosis*.

The ninth dissimilarity between the two gospels centers on the question of human embodiment. Transcendentalists reject the Christian view that we live but one earthly life. To Aquarians such a position seems arbitrary and unfair. They prefer the doctrine of reincarnation. The soul is believed to have evolved upwards through all of the lower orders of nature. Differences among people are explained in terms of the soul's antiquity. More ancient souls are more spiritually developed, so they enjoy ever greater freedom from bondage to circumstance. When the soul finally achieves mystical *gnosis*, it no longer needs to pass through further incarnation. Merged with the All, it loses its particularity. Further existences become superfluous.

Finally, Transcendentalists reject traditional Christianity's linear and brief picture of history. The world was not created by divine fiat 6,000 years ago with all of the species fully formed upon it. The world as we know it has been emerging over millions and millions of years. Our story is the story of an unending forward march. Terrestrial existence will not be terminated by God's apocalyptic intervention. Its future is one of open-ended progress. The nature of divinity becomes progressively manifested in this upward evolutionary spiral.[5]

Notes

In accordance with the conventions of Emersonian scholarship, the following abbreviations are used throughout the chapter to identify often cited sources:

J   *The Journals of Ralph Waldo Emerson.* Edited by Edward Waldo Emerson and Waldo Emerson Forbes. 10 vols. Boston & New York: Houghton Mifflin, 1909-14.

JMN   *The Journals and Miscellaneous Notebooks of Ralph Waldo Emerson.* Edited by William H. Gilman, Alfred R. Ferguson, George P. Clark, Merrell R. Davis, Merton M. Sealts, Harrison Hayforth, Ralph H. Orth, J. E. Parsons, A. W. Plumstead, Linda Allardt, and Susan Sutton Smith. 14 vols. Cambridge: Harvard University Press, 1960—.

LC   *The Early Lectures of Ralph Waldo Emerson.* Edited by Stephen E. Whicher, Robert E. Spiller, and Wallace E. Williams. 3 vols. Cambridge: Harvard University Press, 1959, 1964, & 1972.

W   *The Complete Works of Ralph Waldo Emerson.* Concord Edition. 12 vols. Boston & New York: Houghton Mifflin, 1903.

YES   *Young Emerson Speaks.* Edited by Arthur Cushman McGiffert. Boston: Houghton Mifflin, 1938.

1   Harriette Augusta Curtiss and F. Homer Curtiss, *The Message of Aquaria* (San Francisco: The Curtiss Philosophic Book Co., 1921), 33.

2   Marilyn Ferguson, *The Aquarian Conspiracy: Personal and Social Transformation in the 1980s* (Los Angeles: J. P. Tarcher, Inc., 1980), 120.

3   Ibid., 122.

4   John B. Stallo, *General Principles of the Philosophy of Nature* (Boston: Wm. Crosby and H. P. Nichols, 1848), 44-45.

5   Emerson was better acquainted with critics of Christian thought outside the Church than with those inside it. He had little firsthand

knowledge of either the ascetic or the mystical traditions in Catholic theology. Moreover, during much of his life, Oriental studies were still comparatively undeveloped while critical biblical scholarship had not yet deeply affected Christian thought. Emerson, on a visit to England in 1833, met Carlyle, Coleridge, and Wordsworth, was influenced by all of them, and with Carlyle he formed a close friendship.—Ed.

3 | Mercersburg and Last Things

LOYDE H. HARTLEY

All science must be raised and refined into theosophy, all government into theocracy, all art into divine worship, and the whole of life into a joyful proclamation of the glory of God.
   PHILIP SCHAFF, *The Principle of Protestantism*

Eschatology has again become, as it was in the nineteenth century, a popular aspect of speculative theology. Most religious groups that have emerged in the latter part of the twentieth century offer answers, some of them novel, to the question of what will become of us all. Eschatological hopes spurred some nineteenth-century religious leaders to take action or to make pronouncements. The Millerites, Irvingites, and many others announced dates for Christ's return; the Shakers forbade marriage because the end was near; and some, like Christoph Hoffman, even began to build temples for Christ to occupy on his return. Similar hopes in the twentieth century have produced UFO cults, "pretribulational dispensationalism" (the idea that Christ's faithful will be soon caught up into the clouds before the final judgment), and the "Age of Aquarius."
   Mainstream Christianity often regards such eschatologies with suspicion, sometimes to the point of denying any interest in eschatology at all. For the most part, those proclaiming a radical eschatology have found it necessary to separate themselves from the more orthodox denominations; and in some cases they have been forced out. Nevertheless, from time to time religious thinkers in mainstream Protestant denominations have reflected on the purpose, direction, and end of history—in short, eschatology. Eschatology is never the starting point for theological speculation for these people, nor is the future they envision fantastically spectacular. Rather, their eschatology is derived

37

from their other doctrines and beliefs. Such is the case with the Mercersburg theology.

A "theologically and liturgically creative high church movement"[1] in nineteenth-century American Protestantism, the Mercersburg theology arrived at some eschatological assumptions by way of its Christology, ecclesiology, and view of history. This theology has a developmental understanding of history in which God intervenes supernaturally through the Church in order to bring all people and nations into unity with God, which is the principal characteristic of the end of history.

The purpose of the present paper is first to describe the eschatology of the Mercersburg theology, then to compare it with other eschatologies, and finally to reflect on its worth for contemporary eschatological discussions. Perhaps by reflecting on how orthodox Protestants dealt with eschatology a century ago, contemporary religious thinkers can discover ways to recapture aspects of this religious heritage for twentieth-century mainstream Protestantism. Before proceeding, a brief description of the Mercersburg theology and its leaders will provide background for the discussion of eschatology and the Second Coming as interpreted by the Mercersburg theologians.

The Background of the Mercersburg Theology

Mercersburg, a small town on the eastern slopes of the Allegheny Mountains of Pennsylvania, became the site for what Sydney Ahlstrom calls "one of the most brilliant constellations of religious thinkers in American History."[2] The two principals were John Williamson Nevin (1803–1886), a Presbyterian trained at Union College and Princeton, and Philip Schaff (1819–1893), a Swiss-born and German-educated scholar who came to Mercersburg in 1844. Both were recruited to teach in the German Reformed Theological Seminary then located in Mercersburg. Although Nevin and Schaff in collaboration were to become the key figures associated with the Mercersburg theology, the work of their predecessor, Friedrich Rauch, anticipated the view of history Nevin and Schaff were later to use in their theological interpretations of the Church. Rauch published in 1840 his *Psychology, or a View of the Human Soul, Including Anthropology*. Intended as the first in a series, this book set out to explain conservative Hegelian thought to American readers. Rauch died shortly after Nevin joined the Mercersburg faculty, but the importance of Hegelian views of history and eschatology was to remain a key element in the Mercersburg theology. Nevin's and Schaff's similar views found, at Mercersburg, perhaps the most hospitable reception possible in America at the time, although the whole Mercersburg movement was characterized by conflict with prevailing nineteenth-century American Protestantism.

The details of these conflicts are recorded elsewhere.[3] Suffice it to say here that conflicts centered on the Mercersburg theologians' insistence that Protestantism derived from Roman Catholic roots and that the Roman Catholic Church represents a valid stage in the overall development of the True Church. Prevailing Protestant understanding interpreted the Roman Catholic Church as being apostate and claimed that the True Church was preserved in remnant form through various small groups of the faithful throughout the Middle Ages, such as the Waldensians, to emerge full blown with the Reformation. The Pope was widely thought by Protestants to be the Antichrist. Nevin turned the tables on this view. He called the sectarian spirit in Protestantism (that tendency of Protestants to form new groups over theological disputes through schism) Antichrist.[4] That sectarian spirit is literally Antichrist because it splits apart the incarnate Body of Christ, the Church. Nevin's broadsides against the sects and their "new measures" for saving souls insured substantial conflict. Schaff joined Nevin in condemning the sectarian spirit as being opposed to God's purpose in history. Similarly he was opposed to rationalism as the means of discovering the purpose and direction of history. God's design for history is revealed, not discerned by reason or promulgated by schism.

Nevertheless, the Mercersburg theologians did not set forth a systematic theology over and against rationalism, sectarianism, or the ahistorical biases of the Protestantism of their day. They wrote instead about the Church and wrote liturgies for the Church that were living theology. Their eschatology did not emerge in response to the spectacular eschatologies of groups such as the Millerites (who announced the date of the Second Coming as 1844) or the Mormons (who proclaimed the "Latter Day" even in their name). Rather their eschatology emerged from their affirmation of the centrality of the Church in God's purpose for history, in dispute with mainstream American Protestantism, which was virtually ahistorical.

A thoroughgoing analysis of eschatology in the Mercersburg theology requires tracing the various roots of Nevin's and especially Schaff's thought in nineteenth-century German romanticism. That task is beyond the scope of this paper and has been undertaken, at least in part, elsewhere.[5] Schaff and Nevin were informed by, but not uncritical of, the interpretations of history in general and Church history in particular that emerged in early nineteenth-century Germany. Although in many ways they may be described as Hegelian, some obvious differences with Hegel's assumptions will be noted as this paper progresses.

Mercersburg Eschatology

What, then, is the eschatology that emerged in the Mercersburg movement? It is, in short, a traditional Christian eschatology informed by the creedal heritage and by the thought of Augustine and the Church Fathers combined with a German romantic, ostensibly Hegelian, understanding of development in history. Schaff concludes his *America, a Sketch of the Political, Social, and Religious Character* with a typical eschatological formulation. It is written as a farewell to his readers—Germans to whom Schaff was relating his experiences in America.

. . . in the certain expectation of reunion . . . in the general assembly of the Church of the First-Born, amid an innumerable company of angels, at the grand festival of reconciliation for all nations and confessions in the holy city of God on high, the heavenly Jerusalem, the mother and final home of us all. . . .[6]

One characteristic of the eschaton, then, is union of Christians both nationally and confessionally. Both Schaff and Nevin thought it possible that union of all Christians might be achieved before the Second Coming as a penultimate step to Christ's Second Advent, but always remained open to history as a corrective to such eschatological speculations. Schaff, again in his *America*, wrote:

Now, it is very questionable, whether Protestantism as such and with its present resources, has the capacity and the mission, to produce an external church-organism, possessed of complete unity; or whether the Lord himself has not rather reserved this till his second advent. At all events, however, it is the sacred duty of Evangelical Protestantism, as the voice of one crying in the wilderness, as a Church bearing witness by the pure word and sacraments, as the representative and guardian of personal

Christianity, or direct living intercourse between the individual soul and its Savior, to pave the way for his glorious second coming, and promote, in the most zealous manner, the free inward communion of faith and love, the unity of the spirit in the bond of peace, . . . , till the Lord, by new reformation, or by his personal appearing in the clouds of heaven, gather his people from all the ends of the earth and create a body of such inward unity, that the colossal theocratic organism of Church and State in the Middle Ages . . . and all our boldest ideals of union and confederation will be thrown far into the shade. This much stands immovably firm . . . : the day will come when there will be but one Shepherd and one flock, when all believers will be perfectly one, as He and the Father are one.[7]

Unimaginable glory of the unity of Christ's Body, then, is the sign and seal of the eschaton toward which all history is progressing. Former distinctions (between Catholicism and Protestantism, among Protestant sects, and between sacred and secular) will yield to unity in Christ. This does not mean, however, that present distinctions are unimportant. Schaff and Nevin did not like the idea of syncretic religion based on compromise. The distinctions are important and their value is not to be lost in the unity of Christ. Eschatology, however, is not a point in time, but the basis for the ultimate union of all sects. "We need no new sects; there are already too many. We need no new revelation, the old is sufficient,"[8] proclaimed Schaff.

The two main ideas underlying the Mercersburg theologians' eschatology are their understanding of progress in history and their perception of the Church's role in history. The basic metaphor for their view of history, especially as expressed in Schaff's writing, is that of the biological organism. History is a growing organism going through many stages in its development. Moreover, it can have setbacks in its progress toward its intended maturity. "Diseases" emerge corresponding to every particular stage of historical development,[9] the more serious diseases being more likely to develop at the more advanced stages of history. Nevertheless, history advances. The Roman Church was anticipatory to the "evangelical emancipation of Protestantism,"[10] which in turn will give way to the glorious unity of all Christians in the future. Petrine legalism (Roman Church) was corrected by Pauline freedom (Protestant Church) and both will evolve into Johannine love (Church of the eschaton). This view stands in stark contrast to eschatologies that would restore the True Church only at the end of time without regard for the centuries of development that lie between the First and Second Advent, a view held among Puritan scholars at the time of Schaff and Nevin and by many groups since then. Such a view implies, said Schaff, that "the Lord had not kept his promise to be with the Church always to the end of the world."[11] The Lord had not abandoned the Church, according to the Mercersburg theologians, but was leading it toward a new synthesis: that of "Evangelical Catholicism."

In his early writing, Schaff was eloquent and unrestrained in his enthusiasm for the new society, the ultimate synthesis, which he prophesied:

For the end or scope of all history is this, that the world may resolve itself into the Kingdom of God, reason into revelation, morality into religion, and earth into heaven. All science must be raised and refined into theosophy, all government into theocracy, all art into divine worship, and the whole of life into a joyful proclamation of the glory of God.[12]

Away with human denominations! Down with religious sects! Let our watchword be: One Spirit and one body! One Shepherd and one flock! All conventicles and chapels must perish, that from their ashes may arise the One Church of God, phoenix-like and resplendent with glory, as a bride adorned for her bridegroom.[13]

In later years, Schaff and Nevin perhaps diverged to some extent about the future course of history. Nevin became increasingly interested in the early Church, particularly in Cyprian, while Schaff became increasingly interested in American history and ecumenism as the arenas in which God was unfolding the future. Nevin became ill and seriously considered converting to the Roman Church. The question was "What Church should one die in?" Unlike John Henry Newman, contemporary leader of the Oxford Movement, Nevin finally chose not to convert. Although his writing during this period leaves an inconclusive record of his thinking, there is some evidence that he thought the unity toward which history was moving would occur eventually in a form similar to the Catholicism of the early Church. Schaff disagreed with this, and observed, in correspondence, that Nevin was looking to the past while he was looking to the future. Both Schaff's interpretations of the Civil War and his ecumenism reflect this difference. His ecumenism is demonstrated by his leadership in the Evangelical Alliance, a multinational association of churches promoting Christian union. His last major public address was entitled "The Reunion of Christendom," to be delivered in Chicago at the World Parliament of Religions in 1893. In regard to the Civil War, he wrote that it came "as a righteous judgment of God upon a guilt of South and North reaching through several generations . . . [the] humiliation of an arrogant and boastful nation."[14] Clebsch summarizes Schaff's view of the war succinctly:

In God's characteristic way, working *sub contrario*, the evil of war was made the hour of the great discovery and acceptance of the role of responsible, unifying nationhood, through the suffering of the whole national body. Expunging slavery, developing "the heroic element, the capability of sacrifice," consolidating the government in its force at home and for its duty abroad, purchasing "a priceless wealth of historical traditions," the war was a "very baptism of blood [entitling] us also to hope for a glorious regeneration." Through the dreadful life-and death event came a hopeful death-and-life blessing of real unification of diverse elements of population and geography through the guarantee of harmonious freedom.[15]

Schaff saw God at work in America creating the future toward which all history was moving, and the Civil War as having purged the nation of its sinfulness, so allowing it "first [to enter] the age of manly vigor and independence."[16] God is within history, yet beyond it, guiding it according to the eternal plan. As the result, history (and Christian doctrine as interpretation of history) is ever growing, unfolding, retrogressing, and being corrected. In this regard, Schaff differs from Newman who saw the development of doctrine as cumulative and irreversible.

As noted above, the second main idea underlying the Mercersburg eschatology has to do with the nature of the Church. For the clearest expression of Mercersburg ecclesiology, Nevin's works must be consulted. "History, like nature," he wrote in his *Mystical Presence*, "is one vast prophecy of incarnation, from beginning to end."[17] God is incarnate not only at the points of the First and Second Advent, but is continually incarnate in the Church. Incarnation is permanent with the second phase beginning with the Ascension and enduring until the Last Judgment. Nevin was (and we are) living in the age of the Church, and the Church is the salvific presence of Christ in the world. The Church, however, is not a static dispenser of salvation, but is itself becoming. "In its very nature, the actual Church is in process, which has never yet become complete, but is always pressing forward to its completion, as this will appear in the millennium . . . when the ideal church and the actual church shall have become fully and forever one."[18] In the end, the actual and ideal Church will be one. Now, "the actual is the body of the ideal in growth."[19] The present sects of Christianity, Nevin believed (as did Schaff), will pass away. Denominations are at best defective and at worst "an interimistic abomination."[20]

In the last stage of the Incarnation, when the actual and ideal Church will be one and the Lord will return, the organism (the Church) will have reached maturity:

> In full and final triumph of the process is the resurrection; which is reached in the case of the individual, only in connection with the consummation of the Church as a whole. The bodies of the saints in glory will be only the last result, in organic continuity, of the divine life of Christ, implanted in their souls by regeneration. There is nothing abrupt in Christianity. It is a supernatural constitution indeed; but as such it is clothed in a natural form, and involves itself as regular a law of historical development, as the old creation itself. The resurrection body will be simply the ultimate outburst of the life that had been ripening for immortality under cover of the old Adamic nature before.[21]

History naturally grows toward the Resurrection in "organic continuity" with all that is past. At the Resurrection, the Church will have grown to full maturity with respect to its purpose. Nevin saw this interpretation of the Church and history as the only possible alternative. He named and rejected three other alternatives: (1) a complete disjunction with the past and abandonment of the value of the early and medieval Church, as was the case with the prevailing Protestantism of the nineteenth century; (2) reconciliation with Rome, an alternative Nevin seriously considered during his extended illness but finally rejected; and (3) hope for a new revelation and new apostolic commission, as is illustrated by Swedenborgianism.[22] Nevin chose his idea of the Church as the only one consistent with Protestant faith (in particular, pietistic faith) based on his inquiry into the writings of Cyprian.

Some Comparative Perspectives on Mercersburg Eschatology

Carl Braaten, in his chapter entitled "The Kingdom of God and Life Everlasting," provides a possible conceptual framework that might be useful in developing a comparative perspective on eschatology in the Mercersburg theology even though Braaten's concern is twentieth- not nineteenth-century eschatology. Observing that there is no consensus among twentieth century theologians on how to interpret Jesus' expectation of the Kingdom of God, he then develops a four-part typology of eschatologies based on whether the eschatology is this-worldly or other-worldly and present or future in time.

Did Jesus think of the Kingdom of God as something otherworldly and future (traditional orthodoxy)? Or as something otherworldly and present (Karl Barth and dialectical theology)? Or as something this-worldly and present (Rudolf Bultmann and existential theology)? Or as something this-worldly and future (Christian Marxism and liberation theology)?[23]

Schaff and Nevin are not so easily placed in any of Braaten's categories as might be supposed. At first glance it is tempting to put them with the "traditional orthodoxy" category because of their reverence for orthodoxy or in the last category because of their compatibility with Hegelian views of historical development. They are not aptly characterized, however, in the "traditional orthodoxy" category, for they saw the coming Kingdom as being clearly a part of this world. Yet their view is clearly other-worldly in the sense that all unity will occur "in the clouds" or "in the heavenly Jerusalem." God is in, but clearly beyond, history. Moreover, while the full mature growth of the Kingdom of God in history is a future event, the Church is nevertheless the present fully potent manifestation of the Kingdom. Nevin and Schaff, therefore, saw the Kingdom of God as being both present and future and as being both this- and other-worldly, a position that none of Braaten's categories can easily accommodate, although it participates in some way in all four categories. Because neither Nevin nor Schaff can be easily categorized in this typology constructed for the analysis of twentieth-century eschatologies, there may be some merit in studying Mercersburg to discover ways through impasses in the contemporary discussion of eschatology.

We may use the following five questions as a basis for analyzing differing eschatologies which even more than Braaten's typology, suggest possible areas of eschatological inquiry, drawing on the work of Nevin and Schaff:

(1) *What is lacking in the present order that will be corrected in the eschatological age?* Schaff and Nevin saw disunity of the Church as

the significant missing element in the present order for which history is groping, in contradistinction to eschatologies that identify injustice, powerlessness, personal sins, immorality, or social disorganization as the present ills that are to be redressed in the eschaton.

(2) *What is the level of participation of the historic Church in the last age?* For Schaff and Nevin, the Church is the main eschatological instrumentality. Through the Church, God will bring in the eschaton. There is no participation of individuals in the eschaton apart from the Church. Mercersburg theology is distinguishable from personalistic views of the eschaton and from views that see all churchly bodies as apostate. It is no less distinguishable from a Hegelianism that is vague about individuals' participation in the final synthesis.

(3) *How is the eschatological age brought about? Do human beings participate in the process?* Both Schaff and Nevin decline to theorize about how efforts to bring about unity in the Church might bring about the eschaton, saying only that at that time unity will prevail, even if human beings have failed to accomplish it before the eschaton. There will be unfortunate setbacks in history, painful disappointments and "diseases," but the overall direction is positive and progressive in accordance with God's divine purpose. Every historic age has its particular diseases, which impede the organic growth of the Church and of history. Vatican I illustrated this for Schaff and Nevin by its decreeing Papal Infallibility to be *de fide*— a disappointment but not an insurmountable obstacle to unity. This stands contrary to views that see human sinfulness and social disorganization as signs of the impending eschaton, if not precipitating factors of it.

(4) *How is failure or delay of the Parousia rationalized?* In a sense, the Church is needed because the Parousia is not yet. God is ever with the Church, incarnate in it, and unfolding history through it. Because Nevin and Schaff could not possibly have set a date for the eschaton, no rationalizations of its non-arrival were necessary, as they were with the Millerites' great disappointment. Nor did the Mercersburg theologians need arcane biblical prooftexts for predicting the date or geography of the eschaton. Their eschatology led them rather to work for unity of Christians as history grows and develops under God's divine plan.

(5) *Does history lead to the eschaton or does the eschaton interrupt history?*

For Schaff and Nevin, history leads to the eschaton and the eschaton is the concluding part and fulfillment of history. God is working, fully incarnate in history and does not need or want to employ cataclysmic disruptive interventions to bring about the full purpose and intent of history. In this way, Schaff and Nevin stand in direct opposition to eschatologies that see God's condemnation of a history that is evil and that will be replaced by cosmic intervention. However, in contrast to Hegel, Schaff does not think that the agency of historical development is entirely immanent. God transcends history. Supernaturalism is a key element in Schaff's and Nevin's view of God's revelation in history.

Contribution of Mercersburg Eschatology to the Contemporary Discussion

What, then, is the worth of Nevin's and Schaff's thought on the future for contemporary discussions of eschatology and the Second Coming? Although the Mercersburg theology in its day succeeded only in establishing a theological direction and liturgy for a small denomination (and was not even completely successful in doing that), it does have some far-reaching implications that are only now beginning to be appreciated by mainstream Protestantism. What follows is a list of possible starting points for using Nevin and Schaff's ideas in contemporary discussions about eschatology:

(1) *The idea of progress.* In what circumstances can the myth of progress be considered intellectually respectable in the late twentieth century? Are all linear views of history untenable, given the holocausts? Are all futures bleak? Or, can there be a Christian interpretation of the massive horrors of the twentieth century in the same vein as Schaff's interpretation of the American Civil War? In Nevin and Schaff's future, there is no destruction, no fear, no alienation (an affirmation few twentieth-century observers would dare to make). If the Mercersburg optimism is to be recovered, the question of God's intent in a world filled with massive suffering and injustice must be resolved. Otherwise belief in progress is a cruel hoax.

(2) *The idea of corrections in history's progress.* Clearly, the twentieth century has put to rest all simplistic linear views of history that see one positive development endlessly following another until

the Second Coming. But the Mercersburg theologians, while holding to the idea of development, taught that as history advances, the diseases of history correspondingly worsen. Can some shred of belief in progress be salvaged by contending that the diseases of our century are more severe than deemed imaginable in Schaff and Nevin's time? Some hope may be warranted from the fact that racism, sexism, nuclear madness, holocausts, and massive hunger are seen as disease by conservatives and liberals alike. Is it possible to argue that God is at work even through these diseases? Prevailing opinion today is negative and fearful about the future, but the teachings of Schaff and Nevin reveal that one can discern God's hand at work in real events of history even in our own dark age.

(3) *The idea of historical continuity with the eschaton*. As noted above, Schaff and Nevin's eschatology contradicts any eschatology that sees the Second Coming as an interruption of history. Those who have predicted such an interruption have not been proven right so far. Schaff and Nevin saw God at work in "real" history, that is, in events that actually occurred, not those described in grand schemes, such as "dispensations." Contemporary discussions about eschatology, if they are to prove worthwhile, must do the same. If we are to discern the broad sweep of history we must do so by studying the actual detailed events of history, not by supposing that the detailed events can be predicted by theories about the broad sweep of history.

(4) *The idea of the Church as the embodiment of God for the present age*. A wide range of ecclesiologies are presently being discussed in theological circles. Is the Church an organization that is necessary because of the failed Parousia, or is it the organization through which the Parousia will be brought about, or again, is it a corrupt instrument that must be destroyed by the Parousia? While those alienated from the Church must find the high view of the Church taken by Nevin and Schaff difficult to accept, the idea of God as immanent within the Church continues to have support among some Protestants as well as Catholics. The Church as the Body of Christ has a human and a divine aspect, and thus is susceptible to disease as is history itself.

(5) *The idea of Church union as a theologically desirable outcome rather than simply an administrative convenience*. What, one wonders, would be the result if all the present discussions of Church union and

ecumenical cooperation were conducted with eschatological expectations about the results?

(6) *The idea of subjectivism without personalism*. The Mercersburg theologians were interested not in "my" future but in "our" future as the Church[24]. The logic of proof about which future will obtain does not apply to them; central to their thought about the eschaton is, rather, the logic of discovery, of discernment about how the future unfolds according to God's plan.

(7) *The idea of love and working toward unity as an appropriate interim ethic*. Above all else, Schaff and Nevin were irenic in an age when hostility among religious groups was widespread. We would do well to exhibit their irenic spirit.

Notes

1   Robert T. Handy, *A History of the Churches in the United States and Canada* (New York: Oxford University Press, 1977), 206.

2   Syndey Ahlstrom, *A Religious History of the American People* (New Haven: Yale University Press, 1972), 616.

3   Ibid.,616–19.

4   John W. Nevin, *Antichrist, or the Spirit of Sect and Schism* (New York: John S. Taylor, 1848).

5   Klaus Penzel in John Deschner et al., eds., *Our Common History as Christians, Essays in Honor of Albert C. Outler* (New York: Oxford Press, 1975), 217–60.

6   Philip Schaff, *America, A Sketch of the Political, Social, and Religious Character* (New York: C. Scribner, 1855), 191.

7   Ibid., 289.

8   Ibid., 250.

9   Philip Schaff, *What is Church History?* (Philadelphia: J. B. Lippincott and Co., 1846), 98.

10   Philip Schaff, *The Principle of Protestantism* (Chambersburg, Penn.: Publication Office of the German Reformed Church, 1845), 48.

11   Ibid., 113.

12   Ibid., 145–46.

13   Ibid., 121.

14   As translated in William A. Clebsch, "Christian Interpretations of the Civil War," *Church History* 30, no. 2 (June 1961): 219.

15   Ibid., 220.

16   Ibid.

17   John Nevin, *The Mystical Presence* (Philadelphia: S. R. Fischer Co., 1867), 202.

18   John W. Nevin, *The Church* (Chambersburg, Penn.: Publication Office of the German Reformed Church, 1847), 2.

19   Ibid., 12.

20   Ibid.

21   Nevin, *Mystical Presence,* 177.

22   John W. Nevin, "The Anglican Crisis," *Mercersburg Review* 3 (1851): 393.

23   Carl Braaten, in *Christian Theology: An Introduction to Its Traditions and Tasks*, ed. Peter C. Hodgson and Robert H. King (Philadelphia: Fortress Press, 1982), 278.

24   Compare Dr. Stendahl's Exposition, pp. 211–220.—Ed.

Mormon Millennium
GERALD E. JONES

And because of the righteousness of his people, Satan has no power;
wherefore, he cannot be loosed for the space of many years; for he hath no
power over the hearts of the people, for they dwell in righteousness, and the
Holy One of Israel reigneth.
BOOK OF MORMON

The Church of Jesus Christ of Latter-day Saints proclaims in its
name its eschatological thrust. Known for the first four years of
its existence as the Church of Christ, by revelation it received its
full name on April 26, 1838.[1] This emphasis on the "latter day"
expressed the belief that Christ was to return to the earth during
the last "fullness of times" dispensation. Now toward the end of
the twentieth century, there is still a strong concern for traditional
Mormon eschatology, but a lot has happened in the last century
and a half to deepen the understanding of this aspect of Mormon
teaching in the light of its historical development in Mormon
thought.

The Bible and Latter-day Saint Eschatology

In the current official publication of doctrinal teachings for new
members of the church, biblical prophecies are treated in four
separate chapters: Signs of the Second Coming; The Gathering of
the House of Israel; The Second Coming of Christ; and The Millennium.[2] The biblical references to the signs of the Second Coming,
the Latter-days, begin with Daniel 12:1 prophesying that there will
"be a time of trouble." Matthew 24:6–7 follows with its description
of earthquakes, disease, famines, and "wars and rumors of wars."
These fearful predictions have always had a strong impact on
Latter-day Saints. The Church's welfare program, which urges all
families to have one year's supply of emergency food, fuel,
clothing, and cash to prepare for such calamities that may come in

the latter days, exemplifies the seriousness with which these predictions are taken.

Not all, however, is negative. The description of "another angel flying in the midst of heaven, having the everlasting gospel to preach unto them that dwell on the earth" (Rev. 14:6–7) is interpreted as promising the restoration of the True Church and Gospel by way of the angel Moroni delivering the Book of Mormon to Joseph Smith in 1827.[3] Those who accept this and join the Church may participate in the glorious work of the Kingdom of God in the last days.

Ezekiel also prophesies the coming forth of the Book of Mormon and the gospel in the latter days (Ezek. 37:16–20). Here the Book of Mormon is represented as the stick of Joseph to be put alongside of the Bible, the stick of Judah. Isaiah 29 is frequently used to support the same concept with the "sealed book" coming forth "out of the dust" and being delivered to Joseph Smith, an "unlearned man" who then begins the "marvelous work and a wonder" and causes the eyes of the blind to see and the ears of the deaf to hear in the day when Lebanon shall be turned into a fruitful field again after Solomon's destruction of the forests for his building projects in ancient Israel.

The missionary efforts of the Church in the latter days receive impetus from Matthew 24:14: "the gospel of the kingdom shall be preached in all the world." The Mormons feel they are accomplishing this goal by having about thirty-thousand missionaries in the field at any given time. Spencer W. Kimball, the current prophet of the Church, has emphasized this effort to fulfill the prophecy. As a consequence of the revelation given in 1978, granting the priesthood to all worthy males regardless of race, the work has expanded rapidly in Africa. It has been said that the concern to fulfill Matthew 24:14 was a direct cause of prayerful concern about the issue of priesthood to the Blacks. This recent revelation solved a problem. Efforts at translating the Scriptures and worldwide broadcasts of Church messages further help to fulfill the injunction to spread the Word.[4]

Other important aspects of Latter-day Saint theology are the temple ordinances of baptism and marriage in behalf of the dead. Malachi 4:5–6 is quoted to support this doctrine and a prophecy concerning the latter days. Elijah is to return and turn the hearts of the children to their parents and the hearts of the parents are to turn to their children. The sealing of family members together in the temple is a primary goal of the extensive research into one's ancestors and deceased relatives.[5]

Gospel Principles, the Church's doctrinal handbook, explains how Mormons should view the signs of the latter days:

No one except our Heavenly Father knows exactly when the Lord will come (see Matt. 24:36). However, we can tell that the end is near because many of the signs are already being fulfilled. The Savior taught this with the parable of the fig tree. He said that when we see the fig tree putting forth leaves, we can tell that summer will soon come. Likewise, when we see the signs, we can know that his coming is near at hand (Matt. 24:32–33).

The Lord gave us these signs to help us. We can put our lives in order and prepare ourselves and our families for those things yet to come. We do not need to worry about the calamities, but can look forward to the coming of the Savior and be glad. The Lord said, "Be not troubled, for, when all these things shall come to pass, ye may know that the promises which have been made unto you shall be fulfilled" (See *D&C* 45:35). He goes on to say that those who are righteous when he comes will not be destroyed, "but shall abide the day, and the earth shall be given them for an inheritance . . . and their children shall grow up without sin . . . for the Lord shall be in their midst, and his glory shall be upon them, and he will be their king and their lawgiver. (*D&C* 45:57–59)[6]

The gathering of the House of Israel is related to the missionary activity of the Church of Jesus Christ of Latter-day Saints. One of the two ways this doctrine is taught in the Church is that the gathering of scattered Israel into the Church is accomplished by proselytizing. This refers to the view that most Mormons are descendants of Joseph, son of Jacob/Israel. It is assumed that many of Joseph's sons, Ephraim's descendants, were scattered among the tribes of Europe as they went north with the captured ten tribes who then became lost to the Kingdom of Judah. Jeremiah 16:14–15 as well as Jeremiah 23:3 are cited to validate this doctrine. These are interpreted as bringing the Jews back together into the promised land of Israel or as gathering the "sheep that know the shepherds voice" into the Church from the scattered tribe of Joseph. Both groups are destined to inherit the land promised to their forefathers: For the Jews, Israel, and for the Mormons, the Americas—the land over the water (Gen. 49:22), the land of the everlasting hills (Gen. 49:26). The Latter-day Saints interpret these prophecies as referring to the Andes and Rocky Mountains.[7]

Mormons anticipated the Second Coming of Christ in a special way. They believe that the Second Coming will happen in three stages. In fact the first already occurred when he appeared to the Prophet Joseph Smith in the Sacred Grove theophany, and later to Joseph Smith and Oliver Cowdery in the Kirtland temple. It is also believed that he has appeared to others such as Lorenzo Snow in the Salt Lake City Temple. In short, he has come "as a thief in the night" to the Saints, unknown to the rest of the world.[8]

His second appearance will be to the Jews in the latter days when they are besieged in Jerusalem. Coming to the Mount of Olives, it will split in two, and, by using heavenly armies, God will deliver the Jewish people from destruction by enemy forces. Zechariah 14:1–4 and 12:1–14 are cited in support of this event.

Finally he will come in glory to all the world to usher in the millennial reign of peace and the restoration of the earth to the paradisiacal glory of the Garden of Eden. It will be a terrestrial state, preparatory to the coming of the celestial kingdom at the resurrection of the earth.

The Saints do not profess to know the time frame for these events. Neither do they claim to know how long a time span will separate the various stages of the Second Coming of Christ. But the fact that Christ has begun the process by appearing to Joseph Smith and others in the Church has greatly enhanced the Saints' awareness and anticipation of the future chain of events.

The ushering in of the millennial reign is described in 1 Thessalonians 4:16–17. "For the Lord himself shall descend from heaven with a shout, with the voice of the archangel, and with the trump of God; and the dead in Christ shall rise first; then we which are alive and remain shall be caught up together with them in the clouds, to meet the Lord in the air; and so shall we ever be with the Lord." Most Mormon commentators assume that the righteous dead will be resurrected at this time, while the wicked are to remain in the graves until the end of the Millennium, when they too will be caught up in the clouds to be resurrected. The mortals still living on the earth will be separated into two classes, the wicked and the righteous. The wicked are to be burned at his coming (2 Thess. 2:8) and await their resurrection at the close of the Millennium. The righteous, though, are to be transported heavenward to meet Christ. Afterwards they will dwell on earth under the following conditions:

1 There will be no physical pain or suffering.

2 There will be peace on earth between all living creatures (Isa. 11:6–9).

3 There will be children born on the earth during the Millennium.

4 All will live to the age of a tree, about 100 years (Isa. 65:20).

5 Genealogical research and temple work will be continued.

6 There will be no temptations by the devil.

7 Vegetarianism will be practiced by all creatures since there is to be no death or pain.

8 Missionary work will continue, for not all will yet be members of the True Church.

9 All will speak the same language (Zeph. 3:9).

10 Everyday life will be essentially the same (farming, houses, work, etc.) (Isa. 65:21–23).

After the Millennium of peace, the devil will be loosed for a short time and then cast out forever. The earth itself will then be resurrected, changed into a celestial orb. Joseph Smith revealed that it will be the "sea of glass" spoken of by the writer of the Apocalypse (Rev. 4:6).[9] Only those worthy of the celestial kingdom will dwell upon the earth. Although the others had been allowed to remain on earth during the Millenium, they will now have to leave and will inhabit another planet prepared for them. Only those in the "celestialized" world will be able to enjoy the presence of the Father. Those in the terrestrial kingdom will nevertheless behold the Son of God. The heaven most Christians expect is what the terrestrial kingdom will be according to the *Doctrine and Covenants,* section 76. Only those worthy to live on this earth may become like God, eternally married and capable of producing spirit offspring to inhabit future earths created by these "celestialized" children of God. The end of this world, therefore, is to be the "home for Gods" who enjoy everlasting progress and increase of dominion. In short, the end and glory of both mankind and earth and all that pertains to its paradisiacal state will be jointly inherited and shared together, each in its own sphere of existence.

The Eschatology of the Book of Mormon

The first scripture presented to the world by Joseph Smith was the *Book of Mormon*. It was believed to be a scripture given to prophets in the American continent as had the Bible been given to prophets in the land of Israel. The Book, originally written on gold plates, had been translated by Joseph Smith with divine aid and presented to the world to promote better understanding of Christ and his mission on earth.[10]

Included in the *Book of Mormon* are historical accounts of families and groups who struggled for survival and against disputes with the government. It repeats and expands the teachings of Christ found in the New Testament. The book of Third Nephi is treated by many Mormons as the Fifth Gospel. There are surprisingly few references, however, to the Second Coming of Christ and the Millennium. The only description simply repeats Malachi 3 and 4, and the only other reference recounts signs preceding the Coming such as wars, rumors of wars, famines, apostasy, false churches, and a general state of wickedness and pride, but no specific detail on the Coming of the Lord or of the Millennium is found in Mormon 8:26–32. The Millennium is alluded to only once in the *Book of Mormon* (1 Nephi 22:26), where it is stated that Satan will be bound by the righteousness of the people and the devil will not be loosed for many years. (See also 2 Nephi 30:18).

The Eschatology of The Doctrine and Covenants

In *The Doctrine and Covenants* we learn much more about Mormon eschatology. This collection of revelations given to Joseph Smith and his successors develops the concepts of the Second Coming of Christ and the Millennium in great detail. The theophany of Joseph Smith in the spring of 1820 informed him that he was not to join a church but was to await further instructions for his own mission to establish the work of God. No mention is made of the latter-day return of Christ or of the impending Millennium. The main principles established are the nature of the Godhead and that the heavens are open to revelation from divine beings. It was not until Joseph Smith's second attempt to receive divine guidance that the angel Moroni appeared to him in his bedroom and gave him extensive biblical references. The first revelation recorded in *The Doctrine and Covenants* was of this angelic visitation on September 21, 1823:

Behold, I will reveal unto you the Priesthood, by the hand of Elijah the prophet, before the coming of the great and dreadful day of the Lord. And he shall plant in the hearts of the children the promises made to the fathers, and the hearts of the children shall turn to their fathers. If it were not so, the whole earth would be utterly wasted at his coming (*D&C* 2:1–3).

In this passage is embodied much of the eschatological emphasis of the Latter-day Saints. Elijah returned to the Kirtland temple on April 3, 1836 along with a number of other heavenly visitors including Moses. The "keys" of the Kingdom of God in its various aspects—including that of missionary work, genealogical and temple work, and the return of Israel—were restored. All of this is in preparation for the coming of the Lord which is described as "great and dreadful."

The third section of *The Doctrine and Covenants* begins with the promise that "the works, and the designs, and the purposes of God cannot be frustrated, neither can they come to naught." In fact "it is not the work of God that is frustrated but the work of men." This implies that God's program is unfolding and it is up to the Saints to be participants in a winning activity. This optimistic view is furthered in the fourth section, which begins with the proclamation that "a marvelous work is about to come forth among the children of men. . .for behold the field is white already to harvest." This same concept is repeated in sections 6, 11, 12, and 14 given between April and June of 1829. By August 1830 the Lord had informed Joseph Smith that it is he to "whom I have committed the keys of my kingdom, and a dispensation of the gospel for the last times, and for the fullness of times, in the which I will gather together in one all things, both which are in heaven, and which are on earth" (*D&C* 27:13). This was to "lift up your hearts and rejoice; that ye may be able to withstand the evil day" (*D&C* 27:15). The positive aspect predominates. Furthermore there is no sense of urgency, despite the imminence of the Lord's coming. Yet for the blessing of the missionary and the benefit to the recipient of the missionary's message haste is urged.

In *D&C* 29 (September 26, 1830) we read the encouraging words: "when the Lord will gather his people even as a hen gathereth her chickens under her wings are ye chosen out of the world to declare my gospel with the sound of rejoicing . . . it is his good will to give you the kingdom." It is also here that the dangers are first clearly introduced in Mormon scripture:

> For the hour is nigh and the day soon at hand when the earth is ripe; and all the proud and they that do wickedly shall be as stubble, and I will burn them up, saith the Lord of Hosts, that wickedness shall not be upon the earth. For the hour is nigh, and that which was spoken by mine apostles must be fulfilled; for as they spoke so shall it come to pass; For I will reveal myself from heaven with power and great glory, with all the hosts thereof, and dwell in righteousness with men on earth a thousand years, and the wicked shall not stand (D&C 29:9–11).

Many of the traditional warnings follow: signs in heaven with the sun and the moon darkened and turned to blood, pestilence, and disease. In D&C 45, fifty-five verses are devoted to events of the latter days, the Second Coming and the Millennium. Given March 7, 1831, we read a distillation of earlier scattered hints and details of the latter days. Responding to ideas promulgated by the Shakers, Joseph Smith reported that "the Son of Man cometh not in the form of a woman." Nor did anyone know when he was coming; nor would they know until he came.

More encouragement follows: "He that endureth in faith and doeth my will, the same shall overcome, and shall receive an inheritance upon the earth when the day of transfiguration shall come" (D&C 63:20). Those who die before the Second Coming are promised that "when the Lord shall come, and old things pass away and all things become new, they shall rise from the dead and shall not die after and shall receive an inheritance before the Lord, in the holy city" (D&C 63:49). In this same section is the promise that no one is to die prematurely and that death is to be a sudden change from mortality to immortality. Although the date of the Second Coming is not known, we must observe the signs of the times. Sections 64 and 65 also refer to the Second Coming.

With section 76, given on February 16, 1832, Mormon eschatology took a giant leap. Here is revealed more information about man's ultimate destiny than is to be found in any other revelation given to a latter-day prophet. The basis for this revelation was 1 Corinthians 15:4–42. One hundred verses are devoted to the subject, but no further information has been given since.

Following the above description of life after death in the resurrected state, Joseph Smith inquired of the Lord concerning some difficult passages in the Book of Revelation. The Lord gives answers pertaining to the resurrected earth as the sea of glass of Revelation 4:6, the resurrection of animals, and the seven seals and angels who open the millennial dispensations. Then in section 88 (December 27, 1832) a recounting of calamitous events preceding the Millennium is given in some detail. It is not until March 27, 1836 that we have any significant reference to the Second Coming and events surrounding it (*D&C* 109:73–79).

One of the closing sections of *The Doctrine and Covenants* (130) teaches that the earth will be resurrected in an immortal crystal state and be a huge Urim and Thummim to those who dwell upon it. It also states that the Second Coming will be no sooner than 1890.

The last section added to *The Doctrine and Covenants* was given on October 3, 1918 to President Joseph F. Smith and deals with the activities of people after death while awaiting the Resurrection in the spirit world. Spirits are organized according to their individual capacities and responsibilities. Missionary work is done among those not yet converted to Christ or his Gospel. Opportunity is to be provided for them in the spirit world so that they may attain greater everlasting glory.

Later Developments

Since the doctrine of the Second Coming, the Millennium, and Resurrection were formulated in *The Doctrine and Covenants,* much discussion has ensued. Grant Underwood has done an extensive study of the development of the doctrine as discussed in published speeches.[11] Underwood's study points out the change in views on who would live on the earth during the Millennium. At first early leaders such as Edward Partridge and Sidney Rigdon believed that only the righteous Saints (members of the Church) would remain on earth; all others would be destroyed. Parley P. Pratt and W. W. Phelps expressed poetically the view that blissful rest would ensue. Later developed the notion that work would be done, mainly missionary and temple work, but regular labors would also be undertaken. The idea that Satan is to be bound during the peace period comes to be interpreted thus: The righteous would resist the temptations of Lucifer; in this sense he would be bound. Likewise the notion that government of the Millennium was to be left with Christ reigning during the primary years was modified: "Mortals, both members of the Church and nonmembers, will hold government positions. They will receive help from resurrected beings."[12] A review of the presidents of the Church from Brigham Young to Spencer W. Kimball reveals the scope of comments on the subject. There is a feeling that the righteousness of the people will bring about the Millennium.

Discussion of eschatology diminished dramatically after Wilford Woodruff (1889–1898). David O. McKay (1951–1970) did not change this general trend but Joseph Fielding Smith, his successor (1970–1972) had more published material about the Second Coming of Christ and the Millennium than all other presidents of the Church combined. He believed strongly that we were in the Last Days and that the Second Coming was near (although with an unknown date). He interpreted biblical references to it literally. When asked about the literalness of the burning of the wicked and fire covering the earth, he replied that it was to be just as real as the flood in the days of Noah, which he interpreted no less literally.[13]

The current president of the Church, Spencer W. Kimball (1973–), has not spoken much on the subject, but one of his comments is very similar to Brigham Young's, that man's righteous living may usher in the Millennium. For instance, a certain kind of "family life could bring us back toward the translation experience of righteous Enoch. The Millennium would be ushered in."[14]

Notes

1   *The Doctrine and Covenants of the Church of Jesus Christ of Latter-day Saints* (Salt Lake City: The Church of Jesus Christ of Latter-day Saints, 1981), sec. 115:3–4. Hereafter *D&C*.

2   *Gospel Principles* (Salt Lake City: Deseret Book Co., 1978), vi–362.

3   Ibid., 257. See also Joseph Fielding Smith, *The Restoration of All Things* (Salt Lake City: Deseret Book Co., 1964).

4   Edward L. Kimball, ed., *The Teachings of Spencer W. Kimball* (Salt Lake City: Bookcraft, 1982), 544–93.

5   *Gospel Principles,* 221–54.

6   Ibid., 258–59.

7   Smith, 143–46.

8   Gerald N. Lund, *The Coming of the Lord* (Salt Lake City: Bookcraft, 1971), 13–33. See also Bruce R. McConkie, *Mormon Doctrine* (Salt Lake City: Bookcraft, 1966), 687–98.

9   *D&C* 130:7–9, 77:1.

10 James B. Allen and Glen M. Leonard, *The Story of the Latter-day Saints* (Salt Lake City: Deseret Book Co., 1976), 35–46. Also Leonard J. Arrington and Davis Bitton, *The Mormon Experience* (New York: Alfred A. Knopf, 1979), 8–16.

11 Grant Underwood, "Seminal versus Sesquicentennial Saints: A Look at Mormon Millennialism," *Dialogue: A Journal of Mormon Thought* 14 (Spring 1981): 32–44.

12 *Gospel Principles,* 273.

13 Daniel H. Ludlow, *Latter-day Prophets Speak* (Salt Lake City: Bookcraft, 1948), 241–57.

14 Joseph Fielding Smith, *The Signs of the Times* (Salt Lake City: Deseret Book Co., 1970), 41.

5 | The End of Time in Kermode and Derrida
WESLEY A. KORT

To some extent it can and must be argued that we have fallen into the condition of viewing all things as texts, and even the "thing" itself is textual.
GEOFFREY HARTMAN, *Saving the Text*

Eschatology plays an important role in the work of two recent, major literary theorists, Frank Kermode and Jacques Derrida. Kermode fashions his narrative theory in relation to endings, while writing and texts in the work of Derrida have eschatological implications. These eschatological interests are well worth exploring for their own sake, their wide impact on literary theory and criticism, and their theological implications.

I

Frank Kermode's literary interests center on writings from those decades that immediately precede and follow the turn of the century. This period brought enormous changes to Western culture. Two of the most significant events of the period were the First World War and the rapid urbanization of society; the literature of the time is deeply involved with the traumas, changes, and endings of this period. Marks of this writing, in addition to an explicit interest in the cultural consequences of urbanization and the war, include preoccupation with the question of human temporality and obscurity in style, form, and concepts.

Kermode, in *The Sense of an Ending* and *The Genesis of Secrecy*, has dealt with these salient characteristics of the literature.[1] What is interesting is that in both of these studies he turns to the New Testament and to biblical scholarship for help in understanding the nature of fictional narrative. The reason for his turning to the

New Testament is that writing in this period, especially its preoccupation with time, reveals an intense interest in endings; indeed,
many characteristics of New Testament apocalypticism can be
found in these texts. The contrary relation of these texts to their
surrounding culture and the hermeneutical difficulties they present to the reader give them a somewhat occult and even scrip-
tural quality. Kermode is able, in this comparison between both
the sense of time and the strategies of withholding meaning
characteristic of New Testament texts and the concern with temporality and with textuality in modern fiction, to present some
interesting theories concerning the importance of eschatology for
narrative texts.

Kermode's principal point in *The Sense of an Ending* is that
eschatological interests arise from the human need for temporal
concords. The more that people find their culture to be tor-
mented, fragmented, and uncertain, the greater will be their need
to discover or affirm temporal wholeness. Endings provide this
wholeness. Even when ending is construed as catastrophic, it still
grants time a telos, and events, however arbitrary and pointless
they otherwise may be, can be seen as leading to, or appropriate
for, the approach of an ending.

Kermode accounts for our interest in narrative along these
lines as well. We hear and read narratives gladly because in them
we find time ordered in relation to an ending. The wholeness of
time in narrative is a welcome relief from the sense of time which
we otherwise might have, of time as unordered, merely successive, and unrelated to human interests and needs.

What occurs in the telling or hearing of a story also marks
the way in which we understand the time in which we are living.
We make some kind of narrative out of it, and we do this
primarily by postulating an ending. People have always done
this, and we continue, no matter what our relation to religion
may be, to do the same thing. While some imagine utopian
endings, we typically have in mind endings for our culture that
are dystopic. All the notions we have about the time in which we
are living—that it is transitional, unprecedented, fraught with
danger, awaited for centuries, or headed toward some goal—are
products of fiction-making propensities aroused by our sense
that time may (or does) have no meaning or direction at all.

The *Genesis of Secrecy,* which is primarily a study of the
Gospel of Mark, takes up the problem of those aspects of texts

that resist the concord-producing effects of narrative. If it is true that the purpose of a narrative is to create a sense of wholeness and movement toward completion, why is it that narratives such as the Gospel of Mark or Joyce's *Ulysses* have details that are not tucked into the overall design? The young man who flees naked from the garden in Mark and the man in the macintosh in *Ulysses* are examples of unintegrated detail. Why are these and other such concord-resisting elements found in narrative? The answer is that along with our need for wholeness and direction in time is our recognition, as well, that the meaning of time eludes us. Such narrative texts, then, take to themselves a kind of secrecy or manifoldness which make them endlessly fascinating and tax the resourcefulness of their readers' interpretative skills. For, we should add, the puzzling, unintegrated details of a narrative text are generally taken to be the most important, as having special, hidden meaning. And so it is that the fleeing young man in the garden has often been taken to be Mark himself.

What Kermode has given us in these two books, then, is a theory of narrative texts which is oriented toward the ending of time. It accounts both for the preoccupation with telos in narrative engagement and in our sense of time and for those aspects of our stories and sense of time that we allow to retain anti-concord effects. Our sense of time has both certainty and uncertainty, is both ordered and unintegrated, and is both meaningful and qualified by indeterminate meanings; but basic to time's human qualities is its dependence upon ending.

II

Jacques Derrida's theories have far more to do with texts and writing than with a particular kind of discourse such as narrative. Alert to the psychological and ideological causes and consequences of privilege, Derrida is attentive to the investment we have in thinking of speech as prior to and more important than writing. We tend to posit a series—thought, language, speech, and writing—that is not only chronologically linear but also evaluatively diminishing. Writing is generally taken to indicate descent—speech incarcerated in script. The process of interpretation is a freeing of the soul of meaning, of the original thought, from the prison of its textual body. The philosophical roots of this habit of thought are, of course, Platonist.

We have so much invested in this preferential positioning of speech in relation to writing because of the authority that it may grant. We recognize the cultural/historical relativity of texts. A text can be related to a time, person, purpose, or function. In the world of texts there is no center, although some texts may claim centrality. But the conflicting claims cancel one another. In order to avoid this relativity and uncertainty, we want to think of ourselves or our culture in non-textual terms. We want centrality. While we recognize that we do not live in a geocentric world, we do not have an understanding of our cultural/historical position which resembles our sense of position astronomically.

We want the sense, then, of standing in some non-textual place, some grounding in reality by which we, in our certainty and centrality, can view the relativity and peripherality of texts. The fact of the matter, according to Derrida, is that such grounding is illusory and, in both psychological and ideological ways, repressive.

It is helpful for an understanding of Derrida's assessment of the status of writing to see it in relation to the more familiar philosophical problem of time, especially the question of the relation of past and future to present time. One of our reasons for preferring speech to writing is our preference for present time, which seems real when compared to the other temporal categories. Past time no longer exists, and future time is yet to come. Texts are easily associated with past and future time, for they record what has occurred and predict or prescribe what will or should occur in the future. Consequently, present time and nontextuality, or speech, are closely tied, and to prefer one is to prefer the other. But we are also aware that while present time appears to be real it is also highly elusive. When we speak of it, it is already past. It can be argued, then, that we cannot refer to present time, and that the stress on present time reveals a longing for the end of time. Temporal movement is the exchange of the future for the past. The common "reality," then, to which we refer is the future and the past. Actually, it is textual, even when we refer to it as present time. We refer to the present only in anticipation and memory. Rather than windows looking out onto reality, discourses, whether written or spoken, have a textual quality because they bear the traces of present time or reality. We cannot look through discourse to reality but can infer a reality, which does not yet or no longer exists, from discourse.

A helpful illustration of this point may be derived from the field of high-energy nuclear physics. Accelerators can smash atoms against an obstacle at fantastic speeds, but the process and collision themselves cannot be directly observed. What physicists study are not the events but the tracks of the particles marked and mapped by computer printouts. The present, the shattering of the atom into particles, is inferred from the text; the actual event is long since past and non-existent.

This situation is generally true of our discourse. It refers to what no longer exists and bears the traces of presence and a present now gone. Even speaking itself must become a past event—I must wait until a person has finished speaking in order to know what has been said—before I can refer or respond to it. It is this dimension of discourse—referability—that is at stake in the elevation of writing. We learn about and discuss the world to large degree in its absence. And texts about reality, whether they are scientific studies or philosophical treatises about ontology, refer to texts.

Reversing the hierarchy speech/writing is a strategy on Derrida's part. It is not that, in the long run, he would deny the importance of speech and its relation to present time. But the strategy of reversing privileged relationships or of making the peripheral central is a way of showing that assumptions about authority and finality are inherently at stake. The object of reversing privilege or of decentering is not to create a new privilege or new center, but to reveal that there is no ultimate ground or center. Rather than deny present time and the importance of speech, Derrida calls for a larger view of writing, one which includes speech: "We might speak, as Derrida does of an *archi-écriture,* an archi-writing or proto-writing, which is the condition of both speech and writing in the narrow sense."[2]

It is mistaken to infer, as Gerald Graff does, that for Derrida there is no reality apart from language and that language refers only to itself. While Graff correctly observes that reality "is *always already* interpreted, *already* constructed, *already* constituted by the mythological models, paradigms, sign-systems, conventions, epistemes through which it is given us,"[3] it does not follow that discourse has no relation to reality whatsoever. Although we always know about reality in its absence, we do not therefore lack knowledge of it altogether. Traces are traces of something; absence is the absence of something. This something is so important that we tend to forget how it is that we come to refer to it, how we refer to it when it has already slipped from our hands.

Humanity is marked by a thirst for reality, for a grounding, a center, and a certainty granted by the cessation of time, but humanity is also marked by an inability to have that for which it thirsts. It has only a version, and that version ought not to be mistaken for that which it represents. On the other hand, we cannot do without a sense of the center and of reality. But the center and a sense of reality are merely functional, although their function, says Derrida, "is absolutely indispensable."[4]

We find ourselves, according to this view, in a world constituted by texts. Particular texts—books and essays—are only small parts of this larger textuality in which we live: "The book is not the world," says Derrida, "but the world is in the book."[5] A relation always exists, thus, both between any text and the large textual world of which it is a part and between a text and the textual world of its reader. "To some extent it can and must be argued that we have fallen into the condition of viewing all things as texts, and even the 'thing' itself is textual."[6]

III

For Kermode and Derrida, eschatology arises from our involvement in narrative and in text. For Kermode we need a sense of ending because we are always giving a narrative wholeness to our time; indeed, the more events and experiences seem to defy narrative integration the more we will draw on our resourcefulness to impute to them possible meanings of a most ingenious sort. For Derrida, our putative position apart from texts is really an attempt to transcend time, to be apart from time as the passage of the future into the past. It can also be said that for Derrida (although I do not know of any discussion by him of this point) the future as expectation, plan, or prediction, is textual. The passage from future into past, then, is an exchange of one kind of text for another.

An important ingredient in Kermode's theory is the optional position in which we find ourselves in relation to the meaning and order of time. We all need narratives, and we will produce them for ourselves if they are not provided for us by others. Furthermore, it makes a great deal of difference what kind of narrative we live in. If we live in narratives that are divisive and destructive, we will be compelled by them to exploit divisive and destructive potentials in our experience. A person or a people need not live in such stories, however. Stories are optional and exchangeable. However difficult the move from one story to another may be, it is often well worth the price.

Although he does not use this example, Kermode's treatment of culture and narrative is similar to the status of narrative in psychotherapeutic situations. As James Hillman, Roy Schafer, and others have pointed out, therapy deals greatly in narrative, in bringing to the surface the story the patient is living out and in attempting to modify that story or even exchange it for another.[7] Kermode has a similar view of cultural story. We need not be committed to a narrative of unmitigated division and enmity between people and to the destruction of our world by the terrible powers that we control or that control us. It is possible to live in a different story, to exchange it for one that is positive, healing and reconciling.

Kermode errs, in his narrative theory, by driving a skeptical wedge too deeply between time as he construes it actually to be, namely, without meaning, and those meanings that we impute to time. While this epistemology is common in our culture (Kermode draws it from Hans Vaihinger, and Vaihinger develops it in his attempt to bring together Hume and Kant), it need not be accepted. But while it is not true that events lack inherent meaning and that meaning is only imputed to them by our minds and imaginations, it is also not true that there is no room for variation in the interpretation of events. Surely the line between intransigent and optional meaning is not easily determined, but we seem unduly committed to, even identified with, cultural stories with very unfortunate endings. The eschatological significance of Kermode's literary theory is that we can renege on those commitments and be free from those identifications.

We find in Derrida's theory the arresting point that we posit a present time for ourselves, an ending of time, for the sake of ideological and psychological repression. This apocalyptic move denies our temporality and confers upon us a finality of meaning and authority.[8] If we recognize time as textual and if we recognize both the importance of texts to grant us a common world and the relativity of textuality, we shall not ask the world to find its center and ending in us.

If we search around for reasons why we are committed to a narrative of increased enmity and destruction as marking our goal and ending, we will easily find some. One of them is our desire not to have the world continue after we depart from it. A common reaction of people to termination, whether it is a marriage or a job or life itself, is resentment that the other person, the institution, or society will be able to get along without them. Rather than recognize finitude both in the duration and the significance of our lives, we compensate for finitude by making our own existence and the existence of the world co-terminous. The pride of Western societies is such that the termination of our culture's hegemony and the continuation of the human enterprise are incompatible notions. Better, Samson-like, to bring the whole down on our heads than to recognize the finitude of our cultural duration and significance. The problem is that we have the power, now, to accomplish this. We need not suffer the humiliation of contemplating a world continuing without us. We can save ourselves that sense of replaceability. We are, then, deeply committed to a self-serving story. The question is how we are to deal with ideological and psychological repression of this magnitude and force.

Another point to be derived from Kermode and Derrida is that narrative texts grant us a common world. We generally think of this as the past. H. Richard Niebuhr and others have pointed out that a people has its identity and becomes a community in terms of the story of its own inner life. To become an American, for example, is to accept the story of the Pilgrims or figures like Washington and Lincoln as your own past.[9] But a common world is granted also by the text of expectation. A community is formed in relation to its common sense of the future.

One of the remarkable characteristics of individuals and communities today is their lack of a common world granted by the text of shared expectations. The shared world in Christian communities is provided far more by the sense of a common past, by tradition, than by a common hope or expectation. But this has not always been the case. For example, today we view those who have already died as somehow behind us, in the past. Traditionally, of course, those who died were viewed as having gone before, as belonging to the future. Death was related to what lies ahead rather than to what lies behind.

It is unfortunate for Christians to lose sight of their common situation within time and of the larger story in which they with other people are involved. For the sake of certainty and authority, the Church has too often identified itself with what Jürgen Moltmann calls the "eternal present."[10] It has done so in order to gather authority and centrality for itself. It has also emphasized the past as the source of its common life at the expense of the future. The immediate tasks of Christian eschatology, therefore, are to call Christians away from the denial of time and of the future. We must be taught once again how to affirm our temporality, the time that we share with so many who have gone before us, who follow, and in whose company we live, and the dependability of the God whose creatures we as temporal beings are. Eschatology allows us always to say, with one of Thomas Mann's narrators, "With Him it is always: 'the best is still to come'; He always gives us something to look forward to."[11]

Notes

1   Frank Kermode, *The Sense of an Ending* (New York: Oxford University Press, 1967), and *The Genesis of Secrecy: On the Interpretation of Narrative* (Cambridge: Harvard University Press, 1979).

2   Jonathan Culler, *On Deconstruction: Theory and Criticism after Structuralism* (Ithaca: Cornell University Press, 1982), 171.

3   Gerald Graff, *Literature Against Itself: Literary Ideas in Modern Society* (Chicago: University of Chicago Press, 1979), 193–94.

4   Jacques Derrida, "Structure, Sign, and Play in the Discourse of the Human Sciences," in *The Language of Criticism and the Sciences of Man: The Structuralist Controversy,* ed. Richard Macksey and Eugenia Donato (Baltimore: Johns Hopkins Press, 1970), 271.

5   Jacques Derrida, *Writing and Difference,* trans. Alan Bass (Chicago: University of Chicago Press, 1978), 76.

6   Geoffrey Hartman, *Saving the Text: Literature/Derrida/Philosophy* (Baltimore: Johns Hopkins Press, 1981), 66.

7   James Hillman, "The Fiction of Case History: A Round," in *Religion As Story,* ed. James B. Wiggins (New York: Harper & Row, 1975), 123–74; and Roy Schafer, "Narrative in the Psychoanalytic Dialogue," *Critical Inquiry* 7, no. 1 (Autumn 1980): esp. 35.

8   Jacques Derrida, "Of an Apocalyptic Tone Recently Adopted in Philosophy," in *Semeia Twenty-Three: Derrida and Biblical Studies,* ed. Robert Detweiler (Chico, Calif.: Scholars Press, 1982), 63–97.

9   H. Richard Niebuhr, *The Meaning of Revelation* (New York: Macmillan, 1962), 43–91.

10. Jürgen Moltmann, *Theology of Hope: On the Ground and the Implications of a Christian Eschatology* (New York: Harper & Row, 1975), 29.

11 Thomas Mann, "Joseph the Provider," in *Joseph and his Brothers,* trans. H. T. Lowe-Porter (New York: Penguin Books, 1978), 1119.

6 | Confusions in Christian Eschatology

GEDDES MacGREGOR

When I was a boy, the thought of Heaven used to frighten me more than the thought of Hell. I pictured Heaven as a place where there would be perpetual Sundays with perpetual services, from which there would be no escape, as the Almighty, assisted by cohorts of angels, would always be on the look-out for those who did not attend. It was a horrible nightmare. . . . My opinion is that we shall be reincarnated.

DAVID LLOYD-GEORGE (British Prime Minister, 1916–1922) as recorded by Lord Riddell.

I

The use of the term "eschatology" to designate doctrine about "last things" (final judgment and the afterlife) is a comparatively recent fashion, first coming into vogue in the English-speaking world not very much more than a hundred years ago. A standard biblical dictionary for scholars, edited by Sir William Smith and published in London in 1893, calls it "the name that has of late become common for doctrine concerning both the future state of the indi-vidual . . . and the end of the world with its accompanying events." The term is derived from New Testament phrases such as "in the last day (*en tē eschatē hēmera*)" (John 6:39) and "the last state" (*ta eschata*) (Matt. 12:45). Since all such notions of this kind to be found in the New Testament have deep roots in ancient Hebrew prophecy, messianic expectation, and apocalyptic literature, we must turn first to that literature before attempting to assess the significance of them as they appear in New Testament and other early Christian writings.

The idea of a final day of reckoning, the "Day of the Lord," seems to have had currency even in pre-exilic Israelite religion, for Amos (Amos. 5:18–20) takes it for granted as part of the conceptual scenario of those whom he is addressing. He assures them that it will not be the day of brightness and light that they commonly expect but, on the contrary, a day of blackness. In this way he uses a popular expectation and hope to dramatize his own prediction of the fall of Israel. As the day on which the Lord would manifest himself fully at last, it would seem indeed a day of bright light; but the prophets warn that it will be, on the contrary, a black day, a day of wrath and destruction, with cosmic convulsions, bringing disaster and desolation. Amos predicts that the sun will set at noon, and the face of the earth will grow dark (Amos 8:9); Isaiah promises that on that day Yahweh will bring low all that is now high. Zephaniah tells of crimes being punished and cries being heard all over Jerusalem. Joel and other prophets repeat and develop such language. The Day of the Lord is to be a day of reckoning, when all injustice will come to light and be punished by the avenging hand of God. Without such punishment of injustice, how should justice be victorious as popular hope expected it to be when God would come at last and make his righteousness prevail? How should the right be enthroned unless the wrong be dethroned?

The New Testament writers take over the customary Hebrew imagery almost unchanged, except that to Jesus Christ is assigned the role of divine Judge. The day of God is one on which the heavens are to be destroyed and a new heaven and earth are to appear (II Pet. 3:12). The writer of the Apocalypse sees a battle pitched between the armies of evil and the angels of God (Rev. 16:14). This great and terrible day comes unannounced, "like a thief" (I Thess. 5:2, 4). All followers of the Christian Way must be prepared for it, and they can count on God's strengthening them for the fray (I Cor. 1:8). The coming of the Lord is also aptly called the *parousia,* the ceremonial visit of a king to a city within his domain. The synoptists talk of signs and wonders that are to precede the event: the very stars in heaven are to behave erratically (Matt. 24:29; Mark 13:24; Luke 21:25, 27) and the coming itself is to be like a flash of lightning (Matt. 24:27; Luke 17:24). Yet no one, not even the Son of Man, knows the hour; hence the need to be ever alert, as for a thief in the night. Various parables attributed to Jesus exhibit this motif: the parable of the talents, for instance. Yet texts abound that show the general expectation among first-century Christians that the Second Coming was imminent (e.g., Matt. 10:23; Luke 21:32; I Peter 4:7). This does not mean that Jesus taught, or was believed to have taught, that the Day of

Judgment would come within a specified period, such as ten or a hundred years; it does mean that one went to sleep at night in the knowledge that tomorrow *might* be "The Day" when the sky would darken and the Lord would appear, this time no longer in the guise of a poor man from an obscure region but enthroned, trailing clouds of glory, and manifesting the terrible power of God. The symbolism of kingship is apposite in terms of the Hebrew mould of thought in which it is conceived, for the characteristic function of the Hebrew king was judgment (I Sam. 8:5; II Sam. 8:15). The king was the Supreme Court. In Solomon's palace, one of the rooms was the Hall of Judgment where the king appeared to exercise this function (I Kings 7:7). So kingship is the right quality to attribute to God who is to come to judge everyone according to his or her deeds and who will have the power to execute the judgment, separating the sheep from the goats and sending the latter off to eternal fire while gathering the former to enjoy eternal bliss.

Not all New Testament reference to judgment, however, is directed toward the eschaton. Judgment is such a basic concept in Hebrew thought that it has an ongoing role. We all stand all our lives under the divine judgment. The Christian judges himself daily. "Judgment" implied not only a formal pronouncement by a judicial authority but a kind of moral awareness such as we might have in mind in talking of having something on our conscience. Nevertheless, the implementation of the righteous judgment is to take place in one swoop, and with it is to come the end of the age and the heralding of a new one. So, the old triumphs associated in Jewish tradition with the coming of the Messiah are transferred to the Day of the Lord as Christians conceived it: the Second Coming of Christ. According to Christian belief, the Messiah of Hebrew prophecy has indeed come and gone unnoticed by many; but he will come again and in this Second Coming fulfill the triumphal aspect of the traditional messianic prophecy.

When we come to ask how literally the ancients took such imagery, the answer is by no means as simple as some would like or might expect. That the language (a day in which the sun is darkened and various cosmic convulsions occur) is taken from apocalyptic and other mythological literature can be easily shown; but ascertaining exactly how, throughout centuries of use within prophetic Hebrew and Christian context, it has been interpreted by this or that society or in this or that particular circumstance is impossible. It is true that rural people generally, being close to nature, are very often much less crassly literalistic in their understanding of such language than modern city-dwellers tend to be. It is also true and very demonstrable, that during the Middle Ages, when by modern standards almost the entire economy of Europe was a rural one (since nothing remotely like a modern megapolis such as New York or Los Angeles existed at all and urban centers were so small that nature was never as far away as it is to, say, an apartment-house dweller in Manhattan who works all day in a high rise office building a few blocks away), people were less inclined than we are today to fall into the literalistic trap. The danger was, rather, the reverse. The Bible was so fancifully allegorized that now and then the exegetes had to be reminded (by the Victorines, for instance) to get back to the text. No doubt many a thoughtful peasant in the time of Dante saw beyond the literalistic reading of the words he heard in the priest's homily at Mass and so was less likely to be misled than might be many a well-educated engineer or accountant today as he or she listens to a popular religious telecast about the Second Coming. Literacy, which we all know was not widespread anywhere in the world till comparatively recent times, is in many ways a great boon to humankind; nevertheless, it is not an entirely unmixed blessing. Bible-reading by those whose education is technological rather than literary can result in interpretations so distorted as to blind the reader from the essential insights that the Bible can give to those who come to it with a child's innocence and curiosity and wonder.

Even in the England of the mid-nineteenth-century illiteracy was still quite common. The story is told of a rural vicar who found one of the yokels repeatedly dallying after the service in the parish church. One Sunday the vicar asked him what he was doing when the others had gone, which elicited the reply: "Just finishing the white." Further inquiry disclosed that the old man, not being able to read and not understanding any of the grand words words used in the service, had devised for himself a simpler way. He said that he reduced the whole service to three colors: "Black, that's my sins; red, that's His Blood; white, that's me afterwards." This triple meditation fully occupied the hour of worship. What insights might not a thoughtful, unlettered old man attain about all the mysteries of the Christian Faith by so simple a method of his own devising! After all, that is precisely what the Catholic devotion of the rosary was designed to provide.

By contrast it would not in the least surprise one if a modern geologist, on reading Dante and discovering that the base of the inverted cone of earth encasing the infernal regions had Jerusalem at its center, were to calculate the periphery, knowing that a careful examination of the terrain ought to disclose the location of the gates of hell. I fear that his hope of understanding religion even at the most elementary level should have been abandoned before he ever got going on his mathematical work on that cone!

Yet when all that is said, the fact remains that, for one reason or another, a remarkable proportion of people in every society and throughout all ages seem to be incapable of liberating themselves from their literalistic prison. So we need not doubt that from the time of Amos to our own day millions of people must have listened to the traditional biblical language about the Second Coming and its consequences and understood it in crassly literalistic ways.

II

The consequences of literalistic interpretation of the Second Coming have been only one element in a maze of confusion that has pervaded Christian teachings about the afterlife.

We have already seen that early Christian visions of "last things" had deep Hebrew roots; but in the centuries immediately preceding the Christian era that Hebrew heritage had been saturated with an admixture of foreign ideas: some from Persia, for example; others from the Mediterranean world. The notion of resurrection from the dead, for instance, was alien to classical Hebrew thought; yet by the time of Christ it was one that so influential a group as the Pharisees could espouse. By the time of Jesus a wide variety of speculations on the afterlife had been bandied about. The concept of immortality in the sense of an intrinsically immortal soul, a soul that by its nature is imperishable, was distinctly alien to Hebrew thought but widespread in the Mediterranean world. It had the blessing of Plato. Along with it came, of course, the notion of the transmigration or reincarnation of souls, which Plato had also accepted as part of a Pythagorean inheritance. That by Jesus' time a wide spectrum of such ideas had penetrated even the exclusivistic society of Palestine can be shown from the Gospels themselves. They were resisted, of course, by certain conservative groups: both the Samaritans and the Sadducees, for example, repudiated the idea of resurrection.

The basic mould of most of the New Testament writers was, however, thoroughly Jewish. Paul follows a Jewish tradition in thinking in terms of a plurality of heavens. The Hebrew word is plural: *shamāyim*. Sometimes the third heaven, to which he claimed to have been carried in an ecstatic vision, was identified with Paradise. The word "paradise" (in Greek *paradeisos,* in Hebrew *pardēs*) is a loan-word from the Old Persian, where it was used to designate a walled garden such as one would expect in a royal estate. The Garden of Eden (in Hebrew *gan*) was so conceived and rendered, in the Septaugint, *paradeisos.* Then in later Judaism a tendency to assign the wicked to *sheol* and the righteous to paradise is developed. Sheol, moreover, comes to be distinguished from Gehenna, which by the time of Jesus had been widely accepted as the abode of the wicked. Paradise, however, could be understood in several ways, not only literally as a garden, but also as an intermediate state. The good thief was promised that he would be with Jesus in paradise the very day on which they were hanging together on Calvary. This certainly suggests an intermediate state of some kind: a notion that was not alien to Jewish thought in the century or two before the Christian era, for we read of prayers for the dead: a concept that implies an intermediate state (e.g., II Macc. 12:39–45). The idea of such a state came to be highly developed in Christianity and, in one form or another, plays a central role in all Catholic thought about the afterlife.

Nor was the idea of resurrection clearly defined anywhere in the New Testament. Indeed, Paul expressly discourages speculation upon it. Christians ought not to be wasting their time with such speculations but should be, rather, preparing themselves for the imminent Day of the Lord, the Final Judgment. Wherever a literalistic understanding of that expectation prevailed, Christians were naturally disinclined to develop serious intellectual controversy about the nature of the afterlife. One would know soon enough, perhaps on the morrow. When a holocaust is impending it is plainly better to prepare to withstand it rather than to argue about the exact nature of its results.

Moreover, when Paul speaks of our resurrection to new life in Christ he clearly supposes that such a glorious destiny is by no means due to any intrinsic immortality of the human soul. On the contrary, "the wages of sin is death" and the ordinary expectation of sinful man is and ought to be that death will bring annihilation. In this respect man is no different from other animals. He is, however, *capable* of attaining immortality and this he can accomplish through his acknowledgement of the glorious resurrection of Christ. Christ's resurrection is what makes possible the resurrection of those who truly believe in him. Here is certainly no doctrine of the immortality of the soul. On the contrary, as Cullmann and others have pointed out, a Platonic type of doctrine of the immortality of the soul is the opposite of that which constituted the heart of the early Christian *kerygma*. That kerygma *was* indeed the proclamation of the resurrection of Christ and the inexpressibly glorious consequences flowing from it.

That seems clear enough in the teachings of Paul. Nevertheless, other strands of Mediterranean belief about the afterlife that made their way into early Christian imagery are already of record in the New Testament itself. So we find in the Gospels not only the teaching that the human soul, the *psychē,* is so infinitely precious that to lose it is worse than losing everything else in the world, but that nothing can quench it. So urgent is the recognition of this that failure to appreciate it brings everlasting misery in Gehenna. The soul appears, therefore, in this strand of early Christian thought, to be indestructible. Soon the church was teaching that, glorious in heaven or burning in hell, nothing can destroy the soul. Yet, in the West, at any rate, with its Latin mould of conceptualizing theological notions, the Church came to talk of mortal as opposed to venial sin.

Mortal sin is the kind of sin that kills the soul that is constitutionally unkillable. Category confusion cries out for recognition here; but that is by no means the extent of the trouble. In the fluid state of Christian doctrine of the afterlife in the first century or so of the movement called the Christian Ways, the options were unlimited and the potential for confusion incalculable.

Suppose we go back in imagination to, say, the year A.D. 65 and visit a Christian household in Rome where a bereavement has occurred. A daughter of the house, Felicity, had been tortured and killed in the Neronian persecution. We ask the parents what, as Christians, they believe about the state and the whereabouts of Felicity, their deceased daughter. In all probability they would say she was "asleep in Christ" or "resting in peace," as in the language of the catacombs, where the typical inscription reads *dormit in Christo* or *in pace*. Their daughter, temporarily deprived of a body, was in one way or another preserved in a kind of sleep, protected by Christ from the powers of evil until his return, which might occur any day. When Christ returned she would be awakened from that sleep and they would be united with her again and reign forever with Christ in the power of his resurrection, each clothed in the glorious body that is to be awarded to those who die in the Faith.

Soon, however, some Christians were talking of other temporary arrangements, pending the General Resurrection. The notion of a disembodied sleep is intrinsically difficult to maintain. Perhaps, then, some would conjecture, those who died in the Lord would receive a temporary body of some sort and so be already enjoying heaven. Thence, at the Day of Judgment, they would be recalled with everyone else; only in their case, since their eternal salvation was already assured, they would simply exchange their temporary body for an eternal one.

As hope of a speedy return of Christ faded, the already existing notion of an intermediate state was inevitably developed. We all know that in the West it eventually came to be the focus of enormous ecclesiastical corruption that brought it into extreme disrepute among those who espoused the Reformation heritage. At first, however, it provided a highly intelligible account of the state of good Christians such as Felicity: they were beyond the power of evil and preparing for the final reckoning, the Day of the Lord. Preparation entails spiritual growth, and so indeed they would be growing in that place of refreshment, light, and peace (*locum refrigerii, lucis, et pacis*) to which the Roman liturgy was eventually to allude in the traditional "Commemoration for the Departed." This notion of purgatory, which came to be developed by the English Tractarians in the nineteenth century and in a very different ideological climate, was certainly very unlike the popular late medieval concept of purgatory as a place of punishment by fire. The nature of the fire was disputed: was it physical or spiritual? Either way it was very painful; yet, unlike the fires of hell, it was radically sanctified and blessed by the knowledge that it ineluctably led to everlasting bliss with Christ.

Such were only some of the confusions that arose from marrying Hellenistic ideas to Hebrew ones while the Church's doctrine of the afterlife had been still in a fluid state.

By the time we reach, say, the year 1600, the situation had enormously changed. Let us now visit an English household in that year: one that has suffered recent bereavement. The father of this household had been martyred as a recusant (an upholder of the old Romanist faith in England) who refused to attend Church of England services. Where, we ask, is he now? Some members of the family might reply that he would probably be in purgatory, being punished for certain venial shortcomings so that his soul might be pure enough to go into the full presence of God in heaven. At death he would have already submitted to the Particular Judgment. Whether he would get a temporary body then or would have to wait till the General Judgment might not be clear. At any rate all was well with him and we could all help by praying for his speedy release from purgatory. Other members of the same family, however, would probably feel that he was so saintly and had died such a heroic death and with such perfect contrition for his sins that he would have gone straight to heaven at the Particular Judgment. Our prayers for him, however, would not be wasted; they would be applied in general to the souls in purgatory, benefitting the general reservoir of prayers for these "holy souls" as they came to be called because of the blessed assurance they already had of everlasting bliss.

I say "everlasting" bliss, but even there confusion reigned. For although the medieval schoolmen distinguished eternity (*aeternitas*) from everlasting time (*aeviternitas*), people talked of eternal life and eternal damnation, implying of course a radically different concept. Eternity is outside the order of time, having neither beginning nor end, neither present nor future nor past. Were we to ask the family which it was we should have been extraordinarily fortunate if they had known what we were talking about and would have referred us to their priest on his next round, whose ignorance would in all probability have equalled theirs if not surpassed it.

Suppose, however, that we go across the street to a Protestant household, also bereaved. What have they to tell us of the whereabouts of Aunt Bess? Assuredly she is in heaven, for since there is no purgatory the only alternative is too horrible to think of and could not apply to a saintly soul like Bess. Has she an embodiment? Again, that is unclear, but at the Day of Judgment she will indubitably receive one that is imperishable. But suppose further that we inquire of the status of a scoundrel further down the street who died impenitent toward God and contumacious toward rightful authority on earth. Alas, he must indeed have gone to hell. With a body? Presumably, since the torments of hell are physical as well as mental and spiritual. So even for a temporary stay, pending the Day of the Lord, the body would have to have some asbestos-like quality to withstand so much burning. At any rate he would be ranged eventually with the rest of us at the Throne of Judgment and would receive whatever body was necessary to undergo punishment, eternal or everlasting as the case might be, in the fires of hell. Cheered by the blessed assurance of Aunt Bess's escape from that hideous fate, the bereaved members of the family would be content to remain for the present in a state of considerable ignorance about the celestial geography. In face of hunger and thirst, but assured of a banquet that is even now being prepared, one does not quibble or fuss about the precise contents of the menu.

One might suppose the possibilities of confusion to have been exhausted. By no means. For the mother of the family recently had a baby boy who died a moment after birth and before anyone could baptize him. Since only the baptized could enter heaven and there is no further embodiment, reincarnational or purgatorial, and therefore no further chance of regeneration through baptism, the child's fate is sealed forever. He cannot hope for heaven. Moreover, since by this time the notion of immortality of the soul has come to prevail in both "Catholic" and "Protestant" quarters, the baby must go somewhere. Here the old doctrine of limbo is invoked. He goes to limbo: a place or state that is pleasant but does not confer the bliss (eternal or everlasting) that belongs to heaven alone.

Nor was the doctrine of limbo as simple as that might make it sound. The baby boy would go to the children's limbo: the *limbus infantium*. What sort of body he would eventually receive one could not expect to know with precision, but at any rate it could not be the glorious body that was the right of the redeemed, the blessed in heaven. There was, however another class of person to which reflective minds occasionally turned. What of Plato and Moses? Assuredly they were never baptized, unless Christ himself, during his descent into *hades* (the counterpart of *sheol*) to visit them during the interval between his death and resurrection (as was a widespread traditional belief), had performed that rite and administered that sacrament. Since there seemed to be no firm reason for so supposing, the doctrine of *limbo* was made to do double duty: holy men and women who died before the coming of Jesus Christ would be rewarded by being sent to limbo: in their case the "limbo of the fathers," *limbus patrum*. Intellectual confusion has a remarkable capacity not only for self-perpetuation but for generating more and more broods of confusion, continuing an apparently interminable line.

Even Gregory of Nyssa, one of the most perceptive of the Greek Fathers, in discussing the merits of a reincarnationist as opposed to a resurrection view of the destiny of man, contends that the former presupposes the notion of the soul's "alighting" on one body after another, while in the resurrection view that he prefers one gets back "the same body as before, composed of the same atoms," which are "compacted around the soul." This was indeed a view that seemed to appeal to the medieval as well as to the ancient mind. Some ecclesiastical councils and other assemblies insisted, as did, for instance, the first canon of the Fourth Lateran Council, held in 1215, that both the elect and the reprobate would arise in their own bodies, the bodies they now have, to receive their reward or punishment as the case might be. *Omnes cum suis propriis resurgent corporibus, quae nunc gestant:* "all shall rise with their own bodies, the bodies they now bear." This tenet was acclaimed with the Albigenses in mind and to disown their reincarnationist tradition, which for various reasons had come to be so feared by the ecclesiastical establishment that the Church planned and virtually accomplished their genocide.

Justin, one of the earliest of the Christian apologists, had held that the souls of the righteous were to remain in "a better place" and the wicked in "a worse one" to await the final judgment which no doubt he, like his early second-century contemporaries, expected soon. Papias (*c.* A. D. 60–130) adhered to the view of the writer of the Apocalypse that there was to be a millennium when the righteous who had died would reign under Christ, their Messiah and King. Millenarian views of this type, the advocates of which have usually based their opinion on the Apocalypse, especially chapter 20, literalistically interpreted, have appeared in many quarters throughout the centuries. Justin, Irenaeus, and others in the early Church upheld them in one form or another. Certain medieval sectaries adopted them and at the Reformation likewise certain sects such as the Moravians and the Anabaptists favored millenarian views, as did in more recent times bodies such as the Irvingites and the Adventists. The mainstream of historic Christianity, however, has not taken literally this apocalyptic speculation. Some primitive forms of millenarian teaching persisted in the Church in some quarters till the fourth century; but Origen, in the first half of the third century, and those who followed him opposed it on excellent grounds. Origen was both the most learned biblical scholar in the early Church and its most original thinker. Unfortunately, we do not have a good text of all his writings, because he was a controversial figure whose friends ill served him by "purifying" his works of passages they thought might be more than the Church was ready to accept. Nevertheless, wherever his opinion is unmistakably clear it should command, to say the least, the utmost respect.

III

By way of conclusion little need be said beyond drawing together what has been said already. Quite simply, we may conclude that Christian doctrine on the afterlife is so inchoate and confused, for known historical reasons, that it may be accounted the weakest part of Christian theology. We ought to go back to the roots and see, for instance, what kind of teaching about the afterlife and "last things" would make most sense in terms of central theological positions in Christian thought as expressed in the historic creeds and in Scripture itself. The great classic doctrinal statements of the Church, such as the so-called Apostles' and Niceno-Constantinopolitan Creeds speak only of resurrection followed by "the life everlasting" or "the life of the world to come" without specifying in any detail the nature of that life. While we are assured that the Christian hope is for a fuller and richer life in the nearer presence of God, the interpretations of this are left open. For example, from extensive study I have made in recent years on this subject, I have become convinced that a form of reincarnationism is compatible with a reconstructed Christian view of the afterlife and that it might be identified, for instance, with the traditional Judeo–Christian concept of the intermediate state, especially as understood in terms of purgation, preparation, and growth rather than in penal terms such as prevailed in the medieval Church in the West. (See Editor's Introduction.) It is not a notion specifically taught in Scripture; but neither is the Trinity anywhere taught in the Bible except in isolated passages known by scholars to be spurious additions to the biblical text, notably I John 5:7. Trinitarian doctrine, which of course is generally accounted the focus of classical Christian thought about God can be *extrapolated* from Scripture by learned and at least plausible exegesis. It seems to me that this is also true of reincarnationism.

This is a point I make here without in any way seeking to press it, for there are other viable interpretations. What I do want to press is the fact that no one who has seriously studied the history of Christian teaching on the afterlife and "last things" can escape the conclusion that on these all-important questions there is simply no clear and constant Christian witness. Great historical learning, much philosophical acumen, and profound theological sensitivity are necessary for any attempt at reconstruction.

Proto-Religious Views of Death and Beyond: A Psychological Comparison With Unificationism

MARY JO MEADOW

While the different religions quarrel with one another about which among them has the truth, on our view the truth of religion may be completely disregarded.

    SIGMUND FREUD, *Neue Folge der Vorlesungen zur Einführung in die Psychoanalyse.*

In *The Future of an Illusion* ([1927] 1964), Sigmund Freud declared religious beliefs to be among humankind's most cherished possessions because only they can make life tolerable. He declared that the gods have a threefold task: they must exorcise the terrors of nature, they must reconcile men to the cruelty of Fate, particularly as it is shown in death, and they must compensate them for the sufferings and privations which a civilized life in common has imposed on them.[1]

    While this view of the scope of religious need is certainly narrow, theological explanations of "the end of days" are not readily accepted unless humans share a common "bias of optimism" that things will turn out as hoped. Allport considered religion based primarily on gratification of such hopes to be the product of an immature, undeveloped religious sentiment, appropriate only during childhood.[2]

Proto-Religious Eschatology

To understand proto-religious eschatology involves combining evidence from proto-Indo-European religiousness (PIE), shamanism, and reports of individuals' near-death out-of-body experiences

(NDOBEs). The Indo-European appears to be the only reconstruction of proto-mythology related to a parent language group. Shamanism is a common element in religions of prehistoric peoples. Near-death experiences can be considered primary (not rationally or consciously elaborated) psychological experiences. Such primitive sources can offer us clues as to what the basic human tendencies are regarding hopes and expectations about the "last things."

Proto-Indo-European Eschatology

Proto-Indo-European eschatology is (as is the rest of PIE religiousness) a reconstructed religion. Little evidence remains of the beliefs and practices of those people who inhabited some site in northern Europe from roughly 5500 to 2000 B.C.E. These Kurgan peoples, to give them the name used by Marija Gimbutas[3], a foremost authority on this culture, probably lived on the Russian steppes north of the Black and Caspian Seas. In successive waves of migration they spread to what is present-day Iran and India, to southern Europe where they influenced the Greek and Roman cultures, and across northern Europe, influencing later Germanic and Nordic cultures.

Their religiousness may be reconstructed in a manner similar to that in which we may reconstruct their language: by finding congruences across the various cultures whose development they influenced. When differences can be accounted for either by what we know of the indigenous people overrun by the proto-Indo-Europeans or by other regional influences, a myth can be reconstructed reflecting the "parent" myth. The work is slow and laborious, requiring concurrent reconstruction of the language to determine what words and concepts those people had.

The nature of time

In proto-Indo-European thought, time is seen as going through a series of ages, with each more deteriorated than the one preceding it. Hesiod[4] describes four major ages, if one considers (as do many students of Indo-European cultures) his "age of the heroes" an interpolation into the basic myth. A similar series of ages with declining amounts of goodness are described in the Iranian *Bahman Yasht*[5], Plato's *Politikos*[6], the Hindu (Indic) *Laws of Manu*.[7], and the Jewish *Book of Daniel,*[8] which is very late and influenced by foreign sources. Below the surface differences in these and comparable Germanic/Nordic sources, one sees the world depicted as growing increasingly chaotic and lacking in morals. Throughout all the texts, strife within the family (breaking apart that which should be held together: family solidarity) and incestuous family relationships (bringing together that which should be kept separate: sexuality and family interaction) are seen as indicators of this chaos. Epic battles often mark the transition between these ages. The Indic *Ramayana* and *Mahabharata* describe two of these, the latter ushering in the current last and worst age of the *kali yuga*.

According to some accounts, the age of the gods will begin at the end of the world. Others see a new and similar cycle being born out of the ashes of the old world. Still others[9] conclude that the end of the last age is the end of all. The first opinion is held by some Indo-European scholars to be least likely to reflect the proto–myth, since it reflects messianic ideas that are not compatible with the earliest proto–Indo-European thought.

he end of human physical life

Proto-Indo-European religion suggests that people are to be considered as having two parts, one visible and one invisible: the "solid" parts of their being and the parts that "move" the solid parts. These two parts of the human have different fates at death.

Proto-Indo-European cosmology describes the universe as having been created out of the dismembered body of the first person, offered as sacrifice by the first priest. The various parts of the body go to make up the various parts of the universe. The Indic *Rig Veda* offers one of the many extant samples of this myth:

When they divided Purusa, how many pieces did they prepare?
What are his mouth, arms, thighs, and feet called? . . .
The moon was born of his mind; of his eye, the sun was born;
From his mouth, Indra and fire; from his breath, wind was born.
From his navel there was the atmosphere; from his head, heaven was rolled together;
From his feet, the earth; from his ear, the cardinal directions.[10]

Similarly, the death of any human being was seen as one's last sacrifice to the universe. Any human (or other life form) death replenished and renewed the universe. The elements making up that person's body fuelled the various parts of the universe created from body parts. A constant interchange goes on between universe and human life; the death of either creates and continues the life of the other.

Some myths describe a special kind of paradise on earth to which heroes or other special people may be directly transported. This is depicted as a place of their own apart from the gods. Hesiod[11] gives one description of this, concluding: "Fortunate are these heroes; the grain-giving earth bears them luxuriant honey-sweet fruit three times over." Here is heaven on earth, enjoyed by a chosen few with full human embodiment.

The fate of the soul

In some myths, the soul seems to be equated with the life-breath which disperses to become the wind at death. However, other myths elaborate a geography of the soul's travels at the time of death. Two separate outcomes appear to be delineated: one for the knowing ones and one for the ignorant.[12]

One set of myths describes an elaborate journey made by the soul after death. It usually first must cross a river by boat. *Ger-ont (erosion of substance, or "old man") is the boatman (the asterisk signifies a reconstructed Indo-European word). The soul meets certain figures along the way. Usually there is a dog marked by duality (two heads, two dogs, or speckled coloring). The dog's name is a variant of *ker (Kerberos in Greek, Cerberus in Latin), an animal growling sound. Sometimes the color of the dog—white or black—indicates whether one is to return to life at this point or continue on to death. Once past the dog(s), there is no return. After the dog one meets a maiden or two, beautiful when viewed from the front, but ugly and haggish from behind. She will either lead one gently on, or push one into the bottomless pit. Finally, the otherworld is marked by gates and walls made of heaped up earth.

In many myths the otherworld is described only by negatives: no pain, no suffering, no winter, no hunger, no heat, no cold, no labor, no illness, etc.[13] Some myths describe a paradise with the comforts of human life freely available without any of life's miseries.

The outcome for the enlightened is described simply as a place of light, not a paradise or even another world. The journey may still precede entry into this light. This outcome is posited for a "higher" kind of person. Some scholars[14] suggest that light, which stands for knowledge, is the end for those who know the whole story above to be an allegory. *Ger-ont mediates between life and death. Animal noises are the sounds between the silence of the grave and the speech of humans, as dogs are between wildness—part of the natural world—and domestication—part of the human world. The maiden signifies the process of decay that befalls all that is valuable to human life. Finally, the gated walls are simply the grave itself, the final end of all human life, seen in the mound-like style of the graves in which the Kurgan people buried their dead. In other words, death is the end, there is nothing else. For some Indo-Europeans, fame appears to be the only kind of immortality of which they felt certain. Much of their warrior-like endeavors were in pursuit of fame. Those of whom the poets sing will live forever.

Shamanism

Along with initiation and other rites of passage, shamanism is a key element in the religiousness of preliterate peoples. The word "shaman" is of Siberian origin, and shamanistic elements tend to be stronger farther from the equator. However, shamanism permeates all climates, being an important component, for example, of some California Native American groups.

The person of the shaman

Shamans feel they are called to mediate between the spiritual and the material worlds. Often very early in life they show distinctive behaviors that signify their calling. For some, long and arduous preparation precedes their practice of shamanism; others are spared this. An initiation rite that symbolically signifies the death and resurrection of the potential shaman is commonly performed. Shamans must demonstrate a capacity for visions, for travel between the worlds, for divinistic trance, for healing, and for many varieties of ecstasy or going outside of oneself.[15] The shaman may be male or female; in some societies more often the latter.

The powers of shamans make them able to serve as intermediaries between the spiritual and material worlds in many different situations. They are capable of communicating frequently with spiritual beings, and they can supply helpful information when human affairs are in conflict with the spiritual world. They can also bring messages from the dead, guide the dead to the realm of the spirit, and retrieve the souls of those dead before their proper time. Shamans diagnose spiritual and bodily illness; they prescribe the means necessary for healing and carry out the healing process. They do their work by two chief methods: "traveling" to the spirit world and being possessed by spirits.

The shaman's vocation

Shamans suffer greatly beginning with their "initiatory psycho-pathology"[16] when they receive their call to this vocation from which they cannot escape. They often experience many paranormal phenomena that today would cause them to be diagnosed as psychotic. They suffer mental, bodily, spiritual torment. Potential shamans, thrust into the spirit world, must learn to control their suffering lest they be destroyed. This culminates in the experience of death and rebirth leading to their social acceptance as a genuine member of the shamanistic calling.

Because of their sufferings, their complete devotion to their vocation, and their capacity to mediate between heaven and earth, shamans may be seen as precursors of the "divine redeemers" who could offer salvation to their devotees in the Hellenistic world. The eager thirst for salvation (and for mediators to help one find it) between the third century B.C.E. and the third century C. E. may represent a desire very similar to that of preliterate peoples who felt a need for shamans to institutionalize that role in their societies.

The various mystery cults that developed during the Hellenistic period typically had gods or goddesses (often themselves resurrected from the dead) who offered an immortality of both body and soul to their devotees. The powers of these figures who, like the shamans, could move freely between the spiritual and material worlds were called upon to afford some sense of security regarding personal salvation from the terrors of death.

However, during the Hellenistic period there were thinkers such as Plotinus whose conclusions about "last things" differed, though their thirst for salvation was also strong. Like those Indo-Europeans whose "light" indicated to them that nothing exists after death, these people held that salvation came from perfect understanding and that one must attain this for oneself; there were no messiahs, saviors, or other intermediaries to accomplish the task. Some of these thinkers saw the grave as the end, some considered intuitive knowledge of Ultimate Reality as possible, and some remained agnostic about expectations.

ear-Death Out-of-Body Experiences (NDOBEs)

The publication of Raymond Moody's *Life After Life*[17], telling the stories of individuals who were revived after being clinically dead unloosed an avalanche of reports of similar experiences. Other books appeared, television features were shown, and many individuals expressed relief at being able to report experiences about which they had previously remained silent lest others should think them crazy. Following the rush of descriptions of near-death out-of-body experiences came scientific studies of the phenomenon.[18]

he near-death out-of-body experience

Although variations exist in the stories told, they follow a strikingly similar pattern. The major difference between them depends on how far into the experience one has gone. The NDOBE generally follows this pattern:

1 One experiences leaving the body, often as if floating above it and able to look down upon it.

2 Next is passage through some kind of dark tunnel; sometimes one undergoes a life-review evaluation of one's entire life.

3 One emerges from the tunnel into harmony and peace on the other side. (Some individuals have reported negative experiences; they travel to a "hell" rather than to a "heaven.")

4 One sees beings approaching (often a previously deceased relative or a personally significant religious figure) and they communicate. One is sometimes ordered to go back to life because of work to complete; sometimes one is given a choice, although urged to return to life.

5 One returns to the experience of embodied existence.

People report these as highly positive experiences, and all (except for those who have negative or "hell" experiences) say that their greatest desire was to press onward. All regret loss of the experience and report returning to life with reluctance. People having such experiences typically acquire a deeply religious outlook on life and report that their fear of death is entirely gone. Those with negative experiences interpret their being allowed to return to life as being given a second chance. Some begged for this chance during the NDOBE, while others were freely granted it. Most of these people report many insights on how to live better lives and a resolve to live by them.

Implications of the experience

Scholars argue at both ends of the spectrum regarding the near-death experience. Some say it proves the existence of a spiritual world. Others say that it proves only that the human brain is so constructed that, under the traumatic conditions of physical death, it tends to produce a common type of hallucination which is colored with the particulars of one's own life experiences. Regardless of the objective reality of that which those who have NDOBEs undergo, certain conclusions can be drawn that are interesting to students of religion.

Experiences of this nature might have shaped the understandings of heaven and hell that have developed in many religions. In many faiths, hell is described in terms of the worst that the environment indigenous to the religion can offer. For example in equatorial religions, hell is a place of terrible heat and thirst; in Scandanavian myth, it is typically a place of barren coldness. Heaven is often described in terms of pleasant sensory experiences such as those in the near-death experience. It is reasonable to assume that individuals reporting such experiences may have been taken as authorities on the subject of the afterlife, and that their descriptions crept into the mythology of their religions. By the time human culture became literate, such ideas would exist as a conceptual substratum to religious thought. One version of the "journey" (embellished with its own particular symbolic images) would be that of the Indo-Europeans. Other ancient peoples may have had their own different versions. One who could have such experiences (other than on the occasion of near-death) would have "talent" for being a shaman and would be able to visit the spiritual world and return at will.

A Proto-Religious View of Death and After

We are now ready to develop, from these three sources (proto-Indo-European eschatology, shamanism, and near-death out-of-body experiences), our proto-religious view of death and beyond. It is this: People are at first composed of at least two separable parts, a body and a spirit or soul; then when one dies, the body goes back to the earth, but the soul is capable of having further experiences. A few fortunate people may experience a paradise on earth in both body and soul.

After death the soul must find its way from the material world to the spiritual one; this involves a journey. At the end of the journey, one finds a place free of negative experiences, which may also include some of the pleasures to which one has become accustomed during life; at any rate, all is harmonious.

People are sometimes capable of traveling backward from the spiritual world into the physical world. Those who can do so are people of greater wisdom than those who cannot. One who can move freely between the worlds is often powerful enough to serve as a mediator for those still struggling in earthly existence and to assist them in achieving salvation. Those who do not initially achieve salvation may have an opportunity for a second chance to gain it. Throughout, people may have access to a mediator or mediators whose task is to help them. In this proto-religious eschatology, all comes out right in the end. It argues for what people might most want to attain: universal salvation.

Although the world as a whole appears to be growing worse all the time, there is hope. Things will eventually reach such a bad situation that the world as we know it will collapse. Either a new beginning of the process with a fresh start or else a reign of the gods will probably occur next. This view allows one to acknowledge the disorder one sees around oneself yet still have hope for the world.

In both proto-Indo-European peoples and in the rationalists during the Hellenistic period of craving for salvation, we find those who refuse to be satisfied with comforting stories and insist that attaining the light (or salvation) entails a penetration to the truth. For some proto-Indo-Europeans, this seems to be the "knowledge" that all the stories are allegory and that the grave is the end. For Hellenistic thinkers (representing later elaborations on ideas about salvation) conclusions vary from some that are similar to the Indo-Europeans to others that propose the possibility of direct, intuitive knowledge of the One from which all being comes. Mediatorship is excluded.

Comparison of Unification and Proto-Religious Views

We may now compare such proto-religious views with Unification ideas, noting points of convergence and divergence.

The Nature of the Human Being

Unificationism endorses the idea that the human person is made of two separable parts, a physical self and a spirit self.[19] "Our flesh is like clothes to our spirit; and it is natural for us to discard our flesh when it is old and exhausted. . . . Then our spirit man goes to the invisible world to live there forever. . . . The human body cannot live forever."[20] Unification theology thus agrees with proto-religious thought that the physical part of the human returns to the earth and that the spirit part goes on to further journeys. Unlike much of Christianity, Unification thought also agrees that the physical body ends with its returning to earth: "once it is dissolved into dust, [it] cannot be resurrected to its original state. . . . 'Resurrection' means the phenomena occurring in the process of man's restoration."[21]

Unification thought speaks of what might be considered salvation on the levels of both the world and the individual. In both cases the ultimate outcome is the establishment of a state without negatives, a state of harmony.

Salvation of the World

Restoration refers to the eventual accomplishment of what Unificationism sees as God's plan for the world.[22] Each human individual will perfect himself or herself, reestablishing an appropriate relationship with God. The ideal family will be founded and will serve as the foundation for appropriate relationships among all human beings, culminating in the eventual unification of all peoples as one family. Finally, a proper relationship to nature will be established; nature will become subservient to human needs and there will no longer be worry about natural catastrophes and other environmental disasters. Restoration will thus result in the establishment of conditions on earth similar to those described in the paradise of proto-Indo-European thought and in the experiences of near-death out-of-body travelers.

The Unification view of Restoration provides clear parallels to the special paradises on earth described by some Indo-European myths: those with special earthly paradises set aside for heroes and other important people. In the Unification view, this "paradise on earth" will be experienced by those special people who are involved in accomplishing the full Restoration.

The Unification view of human history, however, posits a

process the opposite of the proto-religious one: Things are getting better all the time. Such an optimism must sometimes be hard to maintain in face of the daily news. The ultimate end (something better for the earth in general than the present situation) is found equally in both proto-religious and Unification thought.

dividual Salvation

According to Unificationism, ideas regarding salvation for the individual soul could never be that of the "rationalists" of either proto-Indo-European or Hellenistic times. "Rationalism" is among the stances opposed to conditions necessary for Restoration. The "rationalists", however, appear to have always constituted a small minority.

Unificationism discusses the last things for the individual soul under the heading of Resurrection, which is equated with the Dispensation for Restoration. "Resurrection means the phenomena occurring in the course of fallen men's restoration to their original nature, endowed at the creation. Therefore, the 'providence of resurrection' means the providence of restoration."[23] The resurrection (purification, perfection) of a person's spiritual self can occur only while inhabiting the physical self, while one is living on earth. The fate of the individual is strongly tied to the fate of the world as a whole; one is unable to attain to heights beyond the level the world has reached.[24] Old Testament people could attain only to the form-spirit-level of the spirit world by the time of their deaths. Since Jesus, people can attain to the life-spirit-level of the spirit world and live in paradise at death. The Messiah of the Second Coming is to usher in the possibility of living in the Kingdom of Heaven in the spirit world. The required self-purification is likely to involve indemnity conditions: paying for one's sins. One may pay a greater or lesser amount of indemnity than one's actual incurred burden.

Unification thought agrees with proto-religious thought not only in holding that embodied existence is necessary for salvation but also in suggesting the possibility of universal salvation. The people who did not complete their perfection while on earth (a possibility open only to those living in the time of completion of the Restoration) can continue their work toward resurrection. They must, however, be earth-embodied to do so. They accomplish this by cooperating with people on earth who have missions similar to their own; a kind of "reincarnation" occurs in which "the physical body of the earthly man serves as the body of the spirit man. The earthly man, receiving the cooperation of the spirit man, would accomplish the mission of the spirit man as well as his own."[25] Evil spirits are not able to return to earth as they wish, but should they meet the indemnity conditions necessary for God to eradicate their sins—in cooperation with earthly persons—they seem able to embark on working for their own resurrection.[26]

Although Unification thought greatly elaborates the twists and turns of the journey to one's eventual resting place (far more than the rather simple proto-Indo-European story of a ferryman, dog, maiden, and gates), it does describe a journeying that must take place enroute to one's final end. The nature of the Kingdom of Heaven in the spirit world is not elaborated, but is declared the abode in the spirit world belonging to divine spirits. Unificationism's "reincarnational" understanding of the return of spirit selves needing further work is similarly more complicated than the more simple proto-religious one derived from near-death accounts.

Mediatorship

Mediatorship is a strong element of Unification thought. Indeed, neither individual resurrection nor the Restoration is possible without mediators. Unificationism describes a long line of individuals fulfilling various aspects of this function throughout history. The two most important mediators are Jesus and the Lord of the Second Advent. Jesus made possible the first step of the Restoration, the perfection of the individual human being. Because of his sufferings, people have to pay a lesser amount of indemnity than they have incurred; this mediator thus directly assists in the salvation of the individual. The Lord of the Second Advent is an individual selected by God to complete the unfinished work of Jesus, that is, to create the perfect family and to reestablish proper human dominion over nature. Mediators in Unificationism are sent by God, and indeed can be seen even as those who have "returned" in some fashion from the beyond in that they may be assisted (inhabited?) by the spirits of earlier mediators.

In contrast, shamans feel themselves called to their vocation but they do not usually see it as a special mission from a god. The spirit world "acknowledges" or "calls" those sensitive to it and in tune with it. No shaman is seen as having a special mission of universal importance. Missions for individual people and/or groups emerge over the course of the shaman's lifetime. Proto-religious mediatorship lacks the cosmic significance that mediatorship has in Unificationist thought.

Summary

In Unification theology as in proto-religious thought, everything "comes out right" in the end. The soul will survive death and all souls have the possibility of salvation. Some souls may experience a "heaven" on this restored earth. For both the individual and the earth, mediators assist the process of making things right. Unificationism rejects any arguments that its ideas about the Last Things may be wishful thinking and that death may be the end of human experience.

Psychological Evaluation of Thought About the Last Things

Except for the occasional person who argues that ideas about the last things are all allegorical, the eschatologies described both posit outcomes that seem to meet the fondest hopes of the human heart. It was from noting how common this is in religion that Freud concluded that religious ideas "are illusions, fulfillments of the oldest, strongest, and most urgent wishes of mankind. The secret of their strength lies in the strength of those wishes."[27] Others have argued that it may show just the opposite: human beings yearn for that for which they are intended.

The correspondence between Unification thought and proto-religious ideas about the last things is indeed striking. Other traditions bear many correspondences to proto-religious positions, but most do so to a lesser extent than does Unification thought.

Thus, in terms of meeting the fondest hopes of the human heart (as they might exist in their earliest, most "primitive" and, therefore, truest form) Unificationism clearly does an excellent job. The extent to which one might really believe that it could all be true is a question of faith, beyond the scope of a social-scientific paper. To this question, individuals will come up with their different answers. Some will reject anything that is comforting simply because such is "too good to be true." Others will dislike the premises from which the conclusions are drawn. Some may be attracted by

Unificationist arguments simply because of their comfort value. Others may feel compelled by the thrust of the arguments. The social scientist cannot rule on the appropriateness of any of these decisions, but can help illuminate personal decisions by pointing out features of the teachings.

Notes

1 Sigmund Freud, *The Future of an Illusion,* trans. W.D. Robson-Scott, ed. James Strachey (Garden City, N.Y.: Doubleday Anchor, 1964), 24.

2 Gordon W. Allport, *The Individual and His Religion* (New York: Macmillan, 1960), 21–22.

3 Marija Gimbutas, "The Indo-Europeans: Archaeological Problems," *American Anthropologist* 65(1963): 815–36; "Proto-Indo-European Culture: The Kurgan Culture During the Fifth, Fourth, and Third Millennia B.C.," *Indo-European and Indo-Europeans* (Philadelphia: University of Pennsylvania Press, 1970), 155–98; "The Beginning of the Bronze Age in Europe and the Indo-Europeans: 3500–2500," *Journal of Indo-European Studies* 1(1973): 163–214; "The First Wave of Eurasian Steppe Pastoralists into Copper Age Europe," *Journal of Indo-European Studies* 5(1977): 277–338; "The Kurgan Wave #2 (c. 3400–3200 B.C.) into Europe and the Following Transformation of Culture," *Journal of Indo-European Studies* 8(1980): 273–316.

4 Hesiod *Works and Days.*

5 Bahman Yasht (Zoroastrian *Avesta*).

6 Plato *Politikos,* 269–74.

7 *Laws of Manu* 1.81–86.

8 Book of Daniel.

9 Steven O'Brien, "Indo-European Eschatology: A Model," *Journal of Indo-European Studies* 4(1976): 295–320.

10 *Rig Veda* 10.90.11–14.

11 Hesiod, *Works and Days,* 167–73.

12 Bruce Lincoln, "Indo-European Religion" (lectures, University of Minnesota, 1983).

13 Ibid.; Bruce Lincoln, "On the Imagery of Paradise," *Indogermanische*

Forschungen 85(1980): 151–64; "Proto-Indo-European Religion," in Charles H. Long, ed., *Ancient European Spirituality,* forthcoming.

14   Lincoln, "Indo-European Religion" (lectures).

15   Mircea Eliade, *Shamanism: Archaic Techniques of Ecstasy,* trans. Willard R. Trask (New York: Bollingen Foundation, 1964).

16   Ibid.

17   Raymond A. Moody, *Life After Life* (Atlanta: Mockingbird Books, 1975).

18   Craig R. Lundahl, *A Collection of Near-Death Research Readings* (Chicago: Nelson–Hall, 1982); Kenneth Ring, *Life at Death: A Scientific Investigation of the Near-Death Experience* (New York: Coward, McCann & Geoghegan, 1980).

19   *Divine Principle* (New York: The Holy Spirit Association for the Unification of World Christianity, 1973), 58–59.

20   *Ibid.* 168.

21   *Ibid.* 170.

22   *Ibid.* 120–29.

23   *Ibid.* 172.

24   *Ibid.* 174–76.

25   *Ibid.* 187.

26   *Ibid.* 186–87.

27   Freud, 47.

Suggested Readings

Allport, Gordon W. *The Individual and His Religion.* New York: Macmillan, 1950. Cited from 1960 paperback edition.

Bahman Yasht (Zoroastrian *Avesta*)

Book of Daniel.

Brihadaranyaka Upanishad

Divine Principle. New York: The Holy Spirit Association for the Unification of World Christianity, 1973.

Eliade, Mircea. *Shamanism: Archaic Techniques of Ecstasy.* Trans. Willard R. Trask. New York: Bollingen Foundation, 1964.

Freud, Sigmund. *The Future of an Illusion*. Trans. W.D. Robson-Scott. Ed. James Strachey. Garden City, N.Y.: Doubleday Anchor, 1964.

Gimbutas, Marija. "The Indo-Europeans: Archaeological Problems." *American Anthropologist* 65 (1963): 815–36.

———. "Proto-Indo-European Culture: The Kurgan Culture During the Fifth, Fourth, and Third Millennia B.C." *Indo-European and Indo-Europeans*. Philadelphia: University of Pennsylvania Press, 1970.

———. "The Beginning of the Bronze Age in Europe and the Indo-Europeans: 3500-2500." *Journal of Indo-European Studies* 1 (1973): 163–214.

———. "The First Wave of Eurasian Steppe Pastoralists into Copper Age Europe." *Journal of Indo-European Studies* 5 (1977): 277–338.

———. "The Kurgan Wave #2 (c. 3400–3200 B.C.) into Europe and the Following Transformation of Culture." *Journal of Indo-European Studies* 8 (1980): 273–316.

Harner, Michael. *The Way of the Shaman*. New York: Harper & Row, 1980.

Herodotus. *History*.

Hesiod. *Works and Days*.

Laws of Manu.

Lincoln, Bruce. "Death and Resurrection in Indo-European Thought." *Journal of Indo-European Studies* 5 (1977): 247–64.

———. "The Hellhound." *Journal of Indo-European Studies* 7 (1979): 273–86.

———. "The Ferryman of the Dead." *Journal of Indo-European Studies* 85 (1980): 41–59.

———. "On the Imagery of Paradise." *Indogermanische Forschungen* 85 (1980): 151–64.

———. "The Lord of the Dead." *History of Religions* 20 (1981): 224–41.

———. "Waters of Memory, Waters of Forgetfulness." *Fabula* 23 (1982): 19–34.

———. "Indo-European Religion." Lectures, University of Minnesota, 1983.

———. "Proto-Indo-European Religion." *Ancient European Spirituality*. Ed. Charles H. Long. In press.

Lundahl, Craig R. *A Collection of Near-Death Research Readings*. Chicago: Nelson-Hall, 1982.

Mahabharata.

Moody, Raymond A. *Life After Life*. Atlanta: Mockingbird Books, 1975.

O'Brien, Steven. "Indo-European Eschatology: A Model." *Journal of Indo-European Studies* 4 (1976): 295–320.

Outline of the Principle: Level 4. New York: Holy Spirit Association for the Unification of World Christianity, 1980.

Plato. *Politikos*.

Ramayana.

Rig Veda.

Ring, Kenneth. *Life at Death: A Scientific Investigation of the Near-Death Experience*. New York: Coward, McCann & Geoghegan, 1980.

Rogers, Spencer L. *The Shaman: His Symbols and His Healing Power*. Springfield, Ill.: Charles C. Thomas, 1982.

Strabo.

Sturluson, Snorri. *Prose Edda*.

Tacitus. *Germania*.

Völuspa.

8 | An African Perception

GILBERT E. M. OGUTU

Millions of spiritual creatures walk the earth
Unseen, both when we wake, and when we sleep.
MILTON, *Paradise Lost*

When I received the invitation to write a paper for the conference on Eschatology and the Second Coming of Christ, I was initially reluctant because of a conflict that has existed at the back of my mind for a long time, between my understanding of the Christian doctrine of the Last Things and my African perception of life as continuing beyond death. And so, when I finally made up my mind to write, I felt I ought to go back to my African forebears' religious experience. That, then, is the background against which my contribution to this symposium is to be read and understood.

In the Christian tradition in which I have been tutored, the eschatological debate began with the resurrection and ascension of Jesus Christ. At the end of Jesus' life it became apparent that his mission was incomplete. The answer he gave to the question "Lord, will you at this time restore the Kingdom of Israel?" (Acts 1:6–8) implies this. The sentiment is also affirmed by the angels' promise to the gazing disciples that "This Jesus . . . will come in the same way as you saw him go into heaven"(Acts 1:11).

Right through the life, ministry, death, resurrection, and even at that crucial moment of Jesus' ascension, the Kingdom he came to proclaim was not a present reality, and yet it was imminent. The unexpected delay of the Second Advent led to the debates and reflections that have lingered on for centuries concerning the words and deeds of Jesus, and the life and hope of the Primitive Church. The desire to understand the nature of the Second Advent has led eminent scholars to advance such theories as "realised eschatology," "inaugurated eschatology," "reinterpreted eschatology," and others.[1]

What, for example, did John mean when he quoted Jesus as having said: "And I, when I am lifted up from the earth, will draw all men to myself" (John 12:32)? What was realized on the cross that led Jesus to say: "It is finished" (John 19:30)? In light of the nature of his mission, how are we to understand that moment in the synagogue when Jesus opened the book of the prophet Isaiah and read: "The spirit of the Lord is upon me, because he has anointed me to preach good news to the poor. He has sent me to proclaim the release of the captives, and recovering of sight to the blind, to set at liberty those who are oppressed [and] to proclaim the acceptable year of the Lord" (Luke 4:18, 19)? The debate on what Jesus came to fulfill continues unabated. What remains basic is that eschatology, as understood from the New Testament narratives, is a Christ-centered phenomenon. We have to look to the life and mission of Jesus and to the life and hope of the Primitive Church to come to some understanding of it, and to fathom the trend it subsequently took.

Be that as it may, the concern about Last Things, is not unique to Christianity. It is found in all the religious traditions of mankind. Both Buddhism and Hinduism lay stress on an ultimate redemption after this world of grief and woe. That ultimate redemption, they claim, is a condition of eternal peace. Zoroastrianism looks to a new creation at the end; while Judaism sees man's redemption as following the pattern of God's plan, which is available only to the elect. In all the religions of the world, ideas about Last Things stand in mutual relationship to the experiences of man here and now. They are part of the environment that shapes human destiny. In the religious traditions of Africa the symbolic meaning of the rites of passage and the understanding of death are governed by a perception of the end. What is significant about the debate on Last Things is that it points to attempts to solve crises in life. This can be seen both in the historical eschatologies of Judaism, Christianity and Islam, on the one hand, and, on the other, in the mythological eschatologies of Africa, which tend to see primordial time regenerated at the end, leading to a timeless world. The problem is to explain what happens to man in the present world and to figure out what holds for man beyond death.

From the foregoing, it should be clear why the nature and consequence of the Second Coming of Christ remains a tricky problem in religious dialogue. Of what significance, then, would perspectives from the religious experience of an African people be?

Let us look at the religious traditions of the Luo of Kenya. The Luo-speaking people live in the geographical area that covers southern Sudan; south-western Ethiopia; north-eastern Zaire; north-

western, northern and eastern Uganda; western Kenya; and northern Tanzania: a corridor that stretches between 12°N to 2°S. For
academic purposes they have been grouped into Northern, Central
and Southern Luo. The northern group, found mostly in Sudan and
Ethiopia include the Nuer, the Dinka, the Anywak, and the Shilluk.
The central group, found in Uganda and Zaire, include the Alur,
the Chope, and the Acholi. And, finally, the southern group, which
is found in eastern Uganda, western Kenya, and northern Tanzania
include the Padhola and the Luo. In Kenya the Luo are the second
largest ethnic community. Although their homeland is in the western part of the country, they are scattered all over Kenya, particularly in the urban centers. They were among the very first
communities to have been introduced by the missionaries to Christianity and literacy. At the time of writing they are figured to be
more then 90 percent Christian. However, their cultural and indigenous values remain deeply rooted in their old religious beliefs and
practices.

According to the Luo, there are two levels of existence, which
together make up the cosmic equilibrium in their ontology: origin
of and life in the physical universe; and death and life in the world of
the spirits (the spiritual universe). As is the case with many other
African societies, the Luo traditions are full of myths loaded with
symbolic meaning. One of their myths of origins paints a picture of
an ideal social universe, in which God was in close relationship to
man; it was created for man as a place to feel at home. But a tragedy
came and man lost his privileged position and his familial relationship with God.

The story goes that in the primordial time, the Luo would take
hoes to the farms in the morning and the plots dug themselves.
They would then fetch the hoes in the evening. But one day, a bride
who was being initiated into the practice was given the sacred hoe
to take to the farm. When she got there, instead of leaving the hoe
there as she had been instructed, she tried to till the land. This
annoyed God. The consequence of this bride's disobedience was
that God withdrew his helping hand and his close relationship with
man. The Luo believe that it is because of this violation of God's
arrangement that human beings have to fend for themselves. This
myth explains the origin of labor and, to some extent, suffering in
general. The myth is often invoked to interpret the Luo saying that
sembe iporo gi nyawadgi, "the past explains the present and directs
the future"; so unfolds human destiny for which the individual

prepares himself by the process known to anthropologists as "rites of passage," namely birth, initiation, marriage, and death. Such rites of passage are not ends in themselves but are turning points in life.

Among the Luo, the individual matters only when he is seen as a part of the group. They often talk of *odwa* (our household); *dalawa* (our homestead); *dhoodwa* (our clan); *ogandawa* (our ethnicity or nationhood); and *pinywa* (our country). There should be no doubt, therefore, why my discussion is biased toward a collective or social destiny, centered on the family, which for the Luo is made up of a man, his wives, children and other relations. The wife and her children constitute the household, while the husband, his wives, children and immediate relations living with him, make up the homestead. The wife is the head of the household; the husband is the head of the homestead. The birth of children is seen as the means of perpetuating and expanding the family. This is why the Luo will say, at the birth of a child, God has blessed the daughter of so-and-so. By raising children, both parents are placed in a state of perfection because they have raised those who will survive them. The men or women who were not blessed with children were as good as dead. This is because their lineages would be terminated by their physical death. In cases where people did not give birth at all, other people did not name children after them. Meanwhile those who had children were never considered dead even when physically they were dead.

The reason behind the unshakable practice of polygamy in Africa has remained baffling to the Christians and others from the western world where polygamy is not countenanced.[2] The idea was not just to raise a large family but to ensure that one was survived by one or more sons when he died. The high mortality rate among infants made it necessary for parents to raise as many children as they could in the hope that at least some would survive. This often led to the marriage of more than one wife by the man or it caused the woman to fetch another wife for her husband from her kinsmen. We should not lose sight of the fact that polygamy was also a sign of wealth and good management. It took a very responsible man to govern his wives and the family affairs as a whole. This not only entailed administrative abilities but very strict adherence to the ethical norms and values. A polygamist had to be very careful how he conducted himself sexually. Violation of the set rules and regulations by the husband often wrecked the fertility of the wives who included *mikaye* (elder wife), *nyachira* (second wife) *reru* (middle wives) and *nyahera* (the last wife, also referred to as the old-age-wife). This explains why the polygamists commanded a lot of respect within the community and why they were often appointed leaders. It also explains why, among the Luo Christians, those who have been appointed to positions of responsibility tend to go polygamous. Most independent churches accord polygamists full membership.

Polygamy had a lot to do with the afterlife as well. It is not rare to hear a dying person complaining: "I have no children who will arrange my funeral. I will be buried like a wild animal. I will have neither fire to warm me nor shelter for my head. I am doomed." These are very sad remarks among the Luo, particularly if they came out of the mouth of one who is about to die. If such a person had only one wife it would not be a surprise to find him wishing he had had more; for maybe he would have had more children. Thus polygamy affects the preparation of the dead for the next world as well as their having a place for their spirits to return.

To the Luo, death, the transition between this world and the next, is an intruder whose arrival has to be explained. Why did so-and-so die? Was it witchcraft? Was he cursed? Did he violate any of the social interdictions that held the society together? Was it the will of God that he died when he did? On the occasion of death, the entire family comes together to participate in burial rituals and ceremonies. The whole family is to bid farewell to the departed in a proper way and to give him a warm send-off. The larger the gathering the better. The rituals are performed according to the age, sex, and social status of the person who has died.

Arising from the attempts of the Luo to explain the meaning of death, and the significance of the ceremonies and rituals that are performed at the funerals, one cardinal question remains: Do the Luo believe in life beyond death? The answer is yes. I have personally attended many funerals in Luoland and participated in burial ceremonies. I have heard wailing women appeal to those whose deaths they were mourning to convey their greetings to the relatives who had died some years back. I have heard the voices of people who died a long time ago as they spoke through the living, stating what they wanted the living to do. I have known of cases where people have consulted diviners about their sick ones and have been told that a relative who died a long time ago needed some food; then, when such food had been provided, the sick got better. I have come across cases where the departed have visited the living in dreams and demanded that children be named after them, and cases where babies have cried endlessly until a diviner advised that so-and-so who had died ages ago wanted the child to be named after him.

These observations go a long way in confirming the Luo belief that the departed are not dead, and that they do come to visit the living either as good or bad spirits. To appease them, the death rituals had to be performed in minute detail in accordance with the traditions of the people. In other words, the physical death of man, although inevitable, does not mark his end. Life continues into the next world, hence the elaborate death rituals that introduce the dead into the world of the spirits.

According to the Luo traditions, at the moment of death *chuny* (the spirit) departs or leaves the body. This is why the Luo will say *ng' ane chunye ochot* (so-and-so's spirit has left him). What remains is *ringruok* (body) which is subsequently buried. Occasionally there are incidents where people who have been declared dead have come to life before burial. In such cases the Luo will say *ng' ane chunye oduogo* (so-and-so's spirit has returned) or *ng' ane ochier* (so-and-so has resurrected). Thus, in the Luo understanding, resurrection occurs where the spirit comes back to inhabit a body it had parted from, before the body is buried, pending a second departure at a later date.

Like most other African peoples, the Luo believe that the dead, being very close to the living, either protect them or cause them to suffer. They are the intermediaries between God and the living. They are as much members of their families as are the living. Children are named after them. Libations are poured to them. Prayers are directed to God through them. The living have to appeal to them for succor and guidance because, apart from being in the spiritual sphere, they formulate the rich traditions and cultural norms and values on which the society is built. Thus, in spite of this otherworldy mode of existence, they still have dominion over the family members born after them. Such familial relationships remain intact as long as the dead continue to be remembered by the living. In fact, violations of social interdictions are seen as offences against the corporate family of both the living and the dead, for which punishments may be meted here and now. Otherwise, beyond death there are no rewards to be coveted and no punishments to be avoided; there is neither heaven to long for nor hell to be threatened with. This outlook underscores the belief that the significance of death lies beyond death.

The decision to name a child after a dead person among the Luo is determined as follows: First, the parents' desire to have the child named after a dead friend, relative or some prominent member of the family of the community who had died. Second, because of dreams or the advice of a diviner, a dead member of the family or community is believed to want the child named after him or her. Third, the identification of certain traits or characteristics of the dead person in a child may suggest a name. For example, I was named after my dead uncle, Ogutu Magenge wuodOtieno, who requested that I be named after him. Those who knew him in his lifetime, look at me and say *Ogutu oduogo mana gi wang'e* (Ogutu has come back in his wholeness). My own father, Achieng' Obedi grew gray hair while he was still a child. All the children he has wanted to be named after him have been known to grow gray hair at very tender ages. The belief is that those are the traits of the dead person that confirm that he really wanted to reincarnate in the child who had been named after him. There is no question, therefore, that the Luo name children after dead people to bring them (the dead) back into physical relationship with the living. In other words, the naming process is a process of reincarnating the ego of the dead individual. The person named after the deceased remains a testimony of the presence of the dead amongst the living. According to the Luo, the individuality of a person is in the name. His spirit (ego) is also identified with the name. This was the significance of the naming process as practiced by my forebears and continues to be practiced by us.

Contemporary African religious experience, however (and the Luo religious experience is no exception), cannot be limited to such traditional beliefs and practices. A lot of changes have taken place as they came into contact with other religious traditions and their conversion to Christianity or Islam. We should notice that dramatic changes began at the beginning of this century when the Luo became converted to Christianity. The idea of a lack of any form of existence immediately after death was introduced, with its gap between death and judgment. The result of such conversion to Christianity was that the afterlife existence, as perceived by the Luo, was thrust aside in the process of bidding farewell to old traditions. The end result was that the christened Luo lost his sense of reincarnation as well as the rich filial pieties, norms and values that had held the society together. We lost the unity of the clan and the centrality of the family. With no past to look to, we were led to accept the unexplained gap between death and the Last Day. Our dead relatives were declared devils whenever they communicated with us. Our names lost their meaning and significance. All this came as a result of the new understanding of the destiny of man that had been presented to us. Yet the enigmas still hold. What happens to a Luo Christian after death? What do the words "life everlasting" in the Apostles' Creed mean to him? What of the gap between death and the final judgment? In his letter to the Corinthians, Paul say that "though our outer nature is wasting away, our inner nature is being renewed everyday . . . from one degree of glory to another" (2 Cor. 3:18). That being the case, one wants to see whether death finds the Christians fully prepared for the Last Day. How does the Luo understand Paul when he says ". . . this perishable nature must put on the imperishable and this mortal nature put on immortality" (1 Cor. 15:53)?

The example I cited on what happens to a Luo at the time of his death, could best be interpreted to mean that the spirit (*chuny*) of the individual frees itself from the body (*ringruok*) (Gen. 35:18). As soon as *chuny* separates from the body it is met by other *chuny* which had separated: the spirit of the dead man is met by spirits of those who died in the past. He joins the world of the spirits where they remain invisible yet present. Life continues into the next world; only the mode of existence has changed. And, to my mind, this mode of existence fills that gap between death and the day of judgment at the Second Coming of Christ. The words of the Creed have not attracted the attention of the Luo theologians because it is the same teaching that they were used to in their traditional setting. As my sister once told me when I was thinking of my dead mother: "Why think of her all the time? Marry and name your first-born after her." Life lasts forever through the naming process.

At the socio-political level we should not forget that in Africa there have been calls for "liberation," "blackness," and "freedom" as factors defining the destiny of man. These have come to be because the African has increasingly found himself physically and spiritually poor, captive, blind, and oppressed as a result of his emulation of western ideas and values. He understandably looks for a moment of liberation and belonging. Such a moment would be fully acceptable only if it were to bring the African back to his roots. All these are consequences of the recurrent oppression and exploitation by external political, economic, and religious forces. Interestingly, the Luo were the first to break away from the established Church because they needed a place to feel at home. A cry is still being heard from that corner of Africa: "O Lord, other lords besides you have been our masters, but your name alone do we acknowledge" (Isa. 26:13).

Christian values have penetrated Luo beliefs and practices. In the New Testament we are called upon to repent for the Kingdom of God is at hand. Our destiny, in this context, depends on the depth of our penitence. Repentance, in Hebrew and Luo traditions, signifies a change of mind and attitude: a turning back. It is not my desire to overstress national, cultural, and racial idiosyncracies. The emphasis here is on ecumenical dialogue, the only means by which "many shall come from the east and west and shall sit down . . . in the kingdom of heaven" (Matt. 8:11). I am convinced that the way humanity responds to its environment and relates to itself is of prime importance. The world as we know it today is close to turning into a nuclear inferno. Perhaps we are in the Last Days. Perhaps the Lord of the Second Advent is telling the human race: "Because the needy are destroyed and the poor cry out, I will arise, says the Lord. I will bring help to him who yearns hereafter" (Ps. 12:15).

I have explored the levels of existence according to an African world view. I have discussed the relationships between the living and the dead. I have attempted to pinpoint the Luo conception of life beyond death as it justifies in them their hope in the Second Advent. My contention is that messianic movements have something to learn and to borrow from the Luo perception of the Last Things. I think we might start with the Luo belief that life continues into the future and that there is the need to return to the lost paradise of filial piety and the centrality of the family. In that spirit I pray: Your kingdom come, O Lord, for we long for that place where we once felt at home.

Notes

1   Among the scholars I have in mind may be mentioned: R. H. Charles, A. Schweitzer, R. Otto, C. H. Dodd, J. S. Mbiti, O. Cullmann, J. A. T. Robinson.

2   See Eugene Hillman, *Polygamy Reconsidered* (Maryknoll, N.Y.: Orbis Books, 1975).

9 | The Teaching of the Unification Church: A Trilogy

Unification Eschatology and Apocalyptic—
ANDREW WILSON

The Unificationist Understanding of
Resurrection—JAMES R. FLEMING

Marriage and the Family as the Key to the Coming
of the Kingdom: A Practical and Pastoral
Approach—THOMAS AZAR

Unification Eschatology and Apocalyptic
ANDREW WILSON

In this way, the whole of mankind will become one people speaking one language, thus establishing one world of one culture.
    DIVINE PRINCIPLE

Central to the teaching of the Unification Church is the proclamation that the world is living in the Last Days, near the moment when God is to enter decisively into human affairs and bring history to its consummation. The Second Advent of Christ is near, and he is to liquidate the power of Satan and inaugurate the Kingdom of God on earth. Out of this proclamation comes the call to commitment and the Church's self-understanding as a harbinger, catalyst, and builder of God's new world.

This orientation has led many to classify the eschatological teachings of the Unification Church with the doctrines of other millenarian Christian sects. Yet close study of Unification teachings raises questions as to whether they are essentially another variation of the apocalyptic traditions which have shaped the doctrines of those Christian groups who look fervently for the Second Coming of Christ. They may in fact diverge from an apocalyptic modality in favor of a more immanent eschatology which had been characteristic of the Hebrew prophets. Therefore we begin with a general discussion of the roots of apocalyptic and its relationship to prophetic eschatology which can serve to illuminate the distinctive features of the Unification doctrine.

Apocalyptic and Prophetic Eschatology

Much recent discussion among biblical scholars has dealt with apocalyptic either as a literary genre or as the literature of an "apocalyptic movement" that flourished from the fifth century

B.C.E. and can be found in both Judaism and Christianity into the second century C.E..[1] It is in the latter sense that one can speak of groups of people holding an apocalyptic eschatology. Eschatology did not begin with apocalypticism; that had been a concern of the prophets, who had warned Israel to expect a coming "day of the Lord" (Amos 5:18). On that day God would act decisively in history. But the apocalyptic movement gave new meaning to eschatological concepts. Hanson has distinguished apocalyptic eschatology from prophetic eschatology as follows:

The prophets, affirming the historical realm as a suitable context for divine activity, understood it as their task to translate the vision of divine activity from the cosmic level to the level of the politico-historical realm of everyday life. The [apocalyptic] visionaries, disillusioned with the historical realm, disclosed their vision in a manner of growing indifference to and independence from the contingencies of the politico-historical realm, thereby leaving the language increasingly in the idiom of the cosmic realm.[2]

The prophets saw God working through the concrete events of history for Israel's benefit, whether it were for judgment, as Jeremiah saw the invasion of Nebuchadnezzar's armies, or for salvation, as Deutero-Isaiah saw the divine will working through Cyrus. They were careful to preserve a dialectical relationship between the divine realm and the earthly one.

The small and powerless communities of visionaries who composed apocalyptic literature lived at a time when Israel was under the yoke of foreign occupation by the Persians, Greeks, and Romans successively.[3] Israel was but a speck in a world of great empires and few could continue to believe that the purposes of God would be achieved in the normal course of political events. Therefore, the apocalyptists hoped for a cosmic intervention of God who, as the Creator of the universe, need not be bound by worldly constraints. In apocalyptic texts God rearranges creation itself, destroying the wicked, exalting the faithful, and establishing God's paradisiacal reign. This theological move, born out of a despair that God could work effectively within history, placed the locus of divine action beyond history. Tearing asunder the vital relationship which the prophets saw between the divine and the human realms, the apocalyptists could see no hope in the world and so placed all their hope in God alone.

Other features of apocalyptic eschatology are a consequence of this orientation. First, while the prophets had recognized the complex and unpredictable nature of human events, apocalyptic oracles followed a stereotyped pattern of tribulation: judgment-salvation that can be traced back to ritual motifs of Temple worship.[4]

Second, in keeping with this stereotyped pattern, apocalyptic literature idealized the eschaton. The age of salvation would be a new age entirely different from the present one. The "new heaven and new earth" will be without sin or any moral ambiguity whatever. According to some writings it will be an earthly paradise; in others death itself will be transcended as the elect are transported into the heavenly realm. The eschaton becomes final, ending temporality as we know it.

Third, apocalyptic literature is often concerned with timetables and predictions of the time of the end. While denying human contingency in its idealization of God's sovereign power, it could focus entirely on divining God's plan. Although the prophet Jeremiah had prophesied of a time period of seventy years from exile until the restoration of Israel (Jer. 25:12, 29:10), it is with apocalyptic speculation such as in the Book of Daniel that concern for timetables becomes a dominant motif.

This determinism is consonant with a fourth characteristic: a moral dualism between the righteous, destined for salvation, and the wicked, bound for destruction. The visionaries were sectarians who suffered oppression and discrimination by the rulers of society. Hence they saw as righteous only their own oppressed community; they saw others, even other Jews, as deserving their fate. The prophets had been concerned with the well-being of all Israel; they lamented over their faithlessness and often held out the opportunity for repentance as a way to avert catastrophe. In contrast, apocalyptic judgment was unconditional and lacked compassion.

Eschatology and the Advent of Jesus

Apocalyptic eschatology was in the ascendant in the Jewish community to which Jesus came. Though the Kingdom of God had its remote origin in pre-exilic times (see Pss. 47, 93, 97, 99), it became a central religious motif of Judaism in apocalyptic literature only shortly before the time of Jesus (Dan. 7:14, *Ass. Moses* 10). John the Baptist, who preached the imminent coming of the Kingdom (Matt. 3:2), led one such apocalyptic sect. Jesus himself spoke out of this context and preached that the Kingdom was already present in his person and the miracles which put Satan to flight (Luke 11:20, 17:20–21)[5] and that its total manifestation would follow shortly (Luke 11:2b–4).[6]

Yet Jesus' preaching differed from the prevalent apocalyptic thought of his age. His words stressed the individual's responsibility to respond to and participate in the Kingdom. In Luke 17:20–21 he criticizes those who would stand by and passively wait for signs. Luke 9:60, Matthew 5:39–41 and Matthew 7:13–14 are proverbs whose ethic is so radical that they demand a total and wholehearted commitment to the Kingdom. Furthermore, the saying in Matthew 11:12: "From the days of John the Baptist until now, the Kingdom of Heaven has suffered violence, and men of violence take it by force" probably implies that by the death of John the Baptist, the work of building the Kingdom would become dangerous and Jesus and his disciples might suffer.[7] Jesus understood the progress of the Kingdom's very unfolding to be contingent upon human events.

Thus Jesus' message, although rooted in the apocalyptic eschatology of his time, moved in the direction of restoring the historicity of divine action characteristic of prophetic eschatology. The historical contingency of the Kingdom is consistent with a notable absence of apocalyptic timetables.[8] Jesus' expectation of the people's response also led him to appeal to all classes, from the Pharisees to the outcasts of society. He did not share the sectarian outlook of most apocalyptists but sought the welfare of all Israel, even praying for his enemies. Here he follows in the tradition of those classical prophets who felt their people's impending doom as their personal tragedy and sought to intercede for them.[9]

Although the Christian tradition has downplayed any contingency with regard to Jesus' mission, Unification theology affirms it in its assertion that the Crucifixion was not the original will of God. *Divine Principle* asserts that had Jesus been able to continue his ministry with substantial support from the people, subsequent history would have looked very different. It reasons that God's purpose for preparing Israel for Jesus' coming could only be that they might receive him, and that had Israel rallied around Jesus, he would not have had to go to the cross. The efforts of Jesus and his disciples during his ministry that the people might believe and follow him, as well as the shock and despondency of the disciples at his execution, indicate that they had hoped for a different outcome. As we shall see, this regard for contingency is also consistent with Unificationist eschatology of the Lord of the Second Advent.

It is generally accepted that in spite of the expectations of the apocalyptists of the day, the Christ event was not the fulfillment of apocalyptic eschatology.[10] Modern theologies that take such a finding of historical-critical scholarship seriously have often not taken contingency as an option; instead they have had to relativize or discount the eschatological thinking of Jesus and his contemporaries either as a metaphor for God's transcendence (Barth), as mythology that can be unpacked as existential encounter (Bultmann), or as an erroneous belief of Jesus who did not understand the true significance of his own mission.

Yet the creedal affirmation that Jesus Christ is truly man implies that Jesus' life and mission be subject to contingency. As the life of a historical person, the Christ event was an eschatological event *within* history and subject to its contingency, not the radical and irresistible inbreaking of God from *beyond* history to judge the wicked and establish God's dominion over the earth as expected by the apocalyptists. Jesus in his ministry restored the broken dialectic between the divine realm and worldly affairs. He brought, for a brief moment, a return to the prophetic mode of eschatology where God works within history.

Christian Apocalypticism

Faced with the human tragedy of the historical Jesus, early Christianity could not maintain a thoroughgoing apocalyptic interpretation of Jesus' life and ministry. The New Testament Churches rapidly ceased to speak about the Kingdom of God which Jesus proclaimed and instead looked to Jesus himself as the focus of faith. They did maintain, as a legacy from apocalyptic eschatology, a total determinism regarding Jesus' mission.[11] However, Jesus' personal example and teaching broke the apocalyptic stereotype of a savior who comes leading heavenly armies (Dan. 7:13) when in his own life he taught the way of self-sacrifice and the cross. To understand this Jesus, the early Christians had to search for new figures such as Isaiah's Suffering Servant which were not usual apocalyptic motifs.

Yet the early Christian community was so schooled in the expectations of apocalyptic eschatology that those traditions rapidly reasserted themselves and became attached to the doctrine of the

Second Coming of Christ.[12] Jesus the apocalyptic Son of Man would return imminently (Mark, Q). The resurrection of Jesus, "first fruits" of the eschaton, became the sign of a general resurrection soon to follow (1 Cor. 15:20).

According to Christian apocalypticism, Jesus' Second Coming would not be constrained by historical reality or even the laws of creation. It would follow the stereotyped pattern of tribulation-judgment-salvation. In the ideal of the New Jerusalem (Rev. 21) or the general resurrection (1 Cor. 15), temporality as we know it would end, "death shall be no more, neither shall there be mourning nor crying nor pain any more, for the former things have passed away" (Rev. 21:4). There was consequently no thought of the responsibilities of the elect who would populate such an ideal world, only an interim ethic as Christians awaited the eschaton.

Neither would there be any contingency in Christ's return; it would be wholly God's doing. The Church would not be the historical agency of world redemption but rather would live only to strengthen itself in anticipation of the blessed day.[13] In New Testament apocalyptic that day could come at any moment (Mark 13:32–37), but later Christian Churches that carried on the tradition of apocalyptic eschatology (from the medieval Joachim of Fiore to nineteenth-century Millerites and twentieth-century dispensationalists) once again speculated about timetables for predicting the day of the Second Advent.

Sectarian dualism also reasserted itself: Christ at his return would come for Christian believers alone, while unbelievers were destined to "the lake of fire" (Rev. 20:14). The wickedness of the age appeared to be so rampant that there was no thought of calling the world to repent; instead the apocalyptist wrote "let the evildoer still do evil, and the filthy still be filthy, and the righteous still do right, and the holy still be holy" (Rev. 22:11; see Dan. 12:10).

These characteristics of apocalyptic eschatology have been part of Christian beliefs about the Second Coming to this day. It is not surprising, given what we know about the social location of apocalyptic, that those churches that emphasize the Second Coming tend to be sectarian and to feel politically powerless.[14]

The Eschatology of Divine Principle

Unification eschatology, like the eschatology of Jesus, grew out of apocalypticism. This is evident from the focus of *Divine Principle* on proclaiming the imminent Kingdom of God, its insistence that

Christianity only finds its completion in the Second Advent, and its preoccupation with timetables. Yet the doctrines of eschatology and the Second Advent in Unification theology depart in important respects from the apocalypticism of most Christian doctrines of the Second Coming, and, again like the eschatology of Jesus, ascribe historicity and contingency to divine activity.

Divine Principle makes this point in several ways. First, it insists that the Second Advent will occur in the same manner as the First. From the standpoint of "providential time identity" the First Advent and the Second Advent are parallel events which follow parallel courses.[15] In asserting the parallel course of the Second Advent and the First, it discounts the biblical sayings that the Second Coming will be an apocalyptic appearance "on the clouds" by arguing that those Jews at the time of Jesus had similar apocalyptic expectations that were in fact disconfirmed by Jesus' actual birth as a human being and ministry subject to contingency.[16] Here Divine Principle is engaged in polemics with "fundamentalist" Protestants who held apocalyptic beliefs about the Second Coming of Christ and who have dominated the religious life of twentieth-century Korea out of which the Unification Church was born.

Second, in its assertion that the Lord of the Second Advent will come and pursue a course in accordance with the Principle of Creation,[17] Unification theology insists that God binds himself to the constraints of creation and history when sending the Lord of the Second Advent. In this regard, apocalyptic eschatology in the Bible is "demythologized" through allegorical interpretation in such a way as to harmonize with a view of God's providential activity always regulated by consistent principles.[18] Consistency of divine activity is a theme throughout Divine Principle, turning up in such places as the discussion of why God did not intervene to prevent the human Fall[19] and of how human contingency can prolong divine providence in history.

Like theologies of many apocalyptic Christian sects, Divine Principle makes extensive use of timetables, and in particular it uses the concept of "time identity" as a way of predicting the time of the Second Advent. Yet these timetables are not indicative of a historical determinism. Each decisive moment of divine activity is conditional; its outcome always depends upon a human portion of responsibility.[20] There is a dialectic between the consistent operation of God's will, as illustrated by the regular cycles of providential history, and the human response required at crucial moments to bring the purpose of that cycle to fulfillment and to avoid its repetition.

The Lord of the Second Advent himself comes as such a divine initiative. Luke 17:25 is cited as prophesying that in the course of his ministry he could be rejected and suffer, just as did Jesus.[21] The text makes it clear that the details of his course are contingent upon whether those Christians whom he calls will receive him. He could be accepted and have a simple course, building the Kingdom upon the inherited Christian foundation, or if he is rejected, he might have to summon a new group of followers who will walk a stormy course of persecution with him on the way to establishing the Kingdom.[22]

Another aspect of Unification eschatology, reminiscent of classical prophecy, is that temporality and history continue after the eschaton. The first chapter of *Divine Principle* contains a detailed description of principles of existence in the ideal world, principles that assert human creativity and responsibility as necessary for the expression of divine love. The finality of the eschaton is understood to be the end of evil and the power of Satan. The conditions at the Fall that allowed Satan to control humanity will be annulled, Satan will lose his hold over the human spirit, and his influence over human events will end. People will continue to be born and to die, to create masterpieces and to make mistakes, to love and to quarrel. Yet as they come to incarnate God's love, the negative aspects of human existence will no longer be dominant. The present world, characterized by violence, oppression and alienation, will give way to the "world of the heart." These are internal changes with many ramifications for human social life, but externally the temporal, physical and biological facts of human existence will remain the same.

Unification eschatology also lacks the moral dualism and sectarian character of apocalyptic. *Divine Principle* was written in the context of sectarian strife and gives an exegesis of many biblical verses about the Second Advent to condemn those Christians who reject and persecute the coming Lord.[23] Yet its description of events of the Last Days includes a universal leavening involving all people and all religions.[24] It describes the role of the Lord of the Second Advent as a central point and a teacher of the unifying ideology—a universal rather than a sectarian modality. Furthermore, it concludes with the hope of universal salvation, of the whole world as one family.[25] The existence of hell itself is an affront to God's perfection, and will be abolished when all its residents are restored to goodness "after a due period of time."[26]

Finally, Unification eschatology is critical of Christian apocalypticism for the same reason Jesus was critical of the Jewish apocalyptists of his day: They seek after observable signs and thereby miss the Kingdom which is dawning in their midst (Luke 17:20–21). Christians who expect a rapture would be blind to the immanent Spirit working among them to bring in the New Age which grows amidst the decline of the old age. Just as many of Jesus' disciples were simple people, able "to receive the Kingdom of God like a child" (Mark 10:14–15) and not overly attached to the dogmas of Old Testament apocalypticism, so those who are able to recognize the Lord of the Second Advent will have freed themselves from old concepts that they may discern where the Spirit of God is working.[27] Paradoxically, because their eschatology leads them to expect a miracle, those other Christians will miss the moment that they seek.

For the Unification Church, as with many apocalyptic sects, discerning the moment is everything. Eschatology functions positively, bringing an urgency which comes from knowing that now is the time. It is a clarion call to action. However, the type of commitment that Unification eschatology engenders seeks not only to evangelize in order to gather more people into the circle of the saved; the destiny of all humanity is bound together, either to transcend the cycle of hate and violence for a new future in God or to destroy itself. The stronghold of one faith cannot prevail in the reality of an interdependent world. There is no assurance of a power that can override the laws of the cosmos and separate the righteous from the wicked.

Instead the Unificationist is called to action with the faith that now, at the time of the eschaton, he or she is participating in the culminating historical work of God who loves the entire world (John 3:16). *Divine Principle* teaches that at the eschaton the destiny of the world hangs in precarious balance. Concerted effort at the proper moment can mean the difference between a bright future and universal catastrophe. The task at the eschaton is to reach out to solve the world's evils and build the Kingdom of God on earth. God has prepared that particular time with all the necessary conditions. The possibility of accomplishing this ideal, previously available for a short time at Jesus' coming, is once again open at the coming of the Lord of the Second Advent. God has raised up a new Messiah and is empowering his movement to take hold of this special opportunity.

Unification theology's thoroughly contingent view of divine activity has its cost. By abandoning apocalyptic eschatology with its lofty view of an omnipotent God who can unilaterally will the Kingdom of God into being, it opens the possibility that the earthly project for the Lord of the Second Advent might end in failure. There is no divine guarantee that the Messiah at the Second Advent will succeed in overcoming the enormous weight of the world's evil, or that some tragedy might not befall him, as befell Jesus. Yet it may be better to face a reality with few guarantees and strive to make it right than either to live without vision or to rest secure in the comforting dreams of apocalyptic. Faith itself is risk in the midst of apparent uncertainty with the confidence that God is a sure support. God's power of resurrection will salvage victory for those who, in the footsteps of Jesus, offer their lives for the Kingdom. The coming of the Lord of the Second Advent is such a call to strive, with faith that conditions are propitious, that God's help may be ever accessible, and that the foundation of human accomplishment is sufficient to sustain the work.

Notes

1   Today many scholars would repudiate the older view that apocalyptic derived from external Persian influences. While a few minor features may have been borrowed, it is essentially an inner-Israelite development. Cf. Paul Hanson, ed., *Visionaries and their Apocalypses* (Philadelphia: Fortress, 1983); Klaus Koch, *The Rediscovery of Apocalyptic* (London: SCM, 1972); John J. Collins, ed. *Semeia Fourteen: Apocalypse: The Morphology of a Genre,* (Missoula, Mont.: Scholars Press, 1979); Paul Hanson, "Apocalypticism," *IDB Suppl.,* 28–34; Michael E. Stone, "Revealed Things in Apocalyptic Literature," in *Magnalia Dei: The Mighty Acts of God,* ed. Cross, Lemke, and Miller (Garden City, N.J.: Doubleday, 1976), 439–43.

2   Paul Hanson, *The Dawn of Apocalyptic* (Philadelphia: Fortress, 1975), 12.

3   See George Nickelsburg, *Jewish Literature between the Bible and the Mishnah* (Philadelphia: Fortress, 1981) for a survey of this literature in its historical context.

4   Ezek. 38–39, Zech. 14, Dan. 7, Rev. 6–22. The prophetic books in their final form also move from tribulation to judgment to salvation, probably because their editors were themselves apocalyptists.

5   These and the following passages are considered to be genuine sayings of Jesus; see Norman Perrin, *Jesus and the Language of the Kingdom* (Philadelphia: Fortress, 1976), 41.

6   This is the minimalist reconstruction of Jesus' understanding of the Kingdom of God. See Johannes Weiss, *Jesus' Proclamation of the Kingdom of God,* trans. R. H. Hiiers and D.L. Holland (Philadelphia: Fortress, 1971); Rudolf Bultmann, *Theology of the New Testament* (New York: Scribner's, 1951), 6.

7   See Perrin, 46. This is the position of *Divine Principle* (New York: Holy Spirit Association for the Unification of World Christianity, 1973), 162.

8   It is remarkable that the early apocalyptic followers of Jesus who transmitted Q and the Markan Apocalypse insisted, in the face of the established apocalyptic interest in predicting the time of the end, that no one may know the time of the Son of Man's advent (Mark 13:32–37, Matt. 25:1–13, Luke 12:35–40). We may infer that Jesus himself opposed those who put their trust in timetables, as he castigated those who waited for signs (Luke 17:20–21).

9   Amos 7:2, Jer. 7:16, 11:14, Isa. 52:13–53:12, Exod. 32:30–32, Deut. 9:18–20.

10   See Rudolf Bultmann, *Jesus Christ and Mythology* (New York: Scribner's, 1958), 14.

11   Of course, the Christian assertion that Jesus' death was predestined was also to counter Jewish polemics that the fact of Jesus' crucifixion was proof that Jesus could not be the promised Messiah.

12   See Norman Perrin, *The New Testament: An Introduction* (New York: Harcourt Brace Jovanovich, 1974), 65–85.

13   This despair with regard to history did not stop apocalyptic communities from seeking converts, based upon their belief that God's will was for as many as possible to be offered the opportunity to join the sectarian group that had assurance of resurrection and life at the impending judgment. In fact, one way in which the early Christians preserved a vestige of the contingency of Jesus' mission was in the notion that the eschaton

would not come until a certain number of converts had filled their ranks (Mark 13:10, Rom. 11:25). Nevertheless, the believing community would not materially affect the inbreaking of God's power at the eschaton through social or political activity.

14   The "Moral Majority" is the exception that proves the rule. It arose as a reactionary coalition of churches that felt besieged by the growing assault of secular values in American life and it has been unable to stem that tide.

15   *Divine Principle,* 532–35.

16   Ibid., 502ff.

17   Ibid., 510–12.

18   Ibid., 113–19, 512–14.

19   Ibid., 95–97.

20   Ibid., 111–12.

21   Ibid., 502.

22   Ibid., 364–65.

23   Ibid., 532–34.

24   Ibid., 120–29.

25   Ibid., 536, cf. 129.

26   Ibid., 190–91. [Here Unification teaching seems to accord with Origen's teaching.—Ed.]

27   Ibid., 133–36.

The Unificationist Understanding of Resurrection
JAMES R. FLEMING

Thus, this age may also be called the "age of justification by attendance."
The spirit men belonging to this age can attain the divine-spirit stage of
perfect resurrection in both spirit and body by believing and serving the Lord
of the Second Advent.
    DIVINE PRINCIPLE

The Unification view of resurrection is based on the ontological assertion that there is a spiritual world populated by spirit persons who are more or less in communication with people on earth. These *Jenseiters* populating the spiritual world are the fore-runners and ancestors of the current inhabitants of the physical world, the *Dieseiters*.

    The spiritual world is not only the home of spirit persons; it is also the ultimate destination of the budding spirit person of each one of us alive on earth today. Furthermore it is a world which is itself in need of restoration. According to Unification theology, both the *Jenseiter* and the *Dieseiter* alike must be resurrected (i.e. re-created according to God's providence of restoration) if the "Kingdom of God on earth and in heaven" is to be realized.[1]

    In the following pages, the notion of resurrection is used as a hermeneutical tool to examine the Unification view of personal eschatology and to elicit deeper and richer meaning within the *Divine Principle,* the speeches of Rev. Sun Myung Moon, and Unification Church praxis.

The Unification View of Resurrection

Unification theology affirms that resurrection is both a "realized" process ongoing in the life of the believer as well as a fervently hoped-for (and worked-for) future event: the complete and final transformation of the self, community, and cosmos, freeing all from the power of sin and uniting all with the Heart of God. While Unification eschatology and faith in human immortality are clearly linked to the doctrine of creation,[2] they are also linked, through the providence of resurrection, to the doctrine of salvation.[3] According to *Divine Principle*, "resurrection means to return to the Heavenly lineage through Christ, leaving the death of the Satanic lineage caused by the fall of Adam."[4] Resurrection does not mean "the restoration of once corrupted and decomposed physical bodies to their original state."[5]

The Unification view of resurrection further stresses these three important ideas, which are biblically based[6] but too often neglected:

1 *The psychosomatic unity of the person.*[7] According to the Principle of Creation,[8] God created an Invisible Substantial World (spiritual world), which exists in relationship to the Visible Substantial World (physical world) as the human mind exists in relationship to the human body.[9] The spiritual world is the home of the spirit self which consists of the spirit mind and spirit body.[10] The spirit self is designed to live for eternity in the spirit world. After a sufficient level of perfection is achieved, it can communicate directly with God. God is said to dwell in the spirit mind which is the essence of the spirit self. The spirit mind continually seeks truth, beauty, and love while it regulates the functions of the spirit body.

The spirit self needs nutrition for its growth and perfection. The nutritional element *Yang* or Life Element is the truth and love supplied by God; the *Um* or vitality element must be generated by the activities of the physical self which, when it acts in accordance with God's will, projects wholesome nourishment for the growth of the spirit self. The spirit self not only receives the *Um* from the physical self, but also projects a spirit element (or spark of life) which energizes and brings joy and a sense of well-being to the physical self. The proper balance in the exchange of life, vitality, and spirit elements, allows the spirit person to grow and mature like a fruit on a vine. The Unificationist believes that at the time of death the physical body (metaphorically the vine) returns to the earth from whence it came, while the spirit person, having both spirit mind and spirit body and thus both personality and personal identity, goes off to live in the spiritual world in relationship with God and other spirit persons.[11]

While Unificationists argue from the doctrine of creation that we are "living in two worlds" simultaneously[12] and are fond of pointing out recent increased interest in mystical experiences and parapsychological experimentation, Unificationism, as a religious path, differs from Spiritualism not in its belief that the individual personality survives the change called death, but in its concern for the *quality* of life after death for the individual, community, and cosmos.

2 *The resurrection of the dead is a giftlike "new creation" rather than a birthright due to the immortality of the soul.* Most Unificationists (to the best of my knowledge) believe that if they were to die today their personal destiny would not radically differ from that of a devout Christian who enters the spiritual world at the same time. Presumably, if the spirit person had grown sufficiently strong during this life on the earth, the Unificationist *Jenseiter* would encounter his righteous ancestors and would be introduced to the saints of Paradise (including Jesus himself) who had worked on earth for the Kingdom of God. The Unificationist, however, would not be content merely to enjoy the gift of Paradise personally, but would continue to work with the saints in the spiritual world to share his or her blessing with others less fortunate. According to *Divine Principle* there would be many such people. As Unificationists like to ask, how could God, Jesus, or the saints of Paradise sit back and enjoy eternal bliss when suffering continues in both worlds and when millions of people enter the spiritual world each year, many of whom have rejected Christianity because of the shortcomings of the Christian Churches? The Unificationist would also attempt to work with the people of earth to inspire them to work for God's Kingdom. He or she would be able to receive vitality elements that would allow spiritual growth to continue in the spiritual world. Such activity is a consequence of the Unificationist emphasis on Universal Restoration.

3 *The resurrection of the dead is a transformation that occurs in the present as well as in the future, on earth as well as in heaven.*[13] God's dispensation for resurrection is based on the people of earth.[14] It

is only earthly people, alive at the time of the coming of the Messiah (the Lord of the Second Advent) who can fully receive the divine Life element (*Yang*) directly from the God–Man and who can then supply the necessary vitality element (*Um*) for the growth of their spirit persons by serving and attending the Messiah as disciples. Yet discipleship is not enough. The God-given mission to build the Kingdom must be taken up by each believer as a personal calling and life-work. In effect all of Rev. Sun Myung Moon's disciples must become "little messiahs,"[15] substantiating God's truth and love in their lives, confronting the evils of this world, and expanding the foundations for the Kingdom of God on earth. They must also become willing and able to share God's blessing universally. Then, through the providence of "returning resurrection,"[16] men and women of the spiritual world of all backgrounds will descend and work with their Unificationist descendants on earth to establish the universal sovereignty of God.[17] Through the providence of God, bodies ruled by sin will be resurrected into bodies ruled by obedience to God, spirit persons will receive new vitality elements, and the Kingdom of God will be established on earth and in heaven.

Resurrection Today: Unification of Theory and Practice

The speeches of Rev. Sun Myung Moon and the practices of the Unification Movement provide us with an opportunity to reflect further on the ways in which church members today experience resurrection. Rev. Sun Myung Moon constantly emphasizes the reality of the spiritual world.[18] Moreover, there is an "untold number" of righteous spirit persons who are intently watching the Kingdom-building activities of earthly Unificationists.[19] All this attention from the spirit world functions to encourage church members to work hard and maintain high standards in order to provide a foundation upon which the spiritual world's assistance can be mobilized:

> The very highest level of the spirit world is occupied by martyrs. If you are going beyond [your limitations]; risking your life, even unto death; committing your life; then all the martyrs, the greatest in the spirit world, will come down on your side. If that happens, all kinds of miracles will happen to you. . . . This is the Principle. In order to mobilize all of the spirit world, we have to be better than their quality or their standard.[20]

But the real purpose underlying these exhortations to hard work and to attain high standards lies in the desire of Rev. Sun Myung Moon to nurture a sense of unselfish and sacrificial love among Unificationists. The love of God, he says, is the "only asset you will have . . . the only thing you can take with you to the spirit world."[21] Conversely, if we go to the spirit world without loving as much as we should, "we must keep repenting and help earthly men and women to do that in our place."[22] The quality and amount of love we experience in this life determines our freedom in the spiritual world:

When you go to the spirit world, that world works like this: . . . the person who experiences a deep sense of love in family life will have much, much freedom to maneuver. He can go horizontally in all directions, everywhere without limitation. In contrast, a person who has no experience of love is narrow-minded. He isolates himself in spirit world and has no freedom at all.[23]

At important church gatherings since the conclusion of his public speaking tour in America in 1976, Rev. Sun Myung Moon, acting as an apostle of God, has proclaimed certain critical junctures in the relations between the spiritual world and the physical world. For example on the Day of the Victory of Heaven, October 4, 1976, Rev. Sun Myung Moon announced that he had mobilized the righteous leaders of the spirit world, "even Jesus himself, as well as Buddha, Confucius, and Mohammed" to come down to their followers on earth and lead them to the Unification movement.[24] And on November 2, 1978, a treaty was negotiated in Korea which breaks down barriers between religions and tribes both on earth and in the spirit world. Since this ceremony, the spirit world no longer recognizes the barriers between religions, clans, and families. Now there is no longer a distinction; it is all one family.[25]

But beyond doctrine, speeches, and startling pronouncements, Unificationism is a religion that stresses orthopraxis over orthodoxy. If the theology is to have meaning, it must become alive in the believers. In the Unification Church, consciousness of the transcendent is not coupled with otherworldliness but with a healthy sense of ecumenicity, which, it is believed, will prepare a worldwide foundation upon which God can act more decisively and dramatically in history. The activities of the International Religious Foundation (IRF) are a case in point: The Youth Seminar on World Religions pursues "world peace through religious dialogue and harmony;" the Interdenominational Conferences for Clergy (ICC) "hopes to promote mutual enrichment, sharing of insights, and exploration among clergy. . .from the widest spectrum of Christianity;" and New ERA "seeks to create a new environment for ecumenical conversation, building bridges of understanding "to encourage a vision of the family of religions and to relate this vision to the transformation of society." These and many other ecumenical activities, staffed and funded by the Unification movement, represent Rev. Sun Myung Moon's personal commitment to orthopraxis.

Conclusion

The mystery of personal eschatology is not an objective problem. The eschatological question, however, as an inquiry into the destiny and meaning of life, remains open as a subject for systematic inquiry. It is hoped that the Unification notion of resurrection, which links personal destiny with providential hope, will provide new religious insights into perennial problems for a growing number of people. Among Unificationists, the biblical expectation of a new heaven and a new earth requires, above all else, the articulation of a new revolutionary theology and the establishment of a new social order.

Here I add a personal confession. I believe that Unification theology and the Unification movement are harbingers of, and may provide the leadership for, this new order of things. If neither the theology as it is currently expressed nor the movement as it currently exists attains this goal, I look to Unification as explored and developed by New ERA. To be able to participate in such an ongoing and enriching process brings me personal fulfillment.

Notes

1   See *Divine Principle* (Washington, D.C.: Holy Spirit Association for the Unification of World Christianity, 1973), 45–46 for the way the Unification notion of the Kingdom of God is rooted in the doctrine of

creation. "If God's purpose of creation had been actualized in this way, [by humans fulfilling the three great blessings] an ideal world, in which no trace of sin could be found, would have been established on this earth. We may call this world the Kingdom of Heaven on earth. Man was created in the beginning to live in the Kingdom of Heaven on earth. At the moment of his physical death, he was to automatically transmigrate into the spirit world where he could enjoy an eternal life in the spiritual Kingdom of Heaven."

2 Young Oon Kim, *Unification Theology* (New York: HSA Publications, 1980), 81; M. Darrol Bryant, "Critical Reflections on Unification Eschatology," in *Exploring Unification Theology,* ed. Bryant and Hodges (Barrytown, N.Y.: Unification Theological Seminary, 1978), 149.

3 *Divine Principle,* 172.

4 Ibid., 171.

5 Ibid., 170.

6 In Acts 23:6–7, Luke seems to suggest that belief in resurrection can provide a bond between Christians and Jews.

7 The Bible has no term that signifies the body existing without the soul. Moreover, the term "soul" always means the whole person existing bodily. Joseph Ratzinger, "Resurrection," in *Encyclopedia of Theology,* ed. Karl Rahner (New York: Seabury, 1975), 1450–53.

8 Ibid., 19–64.

9 The choice of terminology is perhaps unfortunate here in that the Invisible Substantial World is invisible only to fallen people whose spiritual senses have been deadened by sin. Restored individuals would have full spiritual perception.

10 As Macquarrie puts it, "to exist is to be in a world, and it is only by having a body of some sort that one can be in a world." John Macquarrie, *Principles of Christian Theology* (New York: Scribner's, 1970), 324.

11 *Divine Principle,* 60–63. In 1 Corinthians 15:35ff., Paul asserts that it is the *spiritual body* of the Christian believer that is raised and united with the soul at the time of resurrection. This view of the afterlife involves full personal immortality for the believer and includes such corollary beliefs as the maintenance of personal identity, the recognition of other individuals and the possibility of personal relationships in the spiritual world.

12 Kim, 81–86.

13 Two prominent twentieth-century theologians illuminate this point: P. T. Forsyth writes in *This Life and the Next* (New York: Macmillan, 1918), "There are more conversions on the other side than on this." N. F. S. Ferré in *The Christian Understanding of God* (New York: Harper,

1951) calls God "the perfect parent who has no permanent problem children."

14 *Divine Principle,* 173–76.

15 The term is the Reverend Sun Myung Moon's.

16 *Divine Principle,* 181–87.

17 Ibid., 188–91.

18 Sun Myung Moon, "The Spirit World and the Physical World," Speech given 6 February, 1977.

19 Sun Myung Moon, "God's Day Address," speech given 1 January 1974.

20 Sun Myung Moon, "Instructions to IOWC Commanders and Team Members," speech given 31 January 1974. See also "On Witnessing," speech given 3 January 1972.

21 Sun Myung Moon, "Core of Unification," speech given 9 October 1977.

22 Sun Myung Moon, "For the Future," speech given 10 September 1978.

23 Sun Myung Moon, "The Kingdom of God and the Ideal Family," speech given 1 January 1977.

24 Sun Myung Moon, "The Day of the Victory of Heaven," speech given 4 October, 1976.

25 Sun Myung Moon, "Mainstream of the Dispensation of God," speech given 11 November 1978.

Marriage and the Family as the Key to the Coming of the Kingdom: A Practical and Pastoral Approach
THOMAS AZAR

Confucianism has special merit today because it uses the family as a model for society at large. . . . Unificationism differs from Confucianism by interpreting God's plan for mankind in terms of Adam and Eve's purpose. They were created to provide the base for the God-centered family. They were to be true parents for a righteous mankind.
    YOUNG OON KIM, *Unification Theology*

The aim of this paper is pastoral rather than scholarly. Genuine care within the religious family, born of true affection and the Word of God, is the best foundation one can make for understanding and preparing for the eschaton, the Kingdom of God, and for one's own salvation. As a pastor, I see caring as the prime virtue. I have worked in churches black and white; I have served as a hospital chaplain and in the police department of the city of Atlanta for the past seven years. My understanding of eschatology comes, to a great degree, from my confrontation with human life. I have tried to let the experience draw me in; later I have struggled to understand what I have been through. I continually seek to move through the various fields of human relationships. In these relationships can be found the purpose of existence and the basis for the development of human character. I value the interplay of biblical study and pastoral care in the midst of the human crisis. In this context one can better understand one's own theological system and personal commitment, whatever they may be.

According to Unificationist teaching, we ought to be consciously preparing for the Last Days. As I see the situation they are coming non-violently and non-apocalyptically. We are moving toward the future on the basis of God's history, which begins with the family of Adam and Eve. Our hope is rooted in the victorious families to which the Bible, both the Old and the New Testaments, bear witness. The Unificationist understanding of the significance of the family, rooted in the Bible, is that (1) it is the cornerstone of God's building of the Kingdom and the channel of the multiplication of his love, disseminated in the preaching of his Holy Word; (2) it is the pre-Fall or creational institution ordained by God; (3) it serves as the point of intersection for the covenantal relationship between God and humanity; (4) it is where a variety of "loves" grow and develop; and (5) it includes and transcends culture, race, sex, nationality, and even religion itself.

I believe that ecumenical research induces reform. Five hundred years ago, November 10, 1483, Martin Luther was born. His mind and heart were heavy because of the gross discrepancies he saw between the Bible and the teachings of the medieval Church. His early theological studies acquired special meaning for him through his later experience of marriage, with all its distinctive opportunities for spiritual growth.

The purpose of marriage is to allow men and women to live out their faith and love in the freedom of Jesus Christ, within a divinely ordained institution that fulfills the Law and Gospel and thereby establishes a strong social and ethical foundation against Satanic invasion, be it from within the self or outside. Marriage becomes the environment that calls upon parents to overcome their preoccupation with the self and enables them to learn to care, serve, and love their children. Marriage provides the rich soil for faith and love to grow. Furthermore, the family stands between the child's relationship with God on the one hand, and the individual's relationship with human society on the other. Luther boldly states: "Parents cannot earn eternal punishment in any way more easily than neglecting their own children."[1]

Care for one's family is central. Unity, cooperation and happiness are lifegiving aims. Luther opposed the dissidents who, quoting Scripture, taught that one could leave one's family if they were not following the way of the faithful. They, no less than the papacy, were undermining the family. Luther says: "Parents are thus invested with an authority which is prior and superior to all earthly authority—kings and popes included."[2]

Establishing a God-centered family is a divine calling. Unificationists follow Luther in accounting it nothing less. The "Purpose of Creation" set forth in the *Divine Principle* bears much similarity to Luther's sermon on "The Estate of Marriage."

Luther, following Genesis 1:28, taught that the blessings of marriage stem from obedience to God's specific commandment, representing his divine will, which the individual dare not disobey.[3] Unificationist teaching, however, goes further: Salvation and the building of the Kingdom of God begins when the individuals are married by the Lord of the Second Advent. If one works hard and brings results and fulfills certain conditions (one of which is a period of celibacy before marriage), one's marriage can be specially sanctified or blessed. Once again there are similarities. The central model for Christian marriage comes directly out of Luther's theology, with its emphasis on God's love for humanity. The Unification Church follows Luther's use of Paul's image of the bride and bridegroom. Paul's mystical language expresses the nature of the grace-filled union of the believers, first with Christ, then with each other. Luther draws from Ephesians 5:31: "As Christ and humanity become one in God, so the union of two persons, bride and bridegroom, with Christ at the center of the union, becomes a special channel of God's power over sin and death, providing the couple with God's grace and love."[4]

Thus, eschatology finds expression in the family. The "vertical" and "horizontal" relationships intersect in this covenant relationship. As Jesus Christ emptied himself for us on the cross, so in Christian marriage the parties empty themselves, the one to the other in honesty and in sensitive openness. Moreover, as Jesus took upon himself our sins, so husband and wife are to bear each other's burdens for the sake of God, thus growing in love. The believing parties, within the framework of the family, are free to express God's love and grace, the one to the other and both toward their children. Yet Jesus Christ is more than a model to emulate; he is the principal source of the love that sustains the marriage. For Unificationists, moreover, the Lord of the Second Advent and his Bride play a central role in the coming of the "New Age."[5]

How then does one have the "blessed assurance" of salvation? I confess that I have no easy answer to propose. The answer is a mystery deep in the heart of God. Jonathan Edwards states emphatically that no one but God knows. I am content to acknowledge the mystery and to find peace of mind in my awareness of God's love. All affections that are genuine and God-centered are seated in the human heart; God's power is within this heart and inclines the individual to love God and neighbor as Christ did. I believe it is the Holy Spirit of God that fills one and inclines a believer to do God's will. One can feel and experience the grace of God and know for oneself whether one is in relationship with God. But whether I am saved, only God can know.

Both Luther and Jonathan Edwards emphasized the mysterious, surprising, unpredictable nature of God, both in himself and in his work. To me, the recognition of this is a blessed safeguard against the ever-present danger of our making God in our own inflated image. The pretense of knowing everything God thinks and does springs from what theologians call original sin. Although Unificationists may seem inclined to claim to know God's view on everything, they too must be mindful of the biblical report that even Moses saw only the back of God, not his face. Those who stand on institutional doctrine alone should look with openmindedness at the work of biblical scholars and theologians who add their fresh insights as well as their learning to the interpretation of the Bible.

Jesus says: "Fear not, little flock, for it is God's good pleasure to give you the kingdom" (Luke 12:32). The more I learn in the *Divine Principle* of the Last Days and of the Lord of the Second Advent, the more I believe we are offering answers for the enduring questions of history and a salutary prescription for human salvation. I believe, moreover, that we have a very special message to offer. The emphasis on the family in the *Divine Principle* needs to be heard by all believers. Most Christians are concerned only with the salvation of the self. Unificationists are concerned with extending and sacrificing their families to work in an exemplary way for the coming Kingdom of God. Marriage is, of course, a community as well as a private concern. The Unification Church, recognizing this, provides a moral context for the family, not least in our present circumstances, in which the stability of family relationships is very much threatened. We do not claim to have worked out all the details of our vision of the ideal family, but we hope, through openness to criticism and above all through devotion to God's word, to work out these details in time.

Establishing faithful families has been God's effort ever since the Fall. The greatest crimes, the most painful schisms, and the worst corruptions of character tend to take place not among those who do not know each other, but rather among those who do, even within the family. The nature of the Kingdom of God has more to do with restoring relationships within and outside of families than with destroying an old order and building a new one. Jesus often visited families in their homes (Luke 8:39, 10:39 and John 4:53).

According to the *Divine Principle,* Jesus was able to give only spiritual salvation to humanity. Therefore, the third Adam and his bride will come and complete what was left unfulfilled: the physical Kingdom of God on earth. Unificationists believe in (1) an ideal world built through ideal relationships (e.g., Adam and Eve); (2) an apocalyptic ending as the forces of Cain and Abel confront each other, whether through peaceful means or in open global conflict; (3) a new Utopianism; and (4) the Kingdom of Heaven, established in this historical time period through families, clans, and tribes, out to the entire world.[6]

Apocalyptic movements often sound as though they claim a monopoly on God's special directives. Yet although God is mysterious, unknown, and hidden, I do believe there is a covenantal relationship between him and humanity, and that God is moving toward us. We can put our trust and loyalty in him. The Last Days, the Lord of the Second Advent and his Bride, and salvation are all within God's sphere. My experience causes me to humble myself before the unfolding of God's plan for humankind.

Scripture teaches that no one knows but the Father. He alone anoints the Messiah. All I feel I can do is prepare the God-centered family after the creational mandate of God, and in the process of our struggle and growing love, begin to feel in my spirit-filled heart the answer we must give to the question: "Are you he who is to come, or are we to look for another?" (Matt. 11:3). One will know, not by a time chart, but by the genuine love of God, alive and working within the family. Love teaches all things. Faith grows in the rich soil of the God-centered family. The directive "to be fruitful and multiply" is to be taken seriously as believers undertake the working out of their covenantal relationship with God. From his side we are to expect mystery, quiet movement, and love. Recognizing the Messiah and the coming Kingdom depends greatly, I believe, on the sensitivity we acquire in making God's love and truth our own, within the family. Cardinal virtues, sincerely lived out in the lives of spouses and children, and spilling outward to one's neighbors, create more genuine receptivity to God's quiet voice. The primacy of the family is in no way idolatrous; the nature of its love goes beyond itself to the community, where it continues to exercise its holy power.

I recognize that the Unification Church has to demythologize and deorientalize much of its esoteric and apocalyptic teachings and lifestyle. We are not to expect this to come from the elders of the Church. Rather, it will come from the children of the families themselves, as they grow up to accept responsibility for the work initiated by Rev. Sun Myung Moon and the elders of the Church. Statistics show that after marriage many couples move to the background, away from the front line, nevertheless, the Unification Church is a body that can heal itself. So I conclude with what I take to be a fundamental principle in our teaching: The family is the institution of reform for humanity and even for the Unification Church itself.

To this I would add a personal note: My hope is only in an undeceiving God who has been merciful and generous to me, to my family, and to the wider family to whom I minister. I should like to think that whatever I have offered here by way of criticism might be of service to the leaders in the Unification Church.

Notes

1   Martin Luther, *Works,* 6 vols. (Philadelphia: Muhlenberg, 1915–43), 1:256.

2   Martin Luther, *Werke: Kritische Gesamtausgabe,* 58 vols. (Weirman: Bohlau, 1883), 16:354.

3   Martin Luther, *Works,* ed. Jaroslav Pelikan and Helmut Lehman (Philadelphia: Fortress, 1955–), 45:18ff.

4 Ibid., 31:351.

5 *Lifestyle: Conversations with Members of the Unification Church,* ed. Richard Quebedeaux (Barrytown, N.Y.: Unification Theological Seminary, 1982), 5ff.

6 *Divine Principle* (New York: The Holy Spirit Association for the Unification of World Christianity, 1973), 449ff.

PART TWO

Opinions from a Wider Circle of

Scholars

Reincarnation: The Lost Chord of Christianity?

SYLVIA CRANSTON

The idea of reincarnation contains a most comforting explanation of reality by means of which Indian thought surmounts difficulties which baffle the thinkers of Europe.

ALBERT SCHWEITZER, *Indian Thought and Its Development*

Introduction

A theosophical writer of the last century, William Q. Judge, spoke of reincarnation as "the lost chord of Christianity."[1] He probably had in mind, as an analogy, the beautiful soul–evoking song by Sir Arthur Sullivan of Gilbert and Sullivan fame. Published in 1877, "The Lost Chord" was a frequent offering in the concert repertoire of the world's great singers. The words are from a poem by Adelaide Procter. Sir Arthur put them to music at a time of deep sorrow when his younger brother died. For those unfamiliar with the song, I quote:

Seated one day at the organ,
I was weary and ill at ease,
And my fingers wandered idly
Over the noisy keys.
I knew not what I was playing,
Or what I was dreaming then.
But I struck one chord of music,
Like the sound of a great Amen.
It flooded the crimson twilight,
Like the close of an Angel's Psalm,
And it lay on my fevered spirit,
With a touch of infinite calm. . . .
It linked all perplexed meanings,
Into one perfect peace.
I have sought but I seek it vainly,

That one lost chord divine,
Which came from the soul of the organ,
And entered into mine.
It may be that Death's bright Angel,
Will speak in that chord again;
It may be that only in Heaven,
I shall hear that grand Amen.

Chords, we know, serve an immensely vital function in music. There are chords of dissonance that build up tension, turbulence, excitement, conflict, sorrow, and despair; there are chords of harmony that resolve the disturbance, bringing peace and contentment to the human heart. A story is told of Beethoven, who idling in bed one morning, refused to be aroused by a visiting friend. The latter went to the piano and played some spirited music, but just before the closing chord abruptly stopped. To most listeners this would be unsettling, but to the composer's sensitive ear, it was torture. Dashing to the keyboard, he himself played the triumphant notes, and harmony reigned once more.

Application of these thoughts to present-day Christianity, is the main subject of this paper, but first some preliminary considerations.

The notion that reincarnation is the lost chord of Christianity, presupposes that it was once known in the Church, and accepted at least by some members of the faith. The history of reincarnation in Christianity is a long story, and I do not propose to retell it now. It is admirably discussed by Professor Geddes MacGregor in his books *Reincarnation in Christianity* and *Reincarnation as a Christian Hope*.[2] In my own books it is also extensively reviewed.[3] That it became, in effect, anathematized by a sixth-century church council—*unofficially* many scholars now say[4]—is also true. Consequently none of the mainstream Christian Churches today teach it.

It is therefore astounding to learn from the 1981 Gallup Poll on religion that almost one-quarter of professing Christians in the United States affirm belief in many lives.

Statistics of Current Western Belief in Reincarnation

The 1981 Gallup Poll was the subject of a book by George Gallup, Jr., *Adventures in Immortality*.[5] The Gallup Organization describes the census as "the most comprehensive survey on beliefs about the afterlife that has ever been undertaken." It was addressed to adults 18 years old and over. The question on reincarnation was quite explicit: "Do you belive in reincarnation—that is, the rebirth of the soul in a new body after death—or not?" George Gallup reports: "Of those adults we polled, 23 percent, or nearly one quarter, said, they believe in reincarnation." There were 67 percent nonbelievers and 10 percent had no opinion. Among women there were 25 percent believers; among men 21 percent. As to religious denominations, four are listed: Baptist, 21 percent; Catholic, 25 percent; Lutheran, 22 percent; Methodist, 26 percent.

With regard to the 23 percent of adherents among the total adult population, that would mean that over thirty-eight million people believe in reincarnation (using the 1981 U.S. population figures of 166 million adults over the age of 18).[6]

Twelve years earlier, Gallup Poll figures on reincarnation belief for other nations in the West, as well as the United States, were equally revealing. They were published in the February 1969 Gallup census, a "Special Report on Religion" covering the religious beliefs and practices of Protestants and Catholics in 12 countries. The figures for reincarnationists were: Austria, 20 percent; Canada, 26 percent; France, 23 percent; Great Britain 18 percent; Greece, 22 percent; the Netherlands, 10 percent; Norway, 14 percent; Sweden, 12 percent; United States, 20 percent; West Germany, 25 percent.

A later Gallup Poll covering Great Britain alone, revealed that acceptance of reincarnation in that country rose from 18 percent in 1969 to 28 percent in 1979.[7]

It is well known that the current interest in rebirth among young people is enormous. A Pittsburgh piano teacher recently told me of an experience with an eighth-grade pupil. Amazed at the girl's astonishing ability in handling chords, the teacher inquired: "How is it that you know so much about chords?" The girl replied: "I must have learned about them in another life." Aware that the girl had a Catholic background and went to parochial school, the astonished teacher asked: "Where do you hear about such things?" "At school," the girl answered. "My friends and I talk about reincarnation all the time." Similar comments were made to me by other young adults. These girls and boys are the future parents in our society. What will they be teaching *their* children?

The truth of an idea, however, cannot be measured by numbers of adherents. If everyone believed in a plurality of lives that would not make it true.

Wishful, Magical Thinking

Atheists and other non-believers dismiss all teachings concerning an afterlife as wishful thinking. People fear death, they say, and dream up fantasies to cushion the shock of their inevitable demise. However, at least where reincarnation is concerned, its *rejection* could spring from similar thinking: *One does not want it to be true.*

Take the fundamentalists. Would not they prefer an everlasting stay in heaven to the painstaking work of returning to earth to struggle more diligently for their redemption?

Consider next the scientists and psychologists of materialistic persuasions. They may instinctively reject rebirth, because if it were true a lifetime of research based on the theory that matter and energy are the only realities would be undermined.

Then there are the people who are weary and bitterly disillusioned with life. They may say: "What, one more round? Never. I do not want to come back." (This view often rests on a misconception that being reborn means *immediate* rebirth. Most reincarnational philosophies teach that a long period of celestial rest usually intervenes between incarnations—a time for assimilating the harvest of life's experiences. Then, refreshed and spiritually invigorated, the individual returns, not in sadness and despair, but, as childhood attests, in eager joyousness to undertake a new adventure in learning and growing.)

To searchers for truth, neither likes nor dislikes are a legitimate basis for accepting or rejecting reincarnation. "What are the facts?" they will ask. Is there any hard-core evidence supporting the many-lives theory? Yes, there is—not final proofs, but volumes of evidence.

Scientific Investigation of Reincarnation

The leading scientist in reincarnation research is Dr. Ian Stevenson, Carlson Professor of Psychiatry at the University of Virginia Medical School, and former chairman of that department. In an on-going series he has to date five large volumes of case histories—published by the University Press of Virginia—of children around the world who provide evidence, often in amazing detail, that they lived before. Dr. Stevenson's on-the-spot research usually finds their claims to be 90 percent accurate.

In reviewing volume I of Stevenson's *Cases of the Reincarnation Type,* the *Journal of the American Medical Association* (Dec. 1, 1975), spoke of his "meticulous and extended investigations," and that he has "painstakingly and unemotionally collected a detailed series of cases in which the evidence for reincarnation is difficult to understand on any other grounds. . . . He has placed on record a large amount of data that cannot be ignored."

In September of 1977, in the 165th volume of a distinguished psychiatric publication, the *Journal of Nervous and Mental Disease,* almost an entire issue was devoted to Stevenson's research. In May of that year the same journal featured his lengthy paper "The Explanatory Value of the Idea of Reincarnation." What was the reaction of readers? Dr. Eugene Brody, editor of the journal and a psychiatrist at the University of Maryland Medical School, said in an interview: "I must have had three or four hundred requests for reprints from scientists in every discipline. It's pretty clear that there's a lot of interest in this topic."[8]

The children Stevenson investigates prove ideal subjects because most of them claim to have died prematurely just a few years ago; hence their memories of prior parents, friends, and relatives, as well as detailed descriptions of former dwelling places and events, can be verified. In some cases the children recall over fifty items that proved accurate. The optimum time for such past-life recall is between two and four years of age. Between five and eight the memories usually fade.

What is particularly encouraging about this research from a Christian standpoint is that while scholars and theologians speculate endlessly on eschatological matters, never resolving the perplexities arising from a study of the scanty records in the New Testament, acceptable evidence for the possible survival of the human soul is receiving serious attention by the scientific community.

an Human Beings Reincarnate as Animals?

There is a widespread belief in the Orient that human beings can incarnate into lower forms of life. It is interesting that where Dr. Stevenson's subjects reside in India, he has discovered among them an extreme paucity of claims to memories of lives as subhuman animals.[9] This suggests to him that if reincarnations occur, it is a pretense to imagine that human beings so regress.

Unfortunately in the East, the concept of rebirth has suffered from distorting interpretations, far removed from the elevated views of its sages and prophets. The result has often been a hindering, not a fostering of progress. In India, for example, priestly hierarchies have enforced separative caste practices by warning that penalty for violation could be an ensuing birth in an animal or insect. Enlightened reincarnationists teach: "Once a human being, always a human being."[10]

Seven Embarrassments in Church Doctrine

Using "the lost chord" theme, I propose now to consider some of the leading doctrines associated with mainstream Christianity, and which are sources of embarrassment to all learned members of the faith. Over the centuries these embarrassments have driven innumerable persons into hopeless skepticism and atheism. Furthermore, doctrinal disputes thereon have fragmented the priceless message of Christ into hundreds of sects, each claiming to be the true dispenser of his teachings. Can the reincarnational outlook—if valid—create harmony out of this confusion and bring skeptics back into the fold?

What in stark nakedness is now presented as orthodoxy is what appears officially in the creed of the leading churches. It is what vast numbers of people actually believe, not what liberal Christians hold. Many of the latter, lacking other solutions, have become totally absorbed in ameliorating the social and political grievances of the day. Others, as we have seen (almost one-quarter of professing Christians), have already turned to reincarnational teachings.

1 God's Will as involved in human suffering

Innocent children are born maimed, diseased, or mentally retarded; elderly people who have lived exemplary lives meet with dire misfortune and cruel deaths. To materialists this is unanswerable evidence for the non-existence of God. Some years ago the Reverend Billy Graham appeared on BBC in London. He was asked how, in the light of a beneficent, loving God, he could explain the heartaching suffering of children born sick or defective. (How, we might also add, explain the birth of blameless children into filth and squalor, to alcoholic parents, with no opportunities of ever rising out of such an unfavorable beginning?) For once the evangelist did not know what to say. Finally, he lamely replied: "The Bible says there are mysteries."

Wilmon Henry Sheldon, who was Clark Professor of Philosophy at Yale, discussed in his major work *God and Polarity,* how reincarnation and karma (the moral law of compensation), could resolve the foregoing dilemmas. Many people, he said, "suffer untold miseries without any apparent fault of their own. It is the injustice that rankles. Now why do we think these sufferers are punished far beyond their deserts? Because we have no evidence of their having done wrong in anything like the degree of their pains. And in the case of very young children, they could not have done so."

Sheldon then turns to rebirth as a "real alternative to a finite, imperfect deity," that is, God, as an anthropomorphic manipulator of events. If reincarnation/karma "is a true hypothesis," the professor observes, "it at once removes the apparent injustice of so much suffering. . . . For aught we know every single iota of suffering is deserved . . . is the result of grievous sins in some former incarnation."[11]

In the majority of cases, the latter may be true, but there may be exceptions. An aphorism on karma states:

No man but a sage or true seer can judge another's karma. Hence while each receives his deserts, appearances may deceive, and birth into poverty or heavy trial may not be punishment for bad karma, for souls continually incarnate into poor surroundings where they experience difficulties and trials which are for the discipline of the soul and result in strength, fortitude, and sympathy.[12]

In other words, if prior to incarnation a human being realizes it lacks certain qualities and virtues, it may choose an onerous life that is conducive to eliminating deficiencies and thus build a more useful and compassionate character.

A Cambridge philosopher, Professor A. C. Ewing, expressed a similar view in an article on reincarnation. "Granting previous lives, it would seem plausible to suppose where good people live in a specially unhappy environment" this could be "cases of voluntary choice before birth for the same kind of motives as have made exceptionally altruistic people go to live in slums or work among lepers."[13] But even in everyday existence, an easy life is often rejected because it would either be too boring or one would learn little from it. In selecting a school, for example, a young person is not likely to choose one that is too easy; it would offer no challenges.

Nevertheless, according to karma theory, most of life's difficulties and sorrows are caused either by ignorance of the karmic law or by flouting that law by way of self-indulgent actions that negate one's spiritual growth and contravene the rights of others.

A standard theological answer to the problem of injustice, is that in heaven everything will be squared up by God. But why did that almighty, gracious power allow such things to occur in the first place? The transparent flaw in the ecclesiastical reasoning was sensed by a five-year-old one Sunday afternoon when the family boat went aground. The story was reported in the Charleston paper *News and Courier*:

> The Coast Guard commander of the Port of Charleston, South Carolina, received a thank-you note from a family whose small boat had been pulled off a mudbank by the commander's men. The woman who wrote the letter said that, when the boat went aground, her five-year-old daughter started to cry. "Don't worry," a three-year-old daughter comforted her older sister. "God will take care of us."
>
> "Then why did God let us run aground?" sobbed the five-year-old.
>
> "I'm not talking about *that* God," said the three-year-old. "I'm talking about the *Coast* God."

The answer that the rebirth theory offers to the problem of seeming "undeserved" suffering totally exonerates God from charges of injustice, cruelty, or favoritism. It does not put that divine universal power into the role of a policeman, or a punisher of evil deeds, for karma, the law of cause and effect, is self-operative. "Whatsoever we sow we reap." A farmer is not obliged to call upon God to make his crops grow. Unselfish thoughts and deeds in due season shower blessings and grace upon the individual and the whole of life. Selfish, disharmonious causes, operate as hindrances to individual and collective growth. The consequent painful, discordant reactions are not punitive but educative, pointing to wiser, more compassionate paths to tread, leading ever Godward, and to larger spheres of service.

Incidentally, it is the karmic aspect of reincarnation, when understood, that prevents an individual from using rebirth as an excuse to postpone perpetually his salvation to the next life or the next again. The wages of procrastination are heavy enough within one life, and if human beings have future lives, the karmic debt of postponing obligations is likely to be increasingly painful. Appreciating this, who would wish to start his ensuing life plagued with self-caused handicaps?

Communicable sin and a depraved humanity

The orthodox Christian believes in a sinful humanity. We are all born in sin and conceived in iniquity. Because of something we did? No. Because Adam and Eve disobeyed God's command so that in consequence He cursed the entire human race—billions and billions of souls must suffer for one couple's disregard of divine command.

The noted Christian philosopher, Nicolas Berdyaev, speaks of this in *Transmigration of Souls (Pereselienye Doosh),* to which well-known Russian writers and theologians contributed essays:

> The weakness and unreasonableness of theologic teachings concerning the genesis of the soul and its final destiny are responsible for the popularity of reincarnation. It is difficult to reconcile oneself to the traditional teaching according to which the soul is created at the moment of conception and at this moment the primordial sin is communicated as if it were a communicable disease. Also it is difficult to accept the other teaching, according to which the soul is a product of a hereditary process and receives the primordial sin as it would a hereditary disease.*

> Neither of these teachings supply any justification whatsoever for human sufferings and the injustices of individual destiny. . . . The teaching of reincarnation is simple. It makes rational the mystery of human destiny and reconciles man to the [apparent] unjust and incomprehensible sufferings of life . . . man stops comparing his destiny with the happier destiny of other people and accepts it.[14]

In contrast to the concept of a sinful, depraved humanity, the view of Eastern reincarnationist cultures is quite different, as Count Hermann Keyserling observes in his *Travel Diary of a Philosopher*:

> The Indian does not know the feeling of sinfulness. The word "sin" appears often enough in their religious literature, if one can believe the translations, but the meaning to which it corresponds is a different one

---

* Berdyaev refers here to two alternative views: (1) creationism; (2) traducianism. Traducianism was advocated by some of the early Fathers, but creationism was taught by both Aquinas and Calvin.—Ed.

[from ours]. . . . Every action entails, according to the law of karma, its natural and inevitable consequence; every one must bear those for himself; no merciful Providence can remove them. . . .

The Christian consciousness of sin depends . . . upon the commandment to bear it in mind constantly, and this is what the Indian doctrine of salvation forbids. It teaches: as a man thinks, so will be become. If he thinks of himself constantly as bad and low, he will become bad. . . . The man who does not believe in himself is considered to be an atheist in the real sense of the word. The highest ideal would be if a man could think of himself continuously, not as the most sinful of sinners, but as perfect. [15]

—or at least potentially perfect. Did not Christ teach similarly when he said: "You must be perfect, as your heavenly Father is perfect" (Matt. 5:48)? The guilt complex which psychiatrists regard as so disastrous to the human psyche, may have its original source in theological teachings of man's inherent baseness.

3 Doctrine of eternal damnation

A re-examination of reincarnationism, suggests Professor MacGregor, may throw "a vast flood of light on the eschatological muddle that has haunted the history of Christian thought. . . . We cannot overlook the fact that the standard Christian alternative has entailed the horrific doctrine of hell. That doctrine, that those who are not saved are doomed to eternal punishment, does not seem compatible with the fundamental Christian assertion that God is love. . . . We may not boggle at what seems to be the Pauline view that those who fail to win victory with Christ will simply pass out of existence. [The wages of sin is death. Rom. 6:23] What is intolerable is the notion that even one sinner should be punished by everlasting torture." [16]

To attribute to God such "an unappeasable vindictiveness and insatiable cruelty," declares Professor John Hick, "would be regarded as demonic if applied analogously to a human being." [17] Nor would it be in accord with the law of measure for measure that Jesus taught. "Whatever you mete out to others, that will you also receive" (Luke 6:38). How, then, could a lifetime of wickedness, earn an *eternity* of misery and suffering? How could one incarnation of saintly living, earn *everlasting bliss*? The scales of justice do not and are not expected to balance.

"In the Hindu and Buddhist versions of the perennial philosophy," writes Aldous Huxley, "there is no eternal damnation;

there are only purgatories and then an indefinite series of second chances to go forward towards not only man's but the whole creation's final end—total reunion with the Ground of all being. . . . The divine mercy is matched by the divine patience: both are infinite."[18]

The Resurrection of a corpse

For all thoughtful Christians, the Church's teaching concerning the Last Judgment poses a conundrum that the reasoning mind finds impossible to solve. Billions of dead bodies, which in nature's laboratory have been reduced to dust and recycled countless times, will be reassembled and inherit eternal life. And as to the bodies of those who died just prior to Judgment Day, it will not be dust that is transformed and immortalized, it will be a *disintegrating corpse*!

The Church's supporting argument is that what happened to Christ 2,000 years ago when his body ascended to heaven, could also happen to us. In analysing this, Professor C. D. Broad of Cambridge observes: "If the church's teaching is true, though Jesus was human, He was also divine. No other human being resembles Him in this respect." Consequently, Broad points out, the resurrection of one so radically different from ourselves cannot be adduced as evidence that we too will survive. However, he adds, the two cases differ in another way: "The body of Jesus did not decay in the tomb, but was transformed; while the body of every ordinary man rots and disintegrates after his death. . . . Thus the analogy breaks down in every relevant respect. . . ."[19]

If, on the other hand, all human beings are essentially immortal souls, as reincarnationists teach, then bodies are merely temporary instruments for gaining experience in the world—*no need to immortalize them*.

The ceaseless creation of souls

According to Church teaching, at some point in the nine-month pre-birth period, God creates a soul for every human being. For heathen and good Christian, for civilized peoples, savages, and even cannibals, God is daily engaged in this constant task.

Considering the divine economy of life, Benjamin Franklin believed it would be a waste of energy for God to create all these new souls, when through the process of reincarnation He could reuse those already existing:

When I see nothing annihilated and not a drop of water wasted, I cannot suspect the annihilation of souls, or believe that [God] will suffer the daily waste of millions of minds ready made that now exist, and put Himself to the continual trouble of making new ones.

Thus, finding myself to exist in the world, I believe I shall, in some shape or other, always exist; and, with all the inconveniences human life is liable to, I shall not object to a new edition of mine, hoping, however, that the *errata* of the last may be corrected.[20]

In a similar vein, Rudyard Kipling penned these lines:

They will come back, come back again,
As long as the red earth rolls.
He never wasted a leaf or a tree.
Do you think He would squander souls?[21]

Professor C. J. Ducasse observes that there is another reason why reincarnational theory is more rational than the conventional teaching of creation: It is an "alternative to the shocking supposition common among Christians that, at the mating of *any* human pair, be it in wedlock *or in wanton debauch,* an all-wise, almighty, and infinitely loving God creates outright from nothing, or extracts from his own eternal being, an immortal human soul."[22]

Immanuel Kant was also bothered by the thought of "wanton debauch." In his famous *Critique of Pure Reason* he observed that the generation of bodies and souls in the human race, depends on many seeming accidents: "on the views and whims of government, nay even on vice, so that it is difficult to believe in the eternal existence of a being whose life has first begun under circumstances so trivial, and so entirely dependent on our own choice. . . . It would seem as if we could hardly expect so wonderful an effect from causes so insignificant." "But, in answer to these objections," Kant suggests, "we may adduce the transcendental hypothesis, that all life is properly intelligible, and not subject to the changes of time, and that it neither began in birth, nor will end in death. . . . If we could see ourselves and other objects as they really are, we should see ourselves in a world of spiritual natures, our community with which neither began at our birth nor will end with the death of the body" (Part II: i, iii).

The Reverend Leslie Weatherhead in his 1957 lecture, "The Case for Reincarnation," sees additional merit in re-using souls again and again. Weatherhead was former president of the Methodist Conference of Great Britain, and minister of London's historic City Temple for 28 years until his retirement in 1960. Quoting from the lecture:

> If every birth in the world is the birth of a new soul, I do not see how progress can ever be consummated. Each has to begin at scratch. . . . How can a world progress in inner things—which are the most important—if the birth of every new generation fills the world with unregenerate souls full of original sin? There can never be a perfect world unless gradually those born into it can take advantage of lessons learned in earlier lives instead of starting at scratch.[23]

Animals are without souls

The problem here is for what purpose do the lower kingdoms exist. There are millions of species of plants, insects, birds, and mammals. Was each of them created by God, and if so why? Why did He take such infinite pains to do this, when after a brief span of life they are annihilated by death. Fundamentalists are at a loss to handle scientific evolutionary theory, and so must deny its validity. St. Francis of Assisi, if he were alive today, would probably welcome it but would add a spiritual dimension, without which the scientific theory is no more rational and meaningful than the ecclesiastical view. For blind, unplanned evolution of form, without a corresponding evolution of an indwelling intelligence that uses that form and gains experience therefrom, serves no ultimate purpose.

Professor Lynn White, writing in *Science* (March 10, 1967), calls St. Francis "the greatest radical in Christian history since Christ." Why? Because he opposed the arrogance of man as king of creation and sought to establish a democracy of all creatures. In his eyes all living things had souls. "What Sir [Steven] Runciman calls 'the Franciscan doctrine of the animal soul' was quickly stamped out," says White. "Quite possibly the doctrine was in part inspired consciously or unconsciously, by the belief in reincarnation held by the Cathar heretics who at that time teemed in Italy and southern France."

As to how evolutionary and reincarnational theory can work together was outlined by the nineteenth-century American transcendentalist and Boston clergyman, James Freeman Clarke:

> That man has come up to his present state of development by passing through lower forms is the popular doctrine of science today. What is called evolution teaches that we have reached our present state by a very

long and gradual ascent from the lowest animal organizations. It is true that the Darwinian theory takes no notice of the evolution of the soul, but only of the body. But it appears to me that a combination of the two views would remove many difficulties which still attach to the theory of natural selection and the survival of the fittest. . . .

The modern doctrine of evolution of bodily organisms is not complete, unless we unite with it the idea of a corresponding evolution of the spiritual monad, from which every organic form derives its unity. *Evolution has a satisfactory meaning only when we admit that the soul is developed and educated by passing through many bodies.* . . . If we are to believe in evolution, let us have the assistance of the soul itself in this development of new species.[24]

7 "It happens only once" syndrome

This earth, as the orthodox believe, is the only focus for God's attention, and the only place where human beings exist. Here as in items 5 and 6, there appears to be a further inconceivable waste of valuable resources. The astronomer's telescopes and radioscopes reveal that billions of suns exist in our universe. Beyond the Milky Way galaxy are billions of other galaxies. Has all this been created by God? If so, for what purpose? Just to light man's path on a dark night, or guide mariners at sea, as early Christians believed?

As someone cogently observed, orthodoxy appears to be suffering from an "it happens only once" syndrome: one unique world; one unique Christ, who incarnated in human flesh only once; one life on earth for all beings; one chance for salvation; one everlasting heaven and hell.

The universe of the reincarnationist is one of cyclic repetition, cyclic rebirth. Is this not more in accord with the ways of deity as manifested in the natural universe of which that power is believed to be the author? "If You Look Hard, Cycles Are All Over," is the title of an article in *Scientific American* (Feb. 1980). Here the findings of the Foundation for the Study of Cycles, established forty years ago are reviewed. Thousands of biological cycles are also described in the book *The Rhythms of Life,* edited by Edward Ayensu of the Smithsonian Institution, and by zoologist Philip Whitfield. In daily life we observe the alternations of day and night, sleeping and waking, winter's death eternally followed by spring, the ebb and flow of the seas; water rising as vapor to the heavens and descending again as rain. How strange if human beings in their births and deaths should prove an exception? The Bible says "for everything there is a season. . . . A time to be born and a time to die" (Eccles. 3:1–2). But seasons follow seasons, cycles follow cycles—that appears to be God's observable pattern everywhere.

Alternative to Reincarnation: Evolution Proceeds in Higher Worlds

To overcome some of the embarrassments in Church teaching, a few theologians over the centuries have lent a willing ear to the theory of Irenaeus, as described by Professor Hick:

. . . Irenean type of theology sees the divine creation of personal life as taking place through a long and slow process which extends far beyond this present earthly scene . . . it postulates many worlds or spheres of existence in addition to this physical world, and envisages the progress of the soul through them towards a final state of perfection in completely fulfilled relationship both to God and to finite beings.

This view

languished for many centuries, revived again in the thought of the great nineteenth-century protestant thinker, Friedrich Schleiermacher, and has become progressively more widespread ever since in both protestant and, recently, catholic theology.

In comparing the Indian concept of reincarnation with the Irenean view, Hick concedes that

they agree concerning the basic principle of continued responsible life in which the individual may still learn and grow by interacting with other human beings in a common environment or environments. They differ only to *where* this continued life takes place. The Christian belief (in the Irenean tradition) has been that it takes place in other worlds beyond this one. The Indian belief has been that it takes place by means of repeated returns to this world. But this difference seems relatively slight in comparison with the more fundamental agreement.[25]

We may ask, why go elsewhere when planet Earth has still so much to teach? Our earth, from geological and anthropological evidence, has been evolving for millions of years. *All this immense preparation for just one visit to the earth?* Think, too, of the immense variety of experience available to human beings in our world. Lying latent within each of us are vast resources upon which we have never drawn. Why not take advantage of that before going elsewhere?

Is genius the product of a fortuitous combination of genes? Is it a gift of God, who has special favorites among us? Or is it more logical to think that it is the product of experience—of many lives of striving in this field of evolution?

A further consideration is that most people are not sufficiently advanced when they die to benefit spiritually and mentally from a transfer to an advanced world. Thus Albert Schweitzer admitted that:

> By reason of the idea of reincarnation Indian thought can be reconciled to the fact that so many people in their minds and actions are still so engrossed in the world. If we assume that we have but one existence, there arises the insoluble problem of what becomes of the spiritual ego which has lost all contact with the Eternal. Those who hold the doctrine of reincarnation are faced by no such problem. For them that non-spiritual attitude only means that those men and women have not yet attained to the purified form of existence in which they are capable of knowing the truth and translating it into action. . . .
>
> The idea of reincarnation contains a most comforting explanation of reality by means of which Indian thought surmounts difficulties which baffle the thinkers of Europe.[26]

In learning a craft, becoming an artist, a musician, a doctor, the apprentice who succeeds perfects himself in one stage before passing to another. Failing to do so he is in serious trouble, and all his future work will be flawed by such neglect. Would not this be true in the greatest of all arts, the art of living? A house built on sand, said Jesus, will fall. He told the multitudes (not just his advanced disciples): "You must be perfect, as your heavenly Father is perfect" (Matt. 5:48). Only then, it would appear, would they be ready for higher perfections, to rise, as St. Paul said "from one glory to another" (2 Cor. 3:18).

A farmer reaps his harvest in the field where he casts the seed, not in some other field. Is it not natural for souls to do likewise? From this stance, St. Paul's words "as you sow, so shall you reap," connotes "*where* you sow, there too, you shall also reap." Transplanting people to another sphere seems artificial and unnecessary. Could it not also be criticized as an escape philosophy?

William Kingsland observes that the orthodox conception of an eternal heaven also lends itself to objections of escapism: "The

Christian has unfortunately always been taught that he will leave all the disabilities and sin and sorrow of this present world behind him when he dies, and that his 'faith' will ensure him an eternity of bliss 'forever and ever.'" Kingsland questions whether the individual can thus sever himself from the stream of human evolution taking place on earth: "The progress of the race is accomplished only by the progress of the individuals composing it," and if reincarnation is a fact, "this is accomplished by re-peated incarnations."

"It is true," he adds, "that after physical death the individual who has any spiritual nature left in him may enjoy a supreme bliss for a season, in freedom from physical conditions and lim-itations. The 'sleep' of death is simply the equivalent between incarnations of the sleep of the body between one day and an-other." But, this author remarks, "what a difference it would make to this world of ours if each individual realized that he must play his part therein and contribute to the progress of the race from the beginning to end" of its existence, "that he work out, not merely his own salvation, but also that of the race. The Christian scriptures tell us how this must be done."[27]

Notes

1   William Q. Judge, *The Ocean of Theosophy* (1893; reprint, Los An-geles: Theosophy Co., 1915), 64.

2   Geddes MacGregor, *Reincarnation in Christianity* (Wheaton, Ill.: Quest Books, 1978); *Reincarnation as a Christian Hope* (London: Macmillan, 1982; New York: Barnes & Noble, 1982).

3   Joseph Head and S. L. Cranston, eds., *Reincarnation, the Phoenix Fire Mystery* (New York: Crown, 1977), 134–65, 172–86. Sylvia Cranston and Carey Williams, *Reincarnation, a New Horizon in Science, Religion and Society* (New York: Crown, 1984), chap. 13.

4   Head and Cranston, 156–60.

5   George Gallup, Jr., *Adventures in Immortality* (New York: McGraw-Hill, 1982), 137–38, 192–93.

6   U. S. Bureau of Census, *Statistical Abstract of the United States 1982–83,* 103d ed. (Washington, DC, 1982), 30.

7   *Daily Graphic* (London), 15 April 1979.

8   Tom Zito, "The Doctor Studies Reincarnation," *New York Post,* (18 Nov. 1978). See also "The Work of Ian Stevenson, M.D.," in Cranston and Williams.

9   Ian Stevenson, *Cases of the Reincarnation Type* (Charlottesville, Va.: University Press of Virginia, 1976), 1:64.

10   Head and Cranston, 118, 151, 190–91, 204–6, 549–50.

11   Wilmon Henry Sheldon, *God and Polarity* (New Haven: Yale University Press, 1954), 271.

12   "Aphorisms on Karma," *Path* magazine (New York, March 1893): 366–69; reprinted in booklet "Karma" (Los Angeles: Theosophy Co., n.d.).

13   A. C. Ewing, "The Philosophy of McTaggart, With Special Reference to the Doctrine of Reincarnation," *The Aryan Path* (Bombay, Feb. 1957).

14   Essay of Nicolas Berdyaev in *Pereselienye Doosh* (Transmigration of souls) (Paris: YMCA Press, n.d.).

15   Hermann Keyserling, *Travel Diary of a Philosopher,* trans. J. Holyroyd Reece (New York: Harcourt, Brace, 1925) 1:250–52.

16   MacGregor, *Reincarnation in Christianity,* 10, 172.

17   John Hick, *Death and Eternal Life* (New York: Harper & Row, 1980), 200.

18   Aldous Huxley, *The Perennial Philosophy* (New York: Harper, 1945), 213–15.

19   C. D. Broad, *Religion, Philosophy, and Psychical Research* (New York: Harcourt, Brace, 1953), 236–37.

20   *The Works of Benjamin Franklin,* ed. Jared Sparks (Boston: 1856), 10:174, letter to George Whatley, 23 May 1785.

21   Quoted in Eva Martin, *The Ring of Return* (London: Philip Allan, 1927), 217.

22   C. J. Ducasse, *Critical Examination of the Belief in a Life After Death* (Springfield, Ill.: Charles C. Thomas, 1961), 210.

23   Leslie D. Weatherhead, "The Case for Reincarnation" (lecture before the City Temple Literary Society, London, 1957). Booklet published by M. C. Peto in Burgh Heath, Tadworth, Surrey, n.d.

24   James Freeman Clarke, *Ten Great Religions* (Boston: Houghton Mifflin, 1887) 2:ix, 190.

25   Hick, 269–71.

26   Albert Schweitzer, *Indian Thought and Its Development* (Boston: Beacon Press, 1952), 222–23.

27   William Kingsland, *The Gnosis or Ancient Wisdom in the Christian Scriptures* (London: George Allen & Unwin, 1937), 24–25.

Eschatological Implications of the Mesoamerican Ball Games

MANFRED KERKHOFF

The mere fact that ball courts are found only in ceremonial centers is in itself an indication of the religious meaning of the games. . . .

It is one of the great ironies of history that when Cortez stepped on Mexican soil, he soon found himself treated as an "Expected One": by sheer coincidence, the year of his arrival (1519) happened to be the very year ("One Reed") Aztec astronomer-priests had foreseen as the time of the return of the legendary god-king Quetzalcoatl. And as if that—Cortez taken for Quetzalcoatl, the home-coming savior—were not enough, there was another, more fateful coincidence linked to this ominous arrival/return: Aztec culture, according to its own historians, was doomed to inevitable destruction, since it had entered the final stages of the fifth—and last—age of the world. What had *not* been foreseen, was the role the Spaniards would play in this apocalyptical drama: by genocide and evangelization, they fulfilled the Aztec prophecies *their* way.[1]

Six centuries before, another pre-calculated "end of the world"—this time of the fourth age—had prompted the downfall of the classical Mayan culture which had reached admirable peaks of cultural accomplishments between 300 and 900 C.E.; at least this is one of the several possible explanations of the mysterious fact that, almost overnight, the ceremonial centers in the jungles of Guatemala and Chiapas were abandoned.[2] The obsession with time that has been ascribed to the Mayan astronomers had made them

The author wishes to dedicate this chapter to Tom Noel.

project on history the quadripartite space-time-structure of their religious interpretation of nature.[3]

The complicated system of calendars, star-lore, seasonal myths and fertility rites that composed the Mayan *Weltanschauung* was very probably initiated by the Olmec culture that preceded not only the classical Maya but also the Toltec culture of Teotihuacan and Tula (whose destruction had motivated Quetzalcoatl in his emigration to the East—Yucatán—from where he promised to return). The Olmec,[4] who occupied the Gulf Coast, might also be responsible for another eschatological "institution" inherited later by the Toltec, Mayan and Aztec cultures—the ball game, linked—at least esoterically—to their belief in immortality. According to the Aztecs, their very name—Olmeca—identified them as the producers and providers of the rubber (*olli*) that was so abundant in their region and came to be used—among other things—for the balls of that game; to their Quiché-Maya neighbors the Olmec were just that, ball players, and the famous colossal stone heads that appear in Olmec sites, have been interpreted as monuments dedicated to decapitated ball players.[5]

At first sight, it may seem odd to establish a relationship between a ball game and myths and rites concerned with death and afterlife. But from ancient Egypt and Mesopotamia we know that the dead were supposed to play certain games during their way through the underworld, not only for fun, but as a magical rite for overcoming death.[6] So, it is not too far-fetched to imagine that the living, too, at least in certain critical (sacred) periods of time, performed the ball game as a ritual; the mere fact that ball courts are found only in ceremonial centers is in itself an indication of the religious meaning of the games (not to mention the sculptural representations on some ball court panels: the ball identified with a skull, losers of the game sacrificed, etc.).

The evidence for the eschatological meaning of the ball game is twofold (leaving aside the astronomically oriented location of the courts[7]): (1) several Mexican codices (Aztec or Mixtec); (2) the only surviving sacred book of the (Quiché) Mayas, the *Book of Counsel*[8] (*Popol Vuh*). Besides, there are descriptions of the game—in its late form—by Spanish authors, who sometimes mention myths or legends related to the (already professionalized) game.[9] A lot of publications have been dedicated to its various cultural aspects,[10] a few of them only, to the religious symbolism involved;[11] the eschatological meaning itself has only been hinted at here and there—and that is the reason why I shall concentrate on this area.

In the codices,[12] the ball courts are represented in their typical shape: a capital I (or double T), sometimes showing the two lateral rings which belong to the latest form of the game (stone rings set into the lateral walls of the court, "entrances" for the ball which was hit with hips and back only);[13] as to their colour, they are often painted completely in red (symbol of fertility) or divided into four segments painted with the colours of the cardinal directions (and seasons), thereby implying that it was the (annual) course of the sun which was re-enacted during the game.[14] There appear teams of one, two or three players confronting each other, most of the time gods, sometimes men against gods, or symbolic animals against gods or men; the context is predominantly mythical (light against darkness, dry season against rainy season, sun against moon, sun against morning star, etc.),[15] sometimes historical (migrations of the tribe, founding of cities or temples).[16] Special gods are associated with their special type (name) of ball court, sometimes corresponding to stellar constellations,[17] but, in general, to either the night-sky or the day-sky.[18] This division was imitated in many ceremonial centers which had two principal ball courts, for instance, Tenochtitlan itself.[19] Naturally, the gods appearing in the codices could be interpreted as the priests impersonating them on earth[20]—the corresponding temples are often painted near the courts—but the important fact is that the three layers of space (sky, earth, underworld) could be understood as huge ball courts where the decisive powers of nature oppose each other in order to guarantee the regular continuity of the agricultural cycles; the rather profane "exercise" on earth could then be taken for an act of magical "help," on the human side, for the gods who, for our sake, even sacrifice themselves when necessary—expecting the corresponding behaviour from us.

The fertility–aspect of the game (sometimes forgotten by the astronomical reading of the pictographic text[21]) comes out clearly in representations, which show the center-point of the ball court as a hole, from which (as from a fountain) the water, indispensable for vegetation, is thought to spread over the earth.[22] It is noteworthy, in this particular context, that we see the young god of corn (or of the sun, or of both at the same time) celebrating his victory over the forces of winter, death, dryness; or over the stars, the moon, the

morning-star, the night-sky, etc.).[23] We even see the turquoise
serpent (or a double-headed serpent, in the shape of the ball court,
representing the sky) devour or, depending on the context, "vomit"
a ball court: death of the evening or birth of the morning.[24] So, we
should not be surprised to find a ball court too, in the mythical
paradise or place of origin (Tollan; Aztlan), surrounded by symbols
of sprouting vegetation and wealth;[25] and, as this is also the place
where at least some of the dead expect to return (the ancestors are
waiting there, as stars),[26] the idea of having a ball court in the realm
of the dead (*mictlan*) is quite consistent with the concept of cyclical
death and revival, accomplished symbolically by the rite of the
ball game, a game whose principal deity is a twin,[27] the bi-unity
of morning and evening star (or, more popular perhaps, sun
and moon). One of the most impressive passages of the *Codex
Borgia*[28] shows, within the Venus-cycle,[29] the star descending into
the underworld, his playing and losing the game and being
sacrificed in order to be reborn (in the middle of the ball court
and surrounded by skulls) as the morning star which announces
the sun. Out of death itself, that is, out of the dragon-body of
earth, emerges life. No wonder, then, that this twin god
(Quetzalcoatl/Xolotl in Aztec mythology) is considered to be the
special patron of the ball game, and, as such, a *psychopomos,* leader
of the souls of the dead through the regions of torture which
form the several layers of the (Aztec) underworld.[30] This drama,
on the other hand, had to be "imitated" ritually (*Codex Borgia* is a
book of rituals) by the priests, with famous prisoners playing the
game—the role—of their divine archetypes. In the ball court
panels of El Tajin (a Mayan enclave in the Huasteca region of the
Gulf of Mexico), we have this drama sculptured in stone:[31] The
representations, on two ball courts which are thought to be
"continuations" of each other, show, besides the initiation of a
young warrior, the descent and "sin"[32]—Quetzalcoatl having
intercourse with(in) the night (earth) of the star (or the sun) and
its immolation on the ball court itself, sculptured on two panels
of the real ball courts. Likewise, on a ball court panel at Chichen
Itza,[33] the loser of the game, flanked on both sides by seven ball
players, is shown decapitated, with streams of blood "sprouting"
in the form of corn-stalks out of his throat.[34] It has been suggested that before this act of decapitation was enacted, another
rite, with the victim kneeling down was performed: one that
anticipated the transformation of death into life.[35] It comes as no

surprise, then, that golden miniature reproductions of ball courts and their accessories have been unearthed from the tombs of ceremonial centers.[36] In fact, the funeral aspect of the game might have been the most ancient form of the ritualization of the (profane) game, the death of great leaders, and hope for their living-on, either in the sky or in their successors, being the foremost occasion.[37] The sexual connotations of the game,[38] as seen in the context of sexual misconduct cited in the legend of Quetzalcoatl, are connected with the general idea of identifying the head (or heart) of the victim with the seed (of corn) which is fertilized under the earth. Even the later political meaning of the game as initiation into the life of an "eagle" or "jaguar" (night or day sky) may have implied an initiation, in life, of the expected performance after death.

As to the Mayan area, unfortunately there is only one[39] representation of a ball court found in one of the four extant codices; but this lack is compensated by the ball court panels (already mentioned) and by representations of ball players on stelae or stone-markers (of the courts). On the other hand, an attempt has been made to interpret a certain standardized sequence of scenes and inscriptions, painted on funeral vessels, as a sort of "ceramic codex," equivalent to a still undiscovered "Maya Book of the Dead";[40] one extant codex has even been deciphered as such a book, but no agreement has been reached by scholars in this last case.[41] Anyway, the so-called ceramic codex would confirm and even enrich the foregoing display of motifs and concepts: There are ball game scenes from the underworld, and, as a recurrent motif, throne-scenes with the hero-twins, scenes of decapitation in the underworld, and, most important, resurrection-scenes, supposedly belonging to a special "Resurrection-Codex."[42] Accompanying such scenes (or standing isolated), we find inscriptions from which a "Primary Standard Sequence" has been extracted,[43] which not only appears identically on almost all the vases considered—as the gylphic form of funeral hymns—but coincides with identical stone-inscriptions on stelae erected for dead rulers in the ceremonial centers.[44]

Now, as these inscriptions and the related paintings make repeated reference to the destiny of hero-twins (their descent to the underworld, their game against the team of the Realm of Death, their hardships in the torture-chambers, their apparent death and final triumph), it has been suggested that the *Popol Vuh* of the Quiché-Maya, a text which depicts this story, is one of the many versions of the same, but locally modified, eschatological myth; and while questions have been raised as to the authenticity of the book (its transcription and translation to Spanish having taken place under Christian influence[45]) the vast majority of "mayanists" accept it as a valuable source for Mesoamerican eschatology. It should be stated, before entering into details, that the eschatological complex of the book, probably stemming from folk-tales, has been very cannily inserted into the cosmogony[46] which forms the first (mythical) part of the text, followed, in the second part, by the migration-story of the Quiché-Maya. Between the end of the third age of the world and before the beginning of the last attempt of the creation of mankind, the episode of the hero-twins (somewhat interrupting the cosmogonical sequence of the ages), is located at the critical point where the creators have to find the vital stuff (corn) that keeps alive the creatures whose creation has failed three times before finally succeeding. This fitting intercalation might have corresponded to the practical "use" of the cosmogonic myth. Recited (re-enacted) during the critical period of (the five unlucky days[47] before) the beginning of the New Year, it served as an evocation of a renewed beginning accomplished by a previous "traversing" of death; that is why, already in ancient Egypt, the funeral texts coincide with a return to the time of cosmogony. It is to be expected (since corn is the main form of nourishment in Mesoamerica, that is what people, literally, are "made" of) that the twins' story should be connected with the destiny (cycle) of the corn god, and especially with a religious relationship between the events taking place on and under the corn field and the neighboring ball court, both being miniature "copies" of the earth as it was created ("measured") in the beginning.[48] Naturally, this special corn-cycle is closely related to the astral "destinies" of sun, moon, and Venus, whose cycles are the basis for the three calendars which were (and still are) in use among the Maya.

Before being developed as the main motif for the twins' (*Hunahpú* and *Ixbalamqué*[49]) descent to the Underworld, the ball game is mentioned twice in the *"Popol Vuh"*: as the hobby of the giant Zipacná[50] and, more important, as the pastime of the forefathers of the twins.[51] It is precisely *their* daily playing that causes the outrage of the Lords of the Underworld who, besides complaining about the noise "on top of our heads,"[52] seem to defend privileges, as though one would need their permission before playing. But they are especially interested in the magical power of the implements[53] used by the four[54] players on earth. When they "invite" the "Seven hunters" to play against them in Xibalbá,[55] the "Realm of Disappearance," they do not seriously think of playing the game itself, but of killing their enemies before the game and getting the latters' instruments. Knowing this, the twins' ancestors leave their ball on the roof of their mansion as a pledge[56] before descending to death, for this is precisely what happens: After having failed several tests,[57] they are sacrificed on the ball court.[58] But the decapitation of the twins' real father backfires: His skull, thrown into a tree by the Lords of the Underworld,[59] makes the tree blossom and the maiden *Xquic,*[60] daughter of one of the Lords of Death, is attracted by this miracle. Drawn by curiosity, she accepts the sap (spittle, semen) of the skull (fruit) and, trying it, becomes pregnant with the twins. So it comes about that the future victors over Death are themselves begotten in the Realm of Death, by a dead father and Death's daughter as their mother.

Having grown up,[61] the twins discover their father's game attire[62] and, after having worked in the cornfield, begin to play.[63] The same reaction as before on behalf of the Lords of Xibalbá makes them accept the challenge, in order to avenge the death of their ancestors, but before descending they plant a reed in the middle of their grandmother's house as a sign of their death if it dries up, or of their triumph if it sprouts. This gesture is a proof of their role as spirits of vegetation—as was their father's decapitated head.[64] The twins do not commit the errors of their forefathers; they miraculously pass the tests,[65] so that this time the ball game has to take place. Before going into its details, we should note that scholars disagree on the translation and meaning of the decisive passages;[66] I can offer only what seems to me to be the most *probable* account.

Immediately before the start of the game, the twins face three challenges that prove the highly ritualistic character of this clash between life and death. First, they don't reveal their identities, which would have meant a loss of power, while forcing their enemies to do so against their will.[67] Then, in a very important discussion about whose ball will be used (to play with the enemies' ball is almost tantamount to failure) the twins give in, probably because they don't want their ball to get into their enemies' possession.[68] Finally, in a sort of ritual shouting-match, they announce victory in the name of the "head of the jaguar" (an allusion to Ixbalamqué's final triumph)[69] in opposition to their foes' announcement of victory in the name of the "worm."[70]

The game itself begins with a vicious attack by the team of Xibalbá: They kick the ball against Hunahpú's collar (or hip-ring)[71] and, on making contact, the ball cracks and out come splinters of sharp stone, hurting Hunahpú.[72] The twins, feeling betrayed, want to leave the court but are persuaded to stay after Xibalbá's concession that now the twin's ball will be used. The game ends in a draw[73] and the decision is postponed until the next day. During the night, however, besides having to stay in another place of sure death,[74] the twins are challenged to find the winner's prize (a bunch of flowers representing the four corners of the world) in spite of the darkness covering the heavily guarded garden.[75] With the help of aunts they pass this test, too, and by now, their enemies begin to worry. After another draw, the twins have to spend the next night in the House of Bats; and here Hunahpú, protected until then within his blowgun (!), from curiosity about the appearance of dawn, sticks his head out, and is decapitated by a huge "bat from heaven" (*camazotz*). The text seems to imply that this is only an apparent death, a show of magic on behalf of the "Heart of Heaven" (*Huracán*);[76] and indeed, Ixbalamqué forms a substitute head from the carapace of a turtle,[77] while the real head is triumphantly hung over the ball court by the Lords of Xibalbá. When the game begins for the third and last time, they tease Hunahpú, proposing to play with his trophy-head as a ball.[78] But Ixbalamqué, according to a previously conceived plan, kicks the ball outside the court and, by trickery, makes the other team leave the court to chase a rabbit[79] and in the meantime substitutes the real head for the false head. When the adversaries come back with the ball, they seem to realize that now they have lost. When Ixbalamqué crushes the false head into pieces (seeds), they abandon the game.[80] The reinstatement of the decapitated head of the young sun and corn god (the ball/head symbolizing the dying sun or the "decapitated" corn-seed struggling under the earth) means the decisive turn of events: From now on, the twins have the upper hand. They let themselves be sacrificed voluntarily on the pyre;[81] their bones are crushed on a grinding stone ("as corn meal is ground"[82]) and the bone meal thrown into a river, from where they reappear, on the fifth day, as fishmen.[83] Disguised as beggars, they then attract the attention of the Lords by performing strange dances[84] and working miracles.[85] Invited to show their arts to the people of Xibalbá, the twins comply with all the wishes of the Lords and end up sacrificing them, after the Lords had asked for it, without bringing them back to life.[86] After this triumph, judgment is passed against the enemies (among other things, they are forbidden to play the ball game[87]) and, as the last act of their adventure, before they are transfigured into sun and moon,[88] they pay homage to their forefathers,[89] who had died in Xibalbá, assuring them, as the avengers of their death, immortality, that is to say, worship by the noblemen.

Looking back over the whole episode, we must ask: What function could the ball game possibly have in the whole story, if the only intention of the Lords of the Underworld was to kill the twins in order to get their implements? Was it an additional degradation? From the twins' point-of-view, on the other hand, the game was necessary in order to avenge their father's death. In addition, they wanted to secure the privilege of playing the game, that is, of determining *on earth* the corn cycle which is linked to the game; but without the temporary stay in the "womb" of the earth there would be no growing. Now, given the fact that the two motives, vengeance and fight for privileges, appear elsewhere in American mythology in the typical twin adventures,[90] we have to account for a decisive change in the pattern of these narratives, a change which justifies the almost metaphysical importance of what was, before the change, a celebration of athletic abilities. This change, which took place only in Mesopotamia, not in the Caribbean or South America where the game (or variants of it) was also played, must have been the elevation of the pair of culture-heroes to the rank of cosmic powers.[91] It is this reinterpretation in terms of the diurnal or annual course of the sun (moon, Venus), linked to the vegetation cycle on earth, which transforms the ball game into an eschatological rite. Concerned with the rhythms of time (seasonal changes), with its "kairological" rather than chronological qualities,[92] the "philosophers" of Ancient Mexico came to establish the vital analogy between the two cycles already known (stellar bodies and vegetation) and the destiny of man, "originally" *not* cyclic. *His* death and resurrection as star, plant, animal or man,[93] followed the model of the sun or the corn plant, especially since men are made *of* corn.[94] The ball game, then, became a sort of initiation into the eschatological destiny prefigured by the heavenly twins. To be sacrificed in the center of the ball court means to become co-substantial with the corn- and sun-god in his difficult journey of descent and ascent:[95] It is a privilege of high-ranking prisoners only and assures survival.

The full significance of this eschatology could be understood only after a thorough study of the kairomorphic time-concept which lies at the basis of that whole world view; it has to do with the sequence of holy and profane periods of time,[96] with the concept of ripeness of time, so predominant in the calendars, with an intricate system of right placing (ranking) in space and time,[97] the reconstruction of which presents difficulties to a post-mythical mentality.[98] Even in the case of the ball game, an investigation of the times and places it used to be played at, its calendrical anchorage and mythical topography, would contribute much to a more profound understanding of its sacrificial function. Efforts have been made in this direction,[99] but since such an investigation presupposes knowledge of and empathy with kairosophical conceptions[100] all over the ancient world, it is still a task yet to take place.

It is in this context, too, that the "Legend of the Suns," the doctrine of the ages of the world, would have to be interpreted. Fundamentally, it is an "aeonic" amplification of the concept of the year and its god: Xiuhtecutli or Quetzalcoatl,[101] divided by a sequence of "lucky" and "unlucky" days, of the right or wrong time for something to be done or not done. This may sound too *un*scientific to scholars, but unless we take the astrology seriously, not separating it from astronomy,[102] we cannot hope fully to understand Mesoamerican eschatology.[103]

Notes

1   See T. Todorov, *La découverte de l'Amérique* (Paris, 1981). For a general introduction to Aztec culture see B. Cartwright Brundage, *The Fifth Sun: Aztec Gods, Aztec World* (Austin: University of Texas Press, 1979).

2   The apocalyptical interpretation of the end of the Classical Maya is proposed, on the basis of calendrical calculations, by P. Ivanoff, *Découvertes chez les Maya* (Paris, 1968), 235ff. For a general introduction to Mayan culture see Michael D. Coe, *The Maya,* 2d revised and enlarged ed. (New York: Thames & Hudson, 1980), and George E. and Gene S. Stuart, *The Mysterious Maya,* 2d ed. (New York: National Geographic Society, 1983).

3   For the concept time in Mayan religion see J.E.S. Thompson, *Maya Hieroglyphic Writing* (Norman: University of Oklahoma Press, 1960); and M. Léon-Portilla, *Tiempo y realidad en el pensamiento maya. Ensayo de acercamiento* (Mexico City: UNAM, 1978). It is noteworthy that even the Quiché-Maya interpreted the arrival and victory of the Spaniards in Guatemala as a sign of the end of *their* fourth age. On the other hand, the highly apocalyptical character of this interpretation of history survived even in post-conquest times: The famous *Book of the Jaguar Priest,* belonging to the Yucatan-Maya, cites events of the past in the future tense; i.e., in prophetic tones; and one should assume that such a view implies that future events are known from the past.

4   For the Olmec, see Ignacio Bernal, *The Olmec World* (Berkeley: University of California Press, 1969); and Michael D. Coe "Olmec and Maya," in Richard W. Adams, ed., *The Origins of Maya Civilization* (Albuquerque: University of New Mexico Press, 1977).

5   For the identification of the Olmec as ball players cf. Walter Krickeberg, "Das mittelamerikanische Ballspiel und seine religiöse Symbolik," *Paideuma* 3 (Frankfurt, 1949): 118ff. For the interpretation of the colossal heads in the sense here cited see L. Knauth, "El juego de pelota y el rito de la decapitación," *Estudios de Cultura Maya* 1 (1961): 183–98. See also R. Piña Chan, *Spiele und Sport im Alten Mexiko* (Berlin, 1968), 15ff.; and *Quetzalcoatl: Serpiente Emplumada* (Mexico City: UNAM, 1977), 15ff.

6   The expression of "playing at draughts" appears in the title of the famous 17th chapter of E. A. Wallis Budge, *The Egyptian Book of the Dead* (Mineola, N.Y.: Dover Publications, 1967), 28, with the accompanying illustration showing the dead sitting in front of a game-board. More details are presented and explained in Alexandre Piankoff, *The Wandering of the Soul,* ed. Natacha Rambova (Princeton: Princeton University Press, 1974), 115ff.; According to this commentary, the game, *senit,* showed in miniature the way the dead were supposed to follow in order to get to the "Hall of the Double Maat" (place of the judgment). C.L. Wooley, *Ur-Excavations II: The Royal Cemetery,* 221, plate 96, as cited by A. Moortgaat, *Tammuz* (Berlin, 1949), 56, shows the Babylonian variant of the game. For Greek examples see Emily Vermeule, *Aspects of Death in Early Greek Art and Poetry* (Berkeley: University of California Press, 1981), 77ff., 159f.

7 The pioneer work on this subject was done by H. Hartung, *Die Zeremonialzentren der Maya* (Graz: Akademische Verlag Anstalt, 1971), on ball courts, see 26ff., 35f., and notes 213–29, 264–76. From there a new branch of Maya archaeology developed under the title "Archaeo-astronomy." See, as one of the latest publications in this field, Anthony F. Aveni, *Skywatchers of Ancient Mexico* (Austin: University of Texas Press, 1980, on ball courts, esp. 311ff.

8 There are three English translations of the *Popol Vuh:* (1) Delia Goetz and S. G. Morley, *Popol Vuh: The Sacred Book of the Ancient Quiché Maya* (Norman: University of Oklahoma Press, 1950); (2) M. S. Edmonson, *The Book of Counsel: The Popol Vuh of the Quiché Maya of Guatemala* (New Orleans: University of Tulane, 1971); (3) R. Nelson, *Popol Vuh: The Great Mythological Book of the Ancient Maya* (Boston: Houghton Mifflin, 1976), only the first part of the original book.

9 The most famous report is by Fray Diego de Duran, *Book of the Gods and the Ancient Calendar,* trans., F. Horcasitas and D. Heyden (Norman: University of Oklahoma Press, 1971), chap. 23, 312ff. All other pertinent texts are collected in the most extensive study done on the topic: E. Taladoire, *Les terrains de jeu de balle (Mésoamérique et Sud-ouest des Etats-Unis)* (Mexico City: Mission Archeologiaque Ethnologique Francaise au Mexique, 1981), 560ff. For an evaluation of the Spanish chronicles see Taladoire, 31–70.

10 For a complete bibliography of more than 500 titles see Taladoire, 653–89; for a short history of the investigations see Taladoire, 7–22. The main subject of Taladoire's study is a typology of the ball courts (over 600 of them are listed), 125–400. The only other work that has appeared since Taladoire's book is C. Macazaga Ordoño, *El juego de pelota* (Mexico City: UNAM, 1982).

11 Especially concerned with this aspect are the articles of Krickeberg, and Knauth; Taladoire dedicates a chapter to it too, 537–54. See also my first treatment of this subject: Manfred Kerkhoff, "Aspectos escatológicos del Popol Vuh," *Plural* 1, no. 3 (1983): 25–39.

12 Taladoire, 79–120, examines the 62 representations of the ball game, *thachtli,* found on 52 pages of six different codices. See the annex 735ff. for reproductions of these representations. For a detailed interpretation see Krickeberg, 129–69.

13 For the stone-rings see Krickeberg, 120f.; on their sexual meaning as vulvae, Taladoire, 548f.; on the adornments, Krickeberg, 163ff. See Ordoño, 36ff., on the players' outfit and the rules of the game.

14 On this and other interpretations see E. Seler, "Über die natürtliche Grundlage mexikanischer Mythen," in *Gesammelte Abhandlungen* 3 (Berlin, 1908), 313ff. Brundage, *The Fifth Sun,* 8–12.

15   Krickeberg, 130ff, explains the different possibilities, according to the figures appearing in the codices (Codex Borbonicus 27; 19; Codex Fejervary 29; Codex Borgia 21; Codex Magliabecchi 33; 80; the main divinities involved are Quetzalcoatl, Tezcatlipoca, Xochipilli and Xochiquetzal. For the overall meaning see the conclusions of Krickeberg, 136f.

16   Krickeberg, 143ff. mentions the adventures of "Eight Deer" (Codex Vindobonensis and Codex Bodley) as an example, but tends to recognize in this person, rather than a prince-hero, the god of the mountains, Tepeyollotli or Votan (Krickeberg, 145ff.). Krickeberg gives instances of the toponymic use of the ball game hieroglyph.

17   Krickeberg, 129, cites the ball court of Tlaloc, the raingod; Seler, "Über die Mythen," 338, and Brundage, *The Fifth Sun,* 120, mention the *nahuallachco* or ball court of the night-sky (often represented by Tezcatlipoca in the form of the jaguar). Aveni, 29, 36, writes about *citlaltlachtli* or "ball court of the stars," which he identifies with the constellation of the Great Bear. It is interesting that one of the Yucatec-Maya names for the ball game (or court) was *ekel ek* = "jaguar-star." Cf. Ray A. Williamson, ed., *Archaeoastronomy in the Americas* (Los Altos, Calif.: Ballena Press, 1981), 237.

18   For this division see Krickeberg, 153f.

19   Cf. Krickeberg, 139f., on *teotlachtli,* dedicated to Uitzilopochtli, the sun-god; and *tezcatlachtli,* dedicated to Tezcatlipoca, the night-god.

20   We should remember that many god-names are at the same time titles of priests or kings; that is the reason why we find so many Quetzalcoatls or Kukulcan or Gucumatz: different names for the eponym "Feathered serpent."

21   Taladoire, 124, 537ff., stresses this point against the stellar or solar/lunar interpretations of Seler and Krickeberg; Macazaga, 55ff., is even more radical in this respect.

22   See Krickeberg, 135ff. (Codex Borbonicus 19). This fountain-center of the ball court is, at the same time, the entrance to the underworld and therefore its name is also *itzompan* "his place of the skulls." Hartung, *Die Zeremonialzentren der Maya,* note 265, mentions the fact that in the main ball court of Piedras Negras/Usumacinta a tomb was discovered right under the central point of the court. (Krickeberg, 136, cites the Aztec chronicler Tezozomoc for calling this note the "secret meaning of the ball game.")

23   See Krickeberg, 136, on the birth of the sun-god right on the court and his overcoming and killing of the moon-goddess and her 400 companions. Macazaga, 73, interprets the waterhole in connection with the fertilizing blood of the slain stars (prisoners). See Taladoire, 74, 105.

24   See Krickeberg, 152, (Codex Nutall 115).

25 See Seler, vol. 4, 16, 99–106; Krickeberg, 137ff., on the "Magical Ball Court" near the "Serpent Mountain."

26 For the general beliefs concerning the afterlife see Brundage, 188–93 ("Death, Soul, and the Underworld"); more extensive, M. Léon-Portilla *La filosofia nahuatl* (Mexico City: UNAM, 1959), 201ff.

27 *Xolotl* is the double of Quetzalcoatl. See Seler, vol. 4, 43ff., and Brundage, 119ff. (Brundage, 77, a game of Xolotl against Mictlantecutlí, God of the Dead.)

28 Basic for the understanding of this manuscript is the voluminous commentary by E. Seler, *Codex Borgia* (Berlin, 1904–6); re-edited in Spanish translation (Mexico City: UNAM, 1963), 2d ed. 1980, 3 vols. Krickeberg treats the central passage (plates 29–46), 140ff. See also K. A. Nowotny, *Tlacuilolli, Die mexikanischen Bilderhandschiften, Stil und Jnhalt. Mit einem Katalog der Codex-Borgia-Gruppe* (Berlin, 1961), plates 35/36–41/42.

29 On the astronomical aspects of this myth see G. Garces Contreras, *Pensamiento matemático y astronómico en el Mexico Precolombino* (Mexico City: UNAM, 1982), 193ff.

30 See Seler, "Über die Mythen," vol. 4, 8.

31 See Contreras, 233ff.; Krickeberg, 158ff.

32 See Carmen Cook de Leonard, "A New Astronomical Interpretation of the Four Ball Court Panels at Tajín, Mexico," in Anthony F. Aveni, ed., *Archaeoastronomy in Precolumbian America* (Austin: University of Texas Press, 1975), 263ff.

33 See Krickeberg, 161f.

34 See Macazaga, 16: another representation of a decapitated ball player; but instead of cornstalks, there are seven serpents jumping out of the victim's throat. Nevertheless, "Seven Serpent," *Chicomecoatl,* is the goddess of maintenance.

35 See C. Lizardi Ramos, "Rito previo a la decapitación en el juego de pelota," *Estudios de Cultura Nahuatl* 9 (1971): 23ff., who establishes the relationship between the ball/skull and the number 8 which appears in front of it and which symbolizes the corn, as does the flower accompanying the sign *kin* (sun), which can be found near the decapitated players.

36 See Krickeberg, 153ff.

37 Taladoire, 550.

38 Ibid., 554f.

39 Ibid., 739 (Codex Dresden 41A)

40 The discovery of this "Codex" began with Michael D. Coe's

publications *The Maya Scribe and His World* (New York: Grolier Press, 1973) and *The Lords of the Underworld* (Princeton: Princeton University Press, 1978). In the meantime a great number of Codex style vessels have been assembled in thematic groups and published by F. Robicsek and D. M. Hales as *The Maya Book of the Dead: The Ceramic Codex* (New Haven: Yale University Press, 1981).

41   P. Arnold, *Le Livre des morts maya* (Paris, 1978). For more details, see Kerkhoff, "Aspectos Escatológicos del Popol Vuh," 25, 31.

42   Robicsek and Hales, 89–96, and commentary, 117ff.

43   Coe, *The Maya Scribe,* 18ff., see 30 and plate 5 for a representation of a ball player.

44   Hartung, 37ff. reports on such stelae in Piedras Negras. See also D. H. Kelly, "The Birth of the Gods in Palenque," *Estudios de Cultura Maya* 5 (1965): 93–134; Robicsek and Hales, 120 (the dead ruler reborn as a god).

45   For a discussion of the pro and contra of this question see R. D. Bruce, "The Popol Vuh and the Book of Chan K'in," *Estudios de Cultura Maya* 10 (1976–77): 173ff.

46   See Kerkhoff, "Anotaciones sobre la cosmogonía del 'Popol Vuh,'" *Plural* 1, no. 1 (1982): 52–78.

47   On possible allusions, in the context of the *uayeb*-rites, to reincarnation see Kerkhoff, "Aspectos escatológicos del Popol Vuh," 39.

48   See Kerkhoff, "Anotaciones," 60ff., and notes 74–83. For the interpretation of the creation-myth see especially R. Girard, *Le Popol Vuh: Histoire Culturelle des Maya-Quichés* (Paris, 1972), 16–30. For the story of the twins, 160–251.

49   *Hunahpú* means literally "hunter with a blowgun," "shooter"; but the name contains allusions to *Hunabkú* "the only god" and may even represent the sound of the latter. There is, via the calendar, also an allusion to the sun-god as "governor of the cornfield" (Cf. Goetz and Morley, *Popol Vuh,* 78f.). R. Girard, *Origen y desarrollo de las civilizaciones antiguas de América* (Mexico City: UNAM, 1977), 168, identifies H. with the New Sun and his companion with the New Moon; literally the name of the latter could mean "little jaguar" or "she-jaguar"; at the same time, since "jaguar" is also a sign of priesthood, *Ixbalamqué* could mean "little magician." Another possibility is mentioned by Bruce, 184: Imbalamqué could mean "jaguar-deer," and, as such, would have to be related to the planet Venus. Whereas Hunahpú received the Christian name of Santo Tomás, Ixbalamqué had been identified with the god of death by the Mayas of Guatemala; today his name is a synonym of the sun-god, at least for the Kekchi-Maya, while other groups associate him with the moon. See R. M. Carmack, "New

Quichean Chronicles from Highland Guatemala," *Estudios de Cultura Maya* 14 (1982): 87.

50   Goetz and Morley, 95. He is one of the sons of "Seven Macaw" who boasts of being the sun before the rising of the real sun (Hunahpú, in the fourth age).

51   The forefathers of the twins Hun-Hunahpú and Vucub-Hunahpú (Seven Hunters) are the third-age versions or "transforms" of the twins. For this structuralist concept see N. Tarn and M. Prechtel "Metaphors of relative elevation, position and ranking in the *Popol Vuh, Estudios de Cultura Maya* 13 (1981): 105ff. See also Girard, "Le Popol Vuh," 79f.

52   Goetz and Morley, 109. This is an indication that the right place for the ball court has not yet been established.

53   Ibid., 111, mentions leather-pads as protection for the hips and the knees, rings (collars for the neck), gloves, crowns (adornments worn on the head), and masks for the face.

54   Ibid., 109. Girard explains this muliplication as a means to identify the ball court with the cosmic quadrangle, the measuring of which is mentioned in the creation-myth. The four players would correspond to the four skybearers. On the other hand, from the name "seven hunters" we could conclude that the extra three represent the solstitial points and the center. Moreover, this group of seven forefathers is a "transform" of the Seven Creators (Girard, *Le Popol Vuh,* 25, 76f.).

55   From the verb *xibil = disappear (like a phantom); Xibalbá(y) can mean the dead, or the underground region inhabited by the enemies of man or the devil. Sometimes a region in northern Guatemala, descending from the central mountains, was identified with Xibalbá. The word can also mean "cave."

56   Goetz and Morley, 113. See Nelson, *Popol Vuh,* 50.

57   After having crossed a couple of rivers, one of them of blood, they come to a crossroads where, at first, they choose the wrong way (the black one); then they are betrayed by some wooden figures whom they mistake for the Lords of the Underworld, paying respect to them (the third age is the age of wooden men). Next, when invited to sit down, they fail to notice that the bench is of hot stone. Asked to enter the House of Gloom, the first real test, they are offered sticks of pine and cigars and ordered to light them without letting them get burned up; as they fail to succeed in this endeavor, they are spared the rest of the tests, the House of Cold, the House of Jaguars, the House of Bats, the House of Knives (the same places are found in Aztec eschatology) and they are killed at once. On the habit of smoking cigars (even the gods do so) see

F. Robicsek, *The Smoking Gods: Tobacco in Maya Art, History and Religion* (Norman: Oklahoma University Press, 1978).

58   Goetz and Morley, 118, 15.

59   Ibid., 118, interpret the tree as a clabash tree; Nelson, 53, speaks of the "yellow gourds" of the jicaro-tree.

60   *Xquic* means "little blood" or "woman-blood" (she is the daughter of Cuchuma-*quic,* the "gatherer of blood"), but at the same time "rubber," "ball." With this name, she *is* already her future sons, the ball players.

61   The *Popol Vuh* mentions other adventures, typical of young heroes, like the slaying of their rivals, who pretend to be sun and moon, or the punishing of their brothers, who were the favorites of their "ruling" grandmother. See Goetz and Morley, chap. 5–8 of pt. 1 and chap. 5–8 of pt. 2.

62   Goetz and Morley, chap. 6, 131ff., on the circumstances that led to this discovery.

63   Ibid., chap. 7, 136H, on the relationship between work and game. Cf. Tarn and Prestel, on the ritual character of the game, linked to agriculture and the cycle of the seasons.

64   Girard, *Origen y desarrollo,* 143, illustrates the identification of the decapitated head and the grain of corn with the beautiful representation on p. 34 of the Dresden-Codex (decapitation of the Young Corn God). Cf. also the commentary of W. Cordan, *Das Buch des Rates* (Düsseldorf, 1962), 198. The scene refers also to the decapitation of Hunahpú.

65   Goetz and Morley, 139–53.

66   In Kerkhoff, "Aspectos escatológicos del Popol Vuh," notes 63–102, I discuss the different translations of the passage, comparing four Spanish versions with one English, one French, and two German translations.

67   Goetz and Morley, 140f.

68   According to other translations, the team of Xibalbá gives in. In any case, since the ball symbolizes the head, the giving-in could be interpreted as symbolical beheading. Cf. Girard, *Le Popol Vuh,* 164.

69   This is the explanation offered by Cordan, 194f. In other translations there is no "head of the jaguar" even mentioned in the text.

70   Ibid., 194. Cordan denies the existence of a "worm" in the original text; instead, he reads: "soon everything will be over."

71   Goetz and Morley, 144. According to other translators, it is the ring on one side of the ball court.

72   Ibid., 145, translate: "while those of Xibalbá grasped the handle of

the knife of flint." There is a pun with *chaah* = "ballgame" and *chaa* = "knife." Cf. Nelson, 75.

73 Ibid., according to Goetz and Morley, the twins win the game; the other translators either don't mention a result or have a draw.

74 The "House of Knives." Here is another pun: *chaa* = knife and *cha*= talk. The twins *promise* the flesh of all animals to the knives and save their lives.

75 Goetz and Morley, 147ff.

76 *Huracán* is one of the creator-gods mentioned in the cosmogonic myth (ibid., 82); it is *his* timely arrival as triple lightning that "fertilizes" the "Feather Serpent" (*Tepeu Gucumatz*), the primordial waters, and accomplishes the emergence of the earth. Cf. Kerkhoff, "Anotaciones," 62ff. In our context (Goetz and Morley, 149f.), this decapitation has to do with the process of the growing corn; Cf. Girard, *Le Popol Vuh*, 169–86; and Cordan, 90.

77 Goetz and Morley, 151.

78 Ibid., 152.

79 Ibid., 153. The rabbit is a symbol of the moon and as such related to Ixbalamqué, the night-sky.

80 Ibid., 153, let the game end in a draw and have Ixbalamqué throw a stone at the turtle, after the game; this deed is interpreted by the people of Xibalbá as a sign of defeat. According to Girard, *Le Popol Vuh*, 187, the Lords of Xibalbá destroy the false head.

81 Goetz and Morley, 155. The twins embrace each other before jumping into the bonfire.

82 Ibid., 154.

83 Ibid., 155.

84 Ibid., 156.

85 Ibid., 156. (The twins cut themselves into bits and bring themselves back to life; and do the same with other persons.)

86 Ibid., 159.

87 Ibid., 161. Cordan, 99, translates *quic* (-ball) as "pure blood." Xibalbá is denied the status of nobleman. (Goetz and Morley deny both.)

88 Goetz and Morley, 163.

89 Ibid.

90 On the ball game in South America: Krickeberg, 174ff. Special attention is paid to an Uitoto-myth which shows resemblance to the *Popol Vuh;* for the Caribbean ball game (Arawak and Taino), Kricke-

berg, 172; on South America Twin-myths, Cf. R.Alegriá, *Apuntes en torno a la mitología de los indios taínos de las Antillas Mayores y sus orígenes Sudamericanos* (Barcelona, 1978), 95–130.

91 In the South American stories, the twins do not have the stellar signficance we see in the Mesoamerican context.

92 "Kairological" is derived from the Greek *kairos* = "right time." Cf. Kerkhoff, "Zum antiken Begriff des Kairos," *Zeitschrift für Philos. Forschung* 27, no. 2 (1973): 256–74.

93 On the belief in reincarnation among present-day Maya cf. R. Redfield and A. Villa Rojas, *Chan Kom: A Mayan Village* (Washington D.C.: The Carnegie Institution of Washington,* 1934).

94 Cf. Bruce, 201.

95 Cf. Brundage, *The Fifth Sun,* 11, on the sacrifice of 400 prisoners after a ball game in honor of Uitznahuatl.

96 Cf. Kerkhoff, "El Tiempo Sagrado," *Diálogos* 35 (1980):37–59.

97 Cf. Tarn and Prechtel, 117.

98 Cf. H. Neuenswander, "Vestiges of Early Maya Time Concepts in a Contemporary (Cubulco Achi) Community," *Estudios de Cultura Maya* 13 (1981): 125–63.

99 Cf. Barbara Tedlock, *Time and the Highland Maya* (Albuquerque: University of New Mexico Press, 1982). G. Gossen, "Temporal and Spatial Equivalents in Chamula Ritual Symbolism," *Reader of Comparative Religion: Anthropological Approach,* ed. W. Lesa and E. Z. Vogt (New York: n.p., 1972). M. López Baralt, "Tiempo y espacio en Mesoamérica," *Cuadernos Hispanoamericanos,* no. 397 (1983): 1ff.

100 The author is preparing such an investigation under the title *Zeit und Unzeit.* Several chapters of it have been published in Spanish in *Diálogos* 35 (1980): 37–59.

101 See R. Piña Chan (Quetzalcoatl, Mexico, 1977), 27ff.

102 See the excellent work of L. Séjourné, *El pensamiento nahuatl cifrado por los calendarios* (Mexico City: UNAM, 1981), a study of the first three signs of the Aztec Calendar.

103 See R. Ordoñez y Aguiar, *Historia de la creación del cielo y de la tierra. Teología de los Culebras,* ed. Nicolás de León (Mexico City, 1907), 108: (". . . en el juego de pelota simbolizaban la inmortalidad . . ."), written at the end of the eighteenth century!

12 | The Scientific Worldview and a Destiny Beyond Death

JOHN C. POLKINGHORNE

I do not think that they [thoughts of a purpose perfected in an individual human life] are at variance with the insights into the structure of the physical world provided by my experience as a theoretical physicist.

The Christian's belief in a destiny beyond death finds its principal support in the particular event of the resurrection of Jesus Christ, rather than in general considerations about the nature of the world. Yet that particular event is itself credible only if it bears some reasonable relation to the generality of experience. Of course it goes beyond such experience, but if God is more than a celestial magician or arbitrary despot his action in raising Christ from the dead will have to bear some consonant relation to the rest of his action in the creation that he sustains. It is, therefore, not improper to ask if the nature of man as we understand it is compatible with the idea of resurrection, both in the particular instance of Jesus Christ and also as the eventual destiny of all men, "for as in Adam all die, so also in Christ shall all be made alive" (1 Cor. 15:22).

To ask such a question is to be made immediately aware of our limitations in framing any answer. Our understanding of the psychosomatic being of man is rudimentary. Progress with the age-old conundrum of the relationship of mind and brain is minimal. That they are intimately related is clear. Physical damage inhibits mental activity. For me this gives greater credibility to the Christian idea of resurrection, that is, a future existence embodied in some new world of God's creating, rather than the notion of the survival of some tenuous spiritual residue or soul. While we are dependent on the satisfactory working of our physical bodies if we are to maintain and articulate our mental processes, there is nothing special about the material which composes our bodies. The atoms of which we are made are completely changed every few years. It is the pattern they form that provides continuity and preserves our identity. There is, then, no special difficulty in conceiving of that pattern being recreated after death with "physical" components in a different world. In a very crude analogy it would be like running the same computer software program on two different computers. The mathematical notion of mapping from one space to another provides another analogy of what might be involved. Such mappings can be characterized by their invariance properties—the quantities they leave unchanged—and here might be a clue as to how identity could be preserved even if the "matter" of the new world were to exhibit different properties to that of the world with which we are familiar, "for this perishable nature must put on the imperishable," (1 Cor. 15:53) and its organization also to be somewhat different, since it would obviously not be a corpse that was recreated.

These considerations that I have sketched are clearly speculative and far from fully worked out, but they are sufficient, I think, to suggest that the notion of resurrection is neither meaningless nor an irrational possibility. Its credibility is enhanced for those of us who believe that there are signs of a purpose at work in the world, a purpose which nevertheless does not find its final fulfillment within the processes of that world. Strictly speaking science can have nothing to say about such a question, since by its choice of method it abjures the consideration of teleological issues. Nevertheless it is a curious fact that physical cosmology has in recent years exhibited a character that *seems* consonant with the metaphysical notion of purpose and appears to encourage the asking of such questions.

The world is very remarkable structurally. We have to come to realize that a universe in which life can develop has to be extremely close-knit, both in the pattern and in the balance of its basic physical laws and probably also in the initial conditions which specify how that universe started its existence. This insight, that only a universe closely approximating the specific character of the one in which we live (including, incidentally its stupendous size) is capable of evolving complex systems like men, is called the anthropic principle.[1] Is it just our luck that the world is so structured that we can be here or is there some reason for it? Physics of this nature almost suggests metaphysics. Some have supposed that there is a portfolio of different universes and we, of course, simply appear in that particular specimen in which it is possible for us to do so. Such a proposal can be wrapped up in pseudo-scientific language but it is in fact just a metaphysical speculation. More economical, and to me more persuasive, would be the belief that the world is the way it is because it is the creation of a Creator whose will purposes that it should be capable of evolving conscious beings.

If that insight is correct, then the hundred thousand million stars of our galaxy, and the thousand million galaxies of the observable universe, are there to provide an environment in which consciousness can come into existence. Anything smaller would have run its course before that had time to happen. But will it all prove just an interesting but transient episode in the history of the world? The eventual fate of the universe, as we understand it, depends on exactly how much matter it contains. We are not accurately enough informed about that to be able to choose between two possible scenarios. On the one hand, the present expansion may continue indefinitely, leading eventually to a form of heat death as systems condense and decay. On the other hand, the expansion may be reversed and the universe will collapse in on itself. What started as the big bang will end as the big plop. Either way it would not seem that the purpose at work in the world, if indeed there is one, would find fulfillment. On the cosmic scale there would be the same futility that we seem to see individually when hard won gains of character and under-standing are apparently dissolved and dissipated by an indi-vidual's death.

Because I believe that there *is* a purpose at work in the world, I believe that there must consequently be a world and a destiny beyond death, and that this present physical world does not exhaust the intentions of God for his creation:

Of old thou didst lay the foundations of the earth,
and the heavens are the work of thy hands.
They will perish, but thou dost endure;
they will all wear out like a garment.
Thou changest them like raiment, and they pass away;
but thou art the same and thy years have no end (Ps. 102:25–27).

The character of whatever experience awaits us beyond death

is largely beyond our imagining. But if it is true that God's "invisible nature . . . has been clearly perceived in the things that have been made" (Rom. 1:20), then I think there is one reasonable expectation that we can form. The story of the evolution of the world from the big bang of some fifteen thousand million years ago, through the first generation of stars forming heavy elements inside themselves by nuclear cookery, to the second generation of stars and planets on which there could then be found environments in which replicating molecules and eventually conscious beings could develop is awesomely long. Such a story suggests that if there is a Creator he is patient and subtle in his action, content to achieve his purposes by the slow unfolding of the potentialities with which he has endowed the natural laws of the world he sustains. He is certainly not a God in a hurry, achieving his purposes by imperious and sudden fiat, but rather he works through gradual process. If that is so, it lends credibility to the notion of purgatory, a gradual transformation of character beyond death. The crudities of much medieval thought on this subject should not blind us to its inherent plausibility. Nowhere does it find finer articulation than in Dante's *Purgatorio* where the whole mountain resounds to the cry of *Gloria in excelsis Deo* as an individual moves to a higher cornice on the purgatorial mount. It is a noble picture of redemption through process.

While these thoughts of a purpose perfected in an individual human life by means of a destiny beyond death find their motivation in my experience as a believer embracing the hope of the Gospel, I do not think that they are at variance with the insights into the structure of the physical world provided by my experience as a theoretical physicist.

Note

1   See P. C. Davies, *The Accidental Universe* (New York: Cambridge University Press, 1982) for details.

13 | The Church and the Secular Apocalyptic

DAVID H. C. READ

It is ironic that just when the traditional churches had fallen silent on the subject of the Last Things and when for many preachers the apocalyptic note in the Bible had become an embarrassment, we should be experiencing the rise of what could be called "a secular apocalypticism."

This essay makes no claim to original insights into what are curiously called Last Things (if they are really the last, what more is there to be said?); still less am I attempting to assess the vast literature on the subject with only a fraction of which any preacher, or even any theologian, could possibly be acquainted.

I simply want to reflect on the fact that Christian preachers are in the unique position of being expected regularly to voice certain convictions about death and its sequel, about the end of the world, and about the dimension of eternity. The sermon is the point at which the Christian Church proclaims certain convictions about such matters, and traditional liturgies have over the centuries, instilled them in the minds of millions—consciously or unconsciously.

The process of secularization, which was assumed to be steadily eliminating this influence of the Church on popular thought, has run into unexpected cross-currents in recent years: We are witnessing extraordinary signs of re-awakening concern for the spiritual dimension. So it may not be as *passé* as it would have seemed fifty years ago to inquire into the continuing assertions of the Church about these Last Things.

Just how much has the Church, as represented by the major denominations, had to say about these things in recent years? To judge by the impression given by modern novelists and playwrights or the more lurid kind of autobiography, the preachers of the recent past fulminated Sunday by Sunday about the terrors of hell and revelled in spectacular scenarios of final judgment, with a very materialist, if somewhat boring, heaven as the alternative for the elect. It puzzles me where this picture of Christian preaching comes from, since in over seventy years of being exposed to sermons I cannot remember hearing a single one on hell or the Last Judgment and very few on heaven. Of course, there have always been some preachers around who indulged in such homiletical fireworks, but I suspect that most of these writers derive their fictional preachers from one another. On the whole it would be true to say that the twentieth-century mainstream churches have been notable, not for their exuberance, but for their almost total silence about the Last Things. And it seems to have been possible for millions to repeat the final clauses of the Apostles' or Nicene creeds without any noticeable reaction to the tremendous statements they contain. I remember one such, on hearing someone mention the "Second Coming," remarking that she had never heard of such a thing—in spite of having said so many times "from whence he shall come to judge the quick and the dead."

Over the centuries there has been a curious ebb and flow in the emphasis given to beliefs about the Last Things. Apart from some aberrations in a purely secular, this-worldly direction, the Church has stood firm as a witness to the reality of our eternal dimension in its worship and preaching, and few today would doubt that this is an ingredient of Christianity as believed and practiced by its members. But it is only in certain periods that this testimony of the Church coincides with the concerns and fears of the population as a whole. We are, I believe, in such a period now.

The advent of nuclear weapons has unquestionably led to an almost universal and possibly unique consciousness of the precarious position of the human race, faced with the threat of imminent extinction on a global scale. It is useless to point out that our individual existence is, and always has been, extremely precarious, or that there seems little reason to suppose that, since each one of us dies, so the entire human story may not conceivably be brought to a similar end. We are not in the realm of logic. The most fervent Roman Catholic, the most intrepid Calvinist, the most serene Anglican, the most iron-clad fundamentalist is surely, consciously or unconsciously, disturbed by the dawning realization that future events that lurked quietly in the last clauses of their Christian credo, might *really* happen tomorrow and that the lurid images of a Day of Wrath, a *Dies Irae,* might be translated into a global Hiroshima.

It is ironic that just when the traditional churches had fallen silent on the subject of the Last Things, and when for many preachers the apocalyptic note in the Bible had become an embarrassment, we should be experiencing the rise of what could be called a "secular apocalypticism." I am not suggesting that the churches make an instant identification of the prevalent grim forecasts of geno-suicide with the biblical witness to Last Things (still less an exploitation of apocalyptic texts in terms of nuclear physics), but it seems odd that the response of the Church to the new situation has been curiously slow and muffled. Secular apocalypticism has found its voice, not in the eschatology of Jesus but of Prospero in Shakespeare's *Tempest:*

The cloud-capped towers, the gorgeous palaces,
The solemn temples, the great globe itself,
Yea, all which it inherit shall dissolve
And, like this insubstantial pageant faded,
Leave not a rack behind. We are such stuff
As dreams are made of, and our little life
Is rounded with a sleep.

The growing acceptance of the possibility of such an end on a cosmic scale, the fabulism or cynicism with which it is reflected in the philosophy, the poetry and art of our time is in startling contrast to the evolutionist optimism of the pre-1914 era—the confident secular futurism of, for instance, an H. G. Wells or Bernard Shaw.

Thus secular apocalypticism is emerging as a viewpoint that owes nothing to the traditional teachings of the Christian Church. It is pure Prospero (I will not be trapped into saying "Shakespeare"), not a return to the apocalyptic of the Hebrew prophets or the Old Testament. The reservations that often accompany projections into the future today are *"If* humanity is still around," *"If* there is a year 2000," and not "D.V." ("God willing"). The Church's voice has been so inarticulate, the Church's impact on popular philosophy and modern art has been so weak, that no one would be listening if we were to say: "I told you so."

If we take a quick look at the eschatological context of the Christian message as it has been voiced in the pulpit over the centuries, we find remarkable fluctuations. There is no question about its presence (even dominance) in the apostolic age as preserved in the New Testament books. The proclamation of the Gospel, as recorded in the Book of the Acts and in the epistles resounded with references to the Last Things, while the Gospels record a preaching of Jesus (preceded by John the Baptist) which has the accents of an urgency derived from a conviction that the end may be imminent. Few now would doubt that the concept, for instance, of the Kingdom of God has such overtones and cannot possibly be related to the Utopia of modern scientism or the ethical optimism reflected in hymns of the pre-1914 era. The first Christian sermon, on the day of Pentecost, reeked with apocalyptic imagery from the Hebrew prophets, and Jesus is proclaimed not as new prophet or ethical teacher, but as one whom God has made "both Lord and Christ," with all the eschatological weight these words would carry for those hearing them. Even the most philosophical and rational discourse (the sermon attributed to Paul in Athens) ends with the words ". . . because he has fixed a day on which he will judge the world in righteousness by a man whom he has appointed, and of this he has given assurance to all men by raising him from the dead."

The New Testament is alive with a Gospel that speaks of new life, new hope, new expectations based on the irruption into this world of the powers beyond through the incarnation, crucifixion, and resurrection of Jesus Christ. This gives a note of urgency and decisiveness to the message being proclaimed. In Christ "there is a new creation"; he is the Life; he is the Victor over both sin and death; he is the One in whom the world is brought to judgment. Within the canon of the New Testament, there is noticeable variation in the interpretation of the Last Things and in the estimate of how long it would be until the End comes. Already there are signs that the first expectation of an imminent return of Jesus "in glory" was giving way to the possibility that the Christian Church has to be prepared for a "long haul" to the day of triumph.

It is evident that both Jesus and his apostles had to protest a tendency to expect an almost immediate End with a consequent temptation to sit back and do nothing. Jesus warned against speculation as to the "day or the hour," and told the story of the talents (with its violent condemnation of the one who hid the money in the ground and refused to invest) precisely because, as Luke says: "They thought that the Kingdom of God should immediately appear." Paul found some of his converts inclining to the view that, since Jesus was just about to return they might as well abandon their jobs and their families and await the Day. In the Johannine gospel and epistles there is more emphasis on the presence of the Holy Spirit in whom Christ "comes" than on the sudden irruption of the Last Things, although it is here that we find the strongest emphasis on an eternal life that begins now and finds its fulfillment in the resurrection of the dead.

Christianity made its impact on the Greco-Roman world as a convincing and dynamic message of life and hope. For the individual it offers a promise of life beyond death, and the conviction that the human story has a meaning, a direction, and a fulfillment in the dimension of eternity. For society it announced judgment—a "crisis" in which history would culminate in the triumph of God's Kingdom and the elimination of the powers of evil.

As the Church expanded and eventually reached not only the status of a permitted religion *(religio licita)* but of predominance, there was obviously a leveling-off in the proclamation of an imminent End. The teachings about the Last Things were progressively codified and elaborated by the theologians so that there came to be an accepted othodoxy about what happens after death and a conventional expectation of a Last Judgment. Right through the Middle Ages and beyond believers were in the grip of an eschatology in which, if the thoughts of an imminent end of the world had receded, the individual was vividly aware of a very real heaven and hell.

The Reformation did little to alter the general picture of the Last Things, except to eliminate many of the medieval refinements such as the state of purgatory and the claims of the Church to determine the individual's fate in the world beyond. The promise of heaven and the threat of hell were kept alive and supported by the necessary biblical texts. The words of the creeds about the return of Jesus and the judgment of "the quick and the dead" were retained, but the Reformers were not inclined to speculation about the Last Things, or to look for an imminent Second Coming of Christ.

Yet, during these centuries there were constant outbreaks of what one might call "eschatological excitement." Inside and outside the orthodox communions there were sporadic appearances of Christian groups possessed with a vivid sense of the nearness of the End. Speculations, often based on the Book of Revelation, convinced many that the world was about to be dissolved and a fiery judgment inaugurated. The text in the Apocalypse or Book of Revelation about the "thousand year" reign of the saints with Christ gave rise to millenarian movements which have dogged the church from the earliest time to the present. The advent of the year 1000 elicited an excited expectation which we may see repeated in a secular apocalypticism which may culminate around the year 2000.

The Reformers had not only to cope with the struggle against Rome; they fought on another front against sects that were considered dangerous fanatics threatening the established order of both Church and State. Among these apocalyptic visions prophecies were rife. Preachers aroused violent passions with their vivid pictures of an imminent Day of Wrath, and offered various means of escape through participation in groups of the "elect" who would be the heirs of the millennium. As happens today, the historic denominations responded to the "fanatics" by relegating eschatology to the background of their teaching and preaching. During the eighteenth and nineteenth centuries, for instance, both in Britain and the United States, questions about the Last Things and speculations about the return of Christ came to be regarded as the province of sects, revival movements, and intermittent evangelists, while the established churches moved placidly forward toward a Kingdom that came more and more to look like some secular Utopia. So, on the one hand, in the early part of this century the mainstream churches were dazzled by the vision of a church spreading across the world, while the secular dogma of uninterrupted progress was translated into a Christian conviction that the Kingdom of God would be within reach—the product of spiritual and social zeal and enlightenment. In such a worldview there was no room for cataclysmic events and fiery judgments. On the other hand, at this same time, millenarian sects flourished and at least two of them chose 1914 as the date when they predicted the End and the establishment of God's Kingdom.

The two world wars demolished the more optimistic hopes of the historic churches. From 1918 and 1945 theology reflected the collapse of the complacent assumptions of those who had rejected the traditional (if quiescent) doctrines of the Last Things in favor of the hopes of the Enlightenment. Karl Barth had rung the alarm-bell, and it sounded a different note throughout the remains of the Christian West. Crisis, decision, the sovereignty of God over human affairs, the total dependence of a broken humanity on the grace of God, a Church called to serve and to suffer—all these notes coincided with the rise of an existential philosophy and a reversal of the study of the Church Fathers, and of Aquinas, Luther, and Calvin. At last it seemed as though the historic churches were rediscovering an eschatology, re-learning a Word from beyond in Scripture, and re-claiming the territory of the Last Things from the grasp of the fanatics.

Nineteen forty-five might well seem to be a date when, for the Church and the world, the perspective for all futurology, religious and secular, suddenly changed. Dropping the bomb raised the stakes of war enormously and suggested for the first time the possibility of an end to human history devised by humanity itself. After the stunned reaction to the first use of atomic bombs, there was, however, a pause rather than a panic in the reactions of ordinary people. There was even an emerging hope that, at last, war on a global scale had become unthinkable and therefore highly unlikely. But the possessors of the new weapons continued to think and the result has been an escalation of nuclear armaments to such a degree that now, forty years after Hiroshima, the consciousness of an End, sudden, cataclysmic, devastating (one that could *really* happen to the human race), has risen to new heights. A new generation is growing up under a threat that never was before. No future.

So an unprecedented secular apocalypticism is with us. For the first time, without the spur of religious dogma, men and women are living with the conscious or unconscious realization that at any moment, again in Prospero's words, "the great globe itself, yea all which it inherit shall dissolve." Life goes on, more or less as usual, but underneath there is the sense of mortal danger, an awareness that the End is no longer a poetic or theological concept but a reality hovering near. The new apocalyptic broods over our art, politics, literature, and science. It surfaces in casual conversation. It sets a question mark on all plans and projects. It brings back to the human race a fear that seemed to have been exorcized by the achievements of modern medicine and technology, and the philosophies of progress, and the betterment of the human condition. The utopian literature of the last hundred years has given place to the satirical, the horrendous, the mindblowing, and to the fantasies of science fiction. A human family drawn closer together by modern means of communication and transportation shivers in an atmosphere where the absurd seems most likely, terrorism a fact of life, and the veneer of civilization revealed as precariously thin.

This new apocalypticism stirs some to vigorous action. The question of arms control has, for all serious thinkers, become a priority which now unites those who in the era of conventional warfare were divided in their views of the legitimacy of the use of force in conflicts between nations. Arguments about just wars and pacifist convictions have become largely irrelevant in face of a threat that could mean the End. On the other hand we find a widespread paralysis of the will and a new fatalism (che sarà, sarà) by which fears are belied, or disguised, and life goes on as before. Yet Pandora's box has been opened and few believe it can ever be closed.

How is this secular apocalypticism to be related to the traditional eschatology of Christendom or the thoughts and speculations of the fanatical fringe?

The sects, with their claim to an inner knowledge of things to come, with their assurance that Armageddon and the Great Tribulation are infallibly forecast in the Bible, are having a field day. The lurid pictures of the Last Things which used to be dismissed by the average citizen as the product of unbalanced minds are finding a new credibility. A generation of biblical illiterates is easily impressed by arguments based on a literal and materialist interpretation of the apocalyptic imagery of books like Ezekiel, Daniel, and Revelation. The use of words in the Gospels about what immediately precedes the End ("earthquakes, wars and rumors of wars") is impressive to those who never stop to think that such phenomena could be found in every generation of recorded history. It is possible that this identification of prophetic symbols with the potential of nuclear warfare, and this stirring-up of a panic desire to escape the coming holocaust will draw increasing numbers to the fold of the sects and the more extreme of the fundamentalist churches. Perhaps, if we reach and pass the year 2000, the excitement may peak and, as has happened before, the millenarians will dwindle into a muttering minority.

But what of the churches that belong to the mainstream of Christian tradition? They give the impression of having been caught by surprise by this invasion of secular apocalypticism. In the liberal period of Protestantism, and also in the pre-Vatican II rigidity of Rome, eschatology was firmly kept in its place— which was normally the postscript to dogmatics or the last verse of popular hymns. In reaction to what Calvin called the "ravings" of the sects, mainstream churches tended to ignore the Last Things, except in the offering of the conventional consolations to the bereaved and the affirmations of Easter. The major denominations were increasingly reticent about what Reinhold Niebuhr called "the furniture of heaven and the temperature of hell," and thoughts of an end of the world, even in biblical terms, were excluded from most of the theology and preaching of the day. The season of Advent came to be regarded as a warm-up for a cozy Christmas rather than an opportunity to reflect on judgment and the Parousia or Second Coming of Christ.

In the twenties and thirties the demise of evolutionary optimism, the rise of totalitarian ideologies, and, later, the emergence of the Third World, all contributed to a sensitizing of the Church. Crisis theology, existential philosophy, neo-orthodoxy, followed by bold attempts to restate Christian doctrines and realign the Church to the culture of the secular world, were signs that the Christian understanding of the Last Things was again coming to the center of the stage—for none of the very diverse schools of theology was working in a conventional framework. A new note of urgency was being sounded. We were no longer in a world moving slowly and steadily towards the Kingdom of God on earth.

It takes at least a generation for theological changes of climate to be reflected in the preaching of the Church and the thinking of its members. Especially in the great variety of church life and witness in the United States, it is impossible to assess the influence of the new apocalyptic mood. But, at least in the mainstream churches there are signs of an effort to reckon again with the traditional eschatology in the light of refreshed theological thinking. There is a new spirit of realism, meeting the challenge of secular apocalypticism.

In most denominations there are discernible changes in the attitude toward death and what lies beyond. On the one hand the End, in the sense of our personal earthly terminus, has been increasingly deromanticized. The American aversion to the word "death" is disappearing, along with many of the funeral practices that were used to disguise the fact that the End had come. Biblical realism is returning and with it a rejection of the secular illusions about the infinite prolongation of our earthly journey. Only as this happened could the New Testament world of the Resurrection be truly heard. And it *is* being heard, one indication being the gradual restoration of Easter as a festival of life-affirming hope based on the rising of Christ from the dead, instead of being an occasion for a sentimental spring festival in a profusion of flowers. The flowers are still there, but once again they are celebrating the victory of Christ and the triumph of life in him. The realism of "as in Adam all die" is countered with the realism of faith that "in Christ shall all be made alive" and congregations are reminded that "the flowers that bloom in the Spring . . . have nothing to do with the case."

The traditional churches (Catholic, Protestant, and Orthodox) seem to be speaking more clearly with one voice, over and against the despair and cynicism of the secular world. They are also converging on an interpretation of the Last Things that avoids claims to know particulars of the life beyond the grave and concentrates on the thought of fulfillment—eternal life as a dimension into which we can enter now but which, by the resurrection of the whole person means, not an infinite prolongation of life as we know it, but an inexpressible and indescribable heightening of those qualities that illuminate our mortal life as "intimations of immortality" and find their focus in the crucified and risen Christ. This is why, although today's church members may be slightly embarrassed by the imagery of "Jerusalem the Golden," they respond to a sonnet of John Donne:

Since I am coming to that holy room,
Where, with thy quire of Saints for evermore,
I shall be made thy Music; as I come
I tune the instrument here at the door,
And what I must do then, think here before.

In a time when the insecurity of our mortal life is more and more *felt* and not just accepted as a truism (one that somehow applies only to other people) the pastoral work of the historic churches will mean more than ever and will be carried out in the face of a wave of skepticism that has lapped over from the secular world. Since such conviction has its roots in the theology of the living and enduring Church it cannot be sustained if there is an eschatological silence in the pulpit.

That silence has been even more remarkable in the cosmic realm—the traditional doctrines of the Last Things, judgment, heaven, hell, and the End of the World. Mainstream churches have avoided these topics, not only because of a natural and reverent agnosticism about events that must be beyond our scrutiny, but also in reaction to the crudities and arrogance of the increasingly loud voices of the more fanatical sects. It is even more obvious that such voices are appealing to the deep fears of those who are desperate to find some way of escape from the threat of nuclear destruction. The message they hear is simple and comes dressed in the familiar garments of Evangelical Christianity: Yes, the fearful chaos and destruction is coming. It is foretold in Scripture—Armageddon is inevitable—but an experience of conversion, of being born again, will enable you to escape the horrors from which you will be removed ("raptured") to enjoy the triumph of Christ and the company of the saints.

What the traditional churches have to do is to wrestle with the biblical eschatology (with its language and symbols of apocalyptic) and make known the Word that comes to this generation about the Last Things. The un-Christian selfishness of a false eschatology will have to be exposed, and the convictions of the creeds interpreted in the light of the Holy Spirit speaking today.

It is impossible within the scope of this essay to do more than indicate what such convictions are. Let me suggest that they have to do, more than anything else, with the Christian belief in the total sovereignty of God over his creation. The Last Things are *his* things. They cannot be extracted from the Bible by literalist expositors claiming an inside track. They cannot be swept aside by any "liberal theology" that considers them a relic of medieval superstition. They cannot be brushed aside by those who advocate a belief in a limited God—or even announce that he is dead. For questions about the direction and goal of human life are alive as never before. We may not conceive of a Last Judgment in terms of the west-door carvings of a medieval cathedral, but the question of moral choice will not go away and seems to many to be more urgent than ever.

Pictures of a return of Christ in glory as painted either by a primitive or by a glib "televangelist" today may be impossible images for most of us as literal descriptions of an imminent event, but the witness of the entire Church Catholic has been to a climax in history in which Christ appears. For the Christian he must be the Omega as well as the Alpha, and the meaning and climax of the human story is found in him. Secular apocalypticism as we are experiencing it today cannot be crudely christianized, but it will have to be taken seriously as at least a more congenial climate for the proclamation of the God who speaks in the Scriptures, who reveals the Lordship of Christ in Word and Sacrament, and "with whom are the issues of life." The Last Things are hid in him and can neither be penetrated by the believer, nor manipulated by the technology of an unbelieving world.

14 | Time and Eternity in Kairos: Tillich and Religious Socialism

ROBERT P. SCHARLEMANN

It is . . . the property of every living religion to bear within itself a constant opposition toward the religious in itself.
PAUL TILLICH

Perhaps more than in any other movement, with the possible exception of some aspects of recent liberation theology, the question of the relation of the eternal to the temporal was a focus of attention in the religious socialism that appeared in Europe after World War I. This is especially the case for the theology of Tillich, whose debate with socialism in the 1920s provides an instance in which that question became involved in symbols and movements that were both religious and political. One might say that there are three different concepts of the time–eternity relation: according to one, the eternal is what comes at the end of an infinitely extended line of time (it is, literally, at the end of and beyond time); according to a second one, the eternal is the unity of the moments of time, the "eternal now," which, appearing on a time line as the present moment continually moving forward, has an analogy in the unity of memory and anticipation in the consciousness of the present; according to a third, the eternal is the eschatological, that is, the qualitative end and fulfillment of time that can break into time at any moment but that, as such, is equally distant from any particular moment of time. Tillich described his own conception of the relation of time and eternity as that of a line which, like an arc, descends and touches the chronological time line at a certain point and immediately ascends[1]—the intersection of time and eternity has the nature of a mathematical point. This eschatological point is what he means by the *kairos,* or that special moment at which the temporal, intersected by the eternal, becomes itself of eternal significance.

Providing a diagram of such relations is, however, different from elaborating the conceptions themselves and from constructing a theological position with reference to them. Tillich was faced with this latter, constructive task in his dealing with the political, social, and cultural situation in Europe after World War I. In that setting in which criticism of capitalist society was widespread, he was particularly concerned with the symbols *Kingdom of God* and *utopia* and, more generally, with understanding the possibility of a *religious socialism* that was to be different from Marxism on the one side and from quietistic Christianity on the other.[2] For these are the symbols in which the issue of eschatology and history becomes concrete and which contain the question of the relation of time and eternity. One could even say, with justice, that for Tillich's theology the symbol of the Kingdom of God is as basic as is the symbol of the cross, although the latter symbol has been given more attention in the studies of Tillich than has the former. It is generally recognized that the symbol of the cross plays a particularly important role in Tillich's theology because it incorporates the element of self-criticism, and the possibility of self-transcendence, in religious symbols themselves; it is the religious symbol that symbolizes the absolute relativity of all religious symbols. But the religious symbol of the Kingdom of God (and the rational symbol of utopia that is its counterpart) also plays a distinctive role in this theology, being at once one of the most important and one of the most difficult of all symbols because it simultaneously intends something immanent and something transcendent. As a symbol, it has the capacity of expressing both the immanent and the transcendent sides of the historical.[3]

Initially, it might seem that this trait does not make the symbol of the Kingdom of God any different from other symbols. A symbol always has, after all, both a proper and a metaphorical sense, and the proper sense points to the metaphorical and, by doing so, sets the basis for the dialectic of the whole religious symbol. Any such symbol involves something concrete that both calls attention to itself (as unconditionally important) and also points away from itself. In what way is the symbol of the Kingdom of God different from any other religious symbol? This is one question that we shall try to answer in the course of this paper, since the answer has to do with the way the Kingdom of God involves the temporal (the historical and eschatological), or the aspect of time, which is not so fundamentally involved in other symbols.

A second question can be treated by reference to how Tillich interpreted the fact that the movement of religious socialism came to an end, without success, in the latter part of the 1920s. Religious socialism, which tried to steer a path between nationalistic socialism and Marxism, also sought to provide a basis on which Christianity and socialism could be brought together. Despite the fact that the group of religious socialists in Germany to which Tillich belonged was very small, it was conscious of having an important historical role to play, not as a political party but as a circle of philosophical and theological thinkers who endeavored to base their thought on an understanding of the "prophetic principle." For that circle, and especially for Tillich's work in it, the concept of *kairos* ("right time," "time that is ripe for creating something new") became determinative. The concept implied the possibility that, at the right time, a concrete decision concerning a political movement might also be, as such, a decision for or against the Kingdom of God. The idea that there might be such a coinherence of the political and the theological could take one by surprise in view of Tillich's theology otherwise. Indeed, it seems to go contrary to what the *prophetic principle* itself means—namely, that nothing finite or conditional can claim to be of infinite or unconditional importance. As Tillich himself wrote in the *System of Sciences* (1923)[4] and his *Philosophy of Religion* (1925),[5] a decision concerning the unconditional is never one decision among others but rather a *metaphysical* or *transcendental* decision that is made known only through the attitude that is expressed in all one's particular decisions. How, then, is it possible for a particular, political decision to be a theological decision?

The core of Tillich's own answer to this question lies in his concept of the kairos, which contains the notion that "at certain times" (the *kairoi*) there is a convergence between the unconditional and conditional so that the *metaphysical* and the concrete decision are one and the same. Such a time is the coming of the Kingdom of God. That is to say, the Kingdom of God is a symbol of that convergence; it is the symbol in which the kairos is actual. But to say so is to raise another question. What is the nature of the act through which one knows this symbol? To put the question differently: What is the nature of that *spirit of prophecy* (as Tillich called it) which is able to recognize and interpret the kairos? To this question Tillich's own career might offer an answer, which I shall propose here as at least conjecturally plausible. This answer is that it is possible for anyone (though not necessary for everyone) to make such an identification of a kairos only once in a lifetime. It is not possible to do so a second time because the act of making the identification is one in which the self comes completely into its own but, simultaneously, expends itself. The act is eschatological in that the self must put itself so completely at stake that it cannot ever do so again. If that is true, it would offer one explanation of why Tillich, after the breakdown of religious socialism, was never again able in his thinking to become politically engaged.

|

The question of the relation of time and eternity—or the question of the eschatological dimension of history—is at the basis of the way in which Tillich deals with the possibility of a *religious* socialism. He took a stance at the time in opposition both to a socialism without religion and also to a religion without concern for political and social matters. *Religious socialism* served as the name for that stance. It granted that, initially, socialism and Christianity might seem to be incompatible; for the one rests on a belief that it is possible to change the world through technical action, and the other, on the faith that the world can be changed only through the action of God. Yet religious socialism, as Tillich represented it, sought to provide a theoretical foundation for understanding how the apparent incompatibility between human action and divine action is overcome. This involved both a theory of self, which was adapted from neo-Kantian philosophy and Ritschlian theology, and a theory of the dialectic of the divine and the human which has some similarity to, but also major differences from, the dialectic found in the speculative idealism of Hegel.

    This theory is mentioned in an essay entitled "Christianity and Socialism" ("Christentum und Sozialismus," 1919).[6] Tillich, taking up the question of the Kingdom of God from the point of view of how it is possible for Christianity to affirm "the will to change the world immanently" (*den Willen zur immanenten*

Weltgestaltung),[7] set up four points at which Christianity and socialism could come together. What is necessarily excluded here is any conception of Christianity that sees the world as completely lost; for in such a conception the world cannot be improved by human shaping but can be transformed only by a redemption coming from outside it altogether. Such a view would only harden the opposition between shaping the world (technology) on one side and transformation of the world on the other. Yet the intention of the theology of the nineteenth century, particularly in its Protestant form, was to take a course different from one that would harden the opposition. It rested on a dialectical understanding of the unity of such opposites as reason and revelation or the divine and the human. In connection with the question of human shaping and divine transformation, that involves an understanding of the biological and ethical elements in the human self and of the technological and the religious in human activity.

How are the natural or biological and the ethical constitutive of the personal self? Part of the Protestant cultural heritage that Tillich found of particular value for this question was the view that a free personality can be developed only on a natural basis in which there are both psychic and somatic components. That is to say, the natural or biological self includes not only the material individuality of the physical body but also the ethical individuality of the person; both aspects belong to the uniqueness of a human being. But beyond that, it was the dialectical conception of the ego that Tillich found of central importance in neo-Kantianism (though its roots go deeper—to Fichte and Kierkegaard, at least). According to this conception, the self as I is not just an organic unity of psychic and material elements but also a living dialectic in which the contradiction between natural drives and ethical demands is continually being resolved. One might think here of Kierkegaard (who otherwise could not be called a neo-Kantian) and his definition of spirit as the active relating of the self to itself—of its possibility to its necessity, its finitude to its infinity, and so on—instead of as a synthesis of the two. This is to say, in other words, that the apparent contradiction between a Marxist, material and a Christian, spiritual view of the human person is not a final contradiction; for in this dialectical conception of the ego the material and psychic forces are both involved in the activity of the I as such. The human person, or the human spirit, is not essentially a soul inhabiting a material body but is, rather, the continual resolving, on the part of the self as I, of the conflict between the biologically given and the ethically achieved aspects of selfhood.

If one part of religious socialism involves this conception of selfhood, in which both Marxist and Christian views are contained, the other part has to do with the relation between technical, human activity and salvatory, divine action. This is the dialectic of technology and the Kingdom of God. Tillich formulates a theory—again as an alternative to a view that sees them as incompatible opposites—in this way: "The Kingdom of God comes in this world but comes in such a way as simultaneously to place limits on itself. What can be shaped lies in the sphere of the technical, not the ethical; it lies in the sphere of the categories of means and ends and not of the categories of meaning and value. All shaping is a matter of technique, but the technical is not an end in itself. . ."[8] In another formulation, the Kingdom of God is the "nonrational ground" of technical shaping, a ground which appears in the shaping itself but in such a way that it sets its own limits. The formulations may seem somewhat cryptic. But, from the echoes of kenotic theology in them, it is clear that the intention is to provide an alternative both to a nihilism, which a mere technology brings with it, and also to a dual-world supranaturalism, which a pure spiritualism entails; it is clear, too, that in the notion of the self-limiting ground there is a reflection of how Tillich's dialectic of the divine and human differs from that of speculative idealism.

The dialectic involves the contrast between what Tillich otherwise called the cultural form (that is, basically, the self-world relation that constitutes the ontological structure) and the *Gehalt* or depth-content—a contrast that he explicated in his "Idea of a Theology of Culture" from the same year (1919). The depth-content, or the "ground" and "abyss" of the cultural form, is something that "breaks into" the form and is shaped by the form as it breaks in. It is nonrational in the sense that no form is ever adequate to grasp it completely; indeed, the dialectic comes from the tension between the inexhaustibility of that depth and the limited capacity of any and all forms. But it is nonrational also in the sense that it is made known by way of "breakthrough" and not by way of dialectical progression or nondialectical inference. What drives the dialectic is, accordingly, a motive of negation somewhat different from the Hegelian. In the Hegelian dialectic, a finite positive is set over against a finite negative and the two are resolved, or taken up, into a synthesis in which the form of contradiction between the two is removed while the meaning is retained. Thus, in the culminating stage of Hegel's philosophical theology, the religious image of the divine is set over against the philosophical notion of the divine and the two are taken up into a concrete concept that retains the meaning of the image and notion while eliminating the contradiction in form between an image and a notion. The concrete concept is a third, a synthesis, of the other two. In Tillich's understanding of the dialectic, by contrast, the driving impulse comes from the essentially self-negating character of religion as such rather than from an over-arching dialectical reason. It is not that religion is taken up into something else by the force of a dialectic to which it, like other things, is subject. Rather, it is that religion itself has a paradoxical essence—it is the essence of religion to deny itself. Religion posits itself in symbols that claim unconditional significance; but it posits itself as unconditional only in order to deny itself. For the symbol of the Kingdom of God, this means that the divine activity is posited as divine for the sake of denying itself (limiting itself); and this self-limitation is the sphere of the technological.

With this understanding of the relation between technique and the Kingdom of God, Tillich thought it possible to provide a theoretical basis for religious socialism; for the human activity of shaping the world could be understood in the light of the self-limiting of the religious symbol, and political and social activity could be understood as the self-denying activity of God's Kingdom. That is to say, the Kingdom of God does not come in the form of a second kind of reality alongside the worldly reality, but it comes as the dimension of depth which breaks into the human shaping of the world and is made known in the form of its self-limitation—the Kingdom comes in the midst of the technical shaping of the world.

II

At the basis of the eschatological symbol of the Kingdom of God, there is, then, an understanding of the dialectic between ontological form (that is, the self-world structure that is implicit in being anything at all) and religious depth-content (*Gehalt*) which determines the actual vitality of religion by reference to the self-negating essence of religion. Tillich explicated this theory in his essay of 1922 entitled "Overcoming the Concept of Religion in the Philosophy of Religion" (*Die Ueberwindung des Religionsbegriffs in der Religionsphilosophie*).[9] In this essay, a key notion is that religion essentially contains its own negation. As Tillich put it, religion does not intend itself, it intends God. It does not exist for its own sake but for the sake of the one to whom or to which it points. In its relative and conditional character, it intends something absolute and unconditional; and it expresses that intention by containing a relativization of its own absolute positing and a conditioning of its own unconditional claim. This is to say that the form of the religious act is paradoxical, "simultaneously the affirmation and the denial of the autonomous form.[10] A religious act, or a religious thought, has a structure which both employs autonomous forms of action or thinking and also breaks them while employing them.

But how is such a total affirmation and total denial possible simultaneously? How, in other words, is it possible for religion to *exist*—both to have and to have not a form of its own? To make clear how this is possible, one needs to call attention to two notions which are more implicit than explicit in Tillich's own writings but which indicate how this paradoxical existence is possible. First, that religion has a paradoxical form means that the negative aspect of human or earthly existence is *in itself* the positive aspect of the divine presence. It is not merely an empty spot, so to speak, which can be occupied by the divine when God is present; rather, it is itself the presence, or the being-around, of the divine. On this point, Tillich's doctrine of symbol differs from the Thomistic doctrine of analogy: the negation of the negative aspects of the human and earthly is not an indication of what the godly is *like* (as would be the case in a strict doctrine of analogy) but is, rather, itself the coming of the godly; the unconditional that religion intends is actual *as* the negation in that negativity. With regard to the eschatological symbol of the Kingdom of God, this would be to say that the untruth of the prophetic announcement of the Kingdom is itself the mode in which the truth of the Kingdom exists. Second, the "place" at which the dialectic of the divine and the human becomes actual is the kairos, the creative moment. The end of things, the Kingdom of God, comes not as a person or an idea nor as a practice or action but as a right time, a moment of creativity. The unconditional whose

name is God becomes concrete *when* the negativity of the negative is negated, which is to say, when religion, or any religious
symbol, comes into being by negating itself. Nothing is as such
the presence of the Kingdom; but anything can be that presence
positively in the right time.

This conception makes paradoxicality the form not only of
one's knowledge of the divine but also of the real existence of the
divine. That the grasp of the divine has the form of paradox (a
grasp that negates its own grasping) is not due to the finitude of the
human mind and is not of itself an indication of imperfect cognition. It is derivative, rather, from the nature of religion. It is
through a paradoxical form that the very vitality of religion is
grasped, and it is in a paradoxical form that religion actually lives.
The denial of religion is not imposed on religion from without; it is
a phase in the life of religion itself. "It is . . . the property of every
living religion to bear within itself a constant opposition toward
the religious in itself."[11] So, for example, the role played by the
doctrine of predestination, particularly in Calvin's theology, is that
of denying religious value to religion: "neither church nor religion
is a condition of election and of the Kingdom of God, both are at
most divinely ordained means."[12] The same is true of the role
played by religious mysticism and by prophetic criticism. Both the
absolute positing (what Tillich also called the "priestly" or "sacramental" aspect of religion) and the absolute protest (called the
"prophetic" or "Protestant" aspect) belong to the vitality of religion, and both are equally essential to religion as such. Every
living religion, therefore, bears within itself both a positing of
something as unconditional and a protest against the positing.
Religion posits itself in order to deny itself—that is its paradoxical
essence. (One might call this the *imitatio Dei* on the part
of religion.)

With regard to the eschatological symbols, those relations are
conceptually defined in Tillich's first complete systematics, *The
System of Sciences According to Objects and Methods* (1923). There
Tillich makes a distinction between "autonomous" and "theonomous" forms of the "transcendent symbols for the actualiza-
tion of the unconditional."[13] The autonomous forms include such
concepts as happiness, wisdom, vision of the ideas, humanity, and
the kingdom of reason; their theonomous counterparts include the
concepts of beatitude, the Kingdom of God, and the like. The
difference between the autonomous and the theonomous has to do

not with the intention of the concepts or symbols but with the extent to which they explicitly incorporate the self-negating aspect. Autonomous forms of the transcendent symbols run the risk of being taken only in their positive intention, without their self-negation (as, for example, in the case of the idea of a kingdom of reason, from which the nonrational has been excluded); but, even so, they can in their time be the concrete realization of what they mean. In both the autonomous and the theonomous symbols, the real dialectic, which corresponds to the dialectic of knowing what they mean, is that of the unconditional and the conditional; and the real paradox, corresponding to a knowledge of the essence of what they mean, is the paradox of something conditional that is unconditional in its self-denial. The opposition between the unconditional and conditional is, therefore, not a simple one—it is not as though the unconditional were the direct opposite of the conditional in the way that a negative is the direct opposite of a positive. Rather, the unconditional is the opposite of the *opposition* that itself makes up the sphere of the conditional. If, for example, the self as subject is conditional because it is the opposite of the world as object, then the unconditional is the opposite of that whole self-world structure of opposition. What the unconditional means is not just the negation of the self (since the world is already a negation of the self) but a negation of *that* negation, a negation of the negativity that is built into the self-world structure. That is also the case with the Hegelian notion of the infinite—which is not just the negation of the finite but the negation of the negation made by the finite of the finite. But, in Tillich's dialectic, the unconditional appears in a paradoxical form rather than in a dialectical synthesis; it appears when the positing of something as unconditional is accomplished by means of a negation of its unconditionality.

To be conditioned means to be what one is in such a way that one is a *something* (or someone) over against something (or someone) *else*; to be unconditioned means to be what one is not in that way but in such a way that one is both what one is and also what the other is—both what one is and also what one is not. In formal terms, that is the statement of what unconditional being amounts to; for by being what one is not one negates the negative in the relation between the self and the other (or, in terms of Tillich's ontological structure, between the self and the world). The form of the unconditional is the form of conditioning the conditional—conditioning the condition of the one by its other. What kind of thinking, or what kind of cognition, does this entail? How does one come to know the unconditional if the unconditional really has that paradoxical form? How can one tell the difference between the unconditional, so defined, and simply nothing at all? What is the difference between seeing this pattern merely as a formal dialectic (which can be entertaining or irritating, depending on one's mood) and seeing it as a form of knowing something that is really there? The name that Tillich applied to this kind of thinking and knowing was "the spirit of prophecy," or the awareness of the kairos. What makes the difference between an empty dialectic or paradox and a filled one is the ability to read the times—the prophet is one who is able to discern the creativity making itself known in the self-negation of the rational forms, and the prophet points to what is discerned by saying that the truth of the time is to be found in the untruth of the prophet's own announcements. The "spirit of prophecy" is a mentality that is conscious of its own untruth as the medium of the truth which it announces. Unconditional truth is, therefore, a revelation of the untruth of the prophetic word that announces it.

III

Tillich's theory of the paradoxical relation between the form and the depth-content in the recognition and in the reality of the Kingdom of God had a practical dimension in the outcome of religious socialism. In a retrospective essay from the year 1936 ("On the Boundary"), Tillich himself raised the question of whether the religious socialists were right in thinking there was a kairos in Europe after World War I. This question of the truth of the prophetic declaration came up almost as a matter of course, once it had become clear that religious socialism had not succeeded in its battle with national socialism. Did the failure mean that the prophets of religious socialism, including Tillich, were mistaken in their judgment of the times? If they were mistaken, was that very mistake the form in which the reality intended in the symbol of the Kingdom of God was indeed there? Tillich answered with a yes and a no—the prophetic voice was right in its basic criticisms, but it was wrong in its expectation of an immediate social and spiritual transformation.[14]

The reply maintained the view that in a certain period a decision for socialism (or some other political possibility) could indeed be a decision for the Kingdom of God even though a socialist society is, as such, as remote from the Kingdom of God as is any other society. This reasserts the paradoxical relation between the two: No actual reality is, as such, the eschatological, but any actual reality can at the right time coincide with the eschatological. In the kairos, a concrete decision is simultaneously a decision in regard to what is meant in such religious symbols as the Kingdom of God. Something is intended by the symbol and is symbolically presented—that is, presented not as an empirical reality but as an actual power. Normally, it is possible to understand a symbol and to be affected by its power even when it is not identifiable with a concrete reality; in that sense one can say that a symbol has the force of what it represents or "is" what it "means." But in a moment of kairos the power of the symbol is also bound with a concrete reality; then it has not only the force but also the appearance of a reality in the world. That is the case with all symbols. What is peculiar to the eschatological symbol of the Kingdom is that this symbol is *essentially* bound to a kairos. It cannot have actual power if it is not connected with a political and social reality. Even as a religious symbol, it intends something politically actual and not only transcendent; a purely transcendent Kingdom of God would not be the Kingdom of God at all. Hence, although it is true that no society or political realm is, as such, the Kingdom of God, it is also true that the Kingdom (the realm that is meant by the symbol) is really such only when identified with a social and political order, as the demand and expectation present in that order. The Kingdom of God is what it is *as* something that is not it; and the unity of the "is" and "is not" is descried in the prophetic sense of the *demand* to make the Kingdom come and of the *hope* that it will come which the social and political reality awakens. In this way, the Kingdom of God is real as something that is not the Kingdom of God—it is real as the demand and promise that a society bears. Even this form is paradoxical; for the knowledge that the social and political order itself can never be the Kingdom of God is combined with the knowledge that just this is the way in which the Kingdom of God comes—it comes as what is not the Kingdom. Hence, the expectation of the coming of the Kingdom is a refracted one—it understands that what is concretely expected is a refraction of what is really hoped for.

Because the symbol of the Kingdom is essentially tied with historical reality, however, a prophet who summons hearers to decide now for the Kingdom that is in the coming is exposed to the possibility of disappointment in a way that does not apply to other symbols. With other symbols, the depth-content that breaks in makes the other content of the symbol inessential: "The breaking of the form by the *Gehalt* is identical with the content's becoming inessential. The form loses its necessary reference to the content because the content disappears before the fullness of the depth-content breaking in."[15] One confirmation of that description is provided by the hermeneutical principle that no final interpretation can ever be given of a religious symbol; its depth-content, or its religious meaning, can always be formulated anew without ever being exhausted. With the symbol of the Kingdom of God, however, the political and social content is as important as the depth-content. In this case (and perhaps in this case alone) the depth-content makes the ordinary content essential, instead of inessential; the social and political order is essential to the power of the symbol. Tillich's interpretation of the failure of religious socialism is, therefore, of more than biographical interest; it reveals, rather, something of the dynamics of the eschatological symbol itself.

What it reveals I should like to propose in what is only a conjectural thesis—a thesis suggested, however, by Tillich's inability ever again to become so directly engaged in political activity (the one possible exception being his declaration of opposition to Goldwater during the presidential campaign of 1964)[16] as he had been in religious socialism. It is possible, of course, that the inability was due only or chiefly to the difference between politics in mid-century America and politics in the Germany of the teens and twenties. But it is also possible that it has to do with the nature of the "spirit of prophecy" which, in reading the signs of the times, both posits and negates the self of the prophet. In this case, Tillich's later theological period would indicate that recognizing a kairos is possible for anyone only once. By a certain "forgetting" of the unconditional as such, anyone *can* in a theologically responsible way discern a kairos, the coming of the Kingdom in a political and social order, and can accordingly summon others to decide for the Kingdom by deciding for political and social action of a certain kind. But not every time is a kairos, and not everyone is actually such a prophet; hence, no one *must* so discern a kairos. Moreover, no one can recognize more than one such kairos in a lifetime just because the disappointment that inevitably comes afterward, reminding one of having forgotten the unconditional as such, prevents one from ever doing so again. This would offer one explanation of why, despite his continual assertion of the chasm between the unconditional and everything conditional, Tillich could say that a decision for religious socialism was at the time a decision for the Kingdom of God. (As a caution, one needs to bear in mind, however, that Tillich said this of himself and religious socialism only retrospectively. So far as I know, there is no documentary evidence that he made such an assertion during the years of his own involvement with it.) It would also suggest that the impossibility of making such an identification a second time is rooted in the symbol itself and not only in human psychology. When it turns out that the expected did not take place, one can no longer forget the disappointment that accompanied it; that is the peculiarity of the symbol of the Kingdom of God in contrast to other religious symbols. The expectation and the disappointment together constitute the self-positing and self-criticizing of the prophetic act. From that time on, the "prophetic spirit" can understand that the Kingdom of God is always in the coming but is never present as such. But really to understand this, instead of only grasping it abstractly, might require that one does at least once, by a kind of forgetfulness of God's transcendence, actually believe in the identity between the Kingdom of God and a real political and social order; only such an actual belief can provide the concrete aspect of the knowledge of how the Kingdom of God is real even though it is never there as such.

However correct or incorrect this conjecture might be with reference to Tillich himself, it does indicate that the eschatological symbol of the Kingdom of God is distinctive in its dependence on an actual historical reference even for its transhistorical meaning. Furthermore, it indicates how the dialectic of the self as I and of the divine-human relation is fundamentally determined not by a continuing movement of synthesis but by a kairic breakthrough.

Notes

1   Paul Tillich, *Systematic Theology*, 3 vols. (Chicago: University of

Chicago Press, 1951–1963), 3:440. Tillich contrasts this diagram with the Pythagorean circle and the Augustinian straight line.

2   For Tillich and religious socialism, see John R. Stumme, *Socialism in Theological Perspective: A Study of Paul Tillich 1918–1922* ([Chico, Calif.]: Scholars Press, 1978); also his Introduction (pp. ix–xxvi) to Paul Tillich, *The Socialist Decision,* trans. Franklin Sherman (New York: Harper & Row, 1977); and Wilhelm and Marion Pauck, *Paul Tillich: His Life and Thought* (New York: Harper & Row, 1976), 67–74.

3   *Systematic Theology* 3:361.

4   *The System of the Sciences According to Objects and Methods,* trans. Paul Wiebe (Lewisburg, Penn.: Bucknell University Press, 1981).

5   Eng. trans. by James Luther Adams, Konrad Raiser, and Charles W. Fox, in *What Is Religion?,* ed. James Luther Adams (New York: Harper & Row, 1969), 27–121.

6   In *Gesammelte Werke,* ed. Renate Albrecht, (Stuttgart: Evangelisches Verlagswerk, 1962) 2:21–28.

7   Ibid. 2:26.

8   Ibid.

9   In *Gesammelte Werke* (1959), 1:367–88; "The Conquest of the Concept of Religion in the Philosophy of Religion," trans. Kenneth Schedler and Charles W. Fox, in *What Is Religion?,* 122–54.

10   Ibid. 1:381; Eng. trans., 144.

11   Ibid. 1:383; Eng. trans., 146.

12   Ibid.

13   Ibid. 1:270; Eng. trans., 202.

14   *On the Boundary* (1936; reprint, New York: Scribner's, 1966), 79: "The Kingdom of God will always remain transcendent, but it appears as a judgment on a given form of society and as a norm for a coming one. Thus, the decision to be a religious socialist may be a decision for the Kingdom of God even though the socialist society is infinitely distant from the Kingdom of God." "Reply to Interpretation and Criticism," *The Theology of Paul Tillich,* ed. Charles W. Kegley (New York: Pilgrim Press, 1982), 390: "Like those who interpret 'the signs of the time,' we always were both confirmed and refuted. We were refuted with respect to the immediate actuality of the social and spiritual transformation we envisaged, we were confirmed with respect to the basic criticisms of the old and the basic demands for the new period."

15   "On the Idea of a Theology of Culture," trans. William Baillie Greene, in *What Is Religion?,* 155–81, 39.

16   Ronald H. Stone, *Paul Tillich's Radical Social Thought* (Atlanta: John Knox Press, 1980), 128.

5 | Immortality is Too Much and Too Little
KRISTER STENDAHL

Immortality and the concern for immortality appear much too little, too selfish. . . . And immortality is too much since it has a tendency to claim to know more than may be good for us.

Religious man in his faith, in his speaking and singing about God, is actually seeking—and seeking to express—his place in the total universe. He is trying to cope with reality. And religious men and women through the ages have done that within the knowledge of their time, within the science of their time, as well as within other insights and wisdom. The conflict between science and religion has, if I understand it correctly, never been a conflict between science and religion. It has been an unfortunate mistiming or comparing not equal to equal: when religious sanction was given to scientific insights of an earlier time, it often clashed with newer insights in the sciences. Thus the famous clashes between religion and science—theology and science—have usually been clashes between *sciences*. And yet the church has lived through many serious transitions as to world views and scientific insights, and

Editor's note and acknowledgement:

This paper, alone among contributions to the present symposium, has been already published. Permission to reprint it here has been graciously given by Bishop Stendahl and by Gustavus Adolphus College in St. Peter, Minnesota, holders of the copyright. It was first delivered in 1972 at an annual Nobel Conference sponsored since 1965 at that institution, with participation from recent Nobel Laureates, and it was first published in John D. Roslansky (ed.), *The End of Life: Discussion at the Sixth Nobel Conference organized by Gustavus Adolphus College, St. Peter, Minnesota* (Amsterdam and London: North Holland Publishing Company, 1973), 71–83, and then included in Dr. Stendahl's *Meanings: The Bible as Document and Guide* (Philadelphia: Fortress Press, 1984), 193–202.

so have other religious communities. There was one such transition in the time of the early church fathers: the change from the three-story universe to the Ptolemaic view of the world. And then there was the Copernican one. And there is a saying in my homeland that in the first generation the church fights new scientific insights; in the second generation we say that those scientific views are adiaphora, that is, they do not really make a difference to the essence of the faith; and in the third generation we write hymns on the basis of the new scientific insight. You all know that nineteenth-century evening hymn which begins "The day thou gavest, Lord, is ended . . ."In it we sing: "The sun that bids us rest is waking/Our brethren neath the western sky,/And hour by hour fresh lips are making/Thy wondrous doings heard on high." It is a beautiful Copernican hymn.

Now, there has always been, as that dialogue has gone on, a certain tendency of plucking the flowers from the latest scientific insights, and we had a wonderful flower blooming before us here in George Wald's presentation. In this Wald said that actually the entrance of death into this long chain of development coincided with the sexual mode of procreation, which is exactly what it says in Genesis 3, where the awareness of sexuality is combined with the entrance of death into the earlier paradise. But that is exactly the kind of example that preachers should not use glibly for it really is two different modes of speaking. A facile mixing of the language of science and the language of the Bible easily gives the believer the feeling that "science proves the Bible," as if the Bible could not speak for itself in its own language.

I happen to believe that the whole long and glorious Christian tradition of speaking about the immortality of the soul is only a period of the Judeo-Christian tradition, and that period may now be coming to an end. I say this with some trepidation, and my trepidation is not for any other reason than that it is always painful to tear into what is very dear to many. And yet there are times in the history of theology and of the Christian community and the church in which such changes take place. I have always loved the example of the apostle Paul who understood what theologians have great difficulties in understanding: that sometimes there are new problems and new data. It is very hard for a theologian really to have respect for "new data." Partly he is in tune with the historians who always play tricks on us by showing that new data are really just new little twists of the old data. Having as many old data as the historian has: (a) it's easy for him, and (b) he should have some reward for knowing so many data. So he has a tendency always to minimize the new. But tradition, unless it is just museum tradition, living tradition is just as much a way of change as it is a means of continuity. You remember when Paul discusses matters of divorce and things like that in 1 Corinthians 7. Paul says that there are now certain cases of divorce, and Jesus said that there should not be any. Then Paul quotes a word from the Lord, but then he says, "Now how is it then in special cases?" and mentions certain special cases. Finally, Paul says, "On this one I have no word from the Lord." And I think he was the last preacher in Christendom who had the guts to admit that. But what is really involved in that is a respect for the new. He could just as well—could he not?—have done what we all do: "Now, of course, we don't have exactly a word for that but it follows from what we have—etc. . . ." That way one will always smother the newness.

The new insight, the new experience, is something to be taken seriously, and I happen to believe that this should be our first observation when we think about immortality and the end of life in the perspective of the Christian tradition. Now, to outsiders this kind of speaking about new interpretations does not go over very well, because it always sounds as if: "Oh, those tricky theologians. Of course, they really have lost their faith but they have to somehow make something of it. So they are clever manipulators. Of course, they do not believe but after all they earn their living on belief so they have to do something."

There is an attitude which I always have called "the funda-mentalism of the nonbeliever," and that is the worst kind because it is one that takes for granted that "the Christian faith," or "the meaning of the Bible," is always the most sterile, unchangeable orthodoxy that could ever be imagined. That is at least honest, as they say. But as the rabbis already knew, there comes a moment, as they said, when there is time to do something for the Lord, and by that they meant a time for a new interpretation. Now, that is a little arrogant but it points in the right direction.

The question about immortality of the soul is interesting for someone who is primarily a biblical scholar because he specializes in sixty-six so-called books that do not know of immortality of the soul. The word occurs in two places in the NT: once about God "who alone has immortality" (1 Tim. 6:16), and once in a very special setting, where it is perhaps borrowed from other people whom Paul quotes when he speaks of how the mortal nature must put on immortality (1 Cor. 15:53ff.). But perhaps the almost complete absence of the word "immortality" is not really the point. The point is that the whole world that comes to us through the Bible, OT and NT, is not interested in the immortality of the soul. And if you think it is, it is because you have read this into the material. In terms of the OT it is very clear that Abraham, Isaac, and Jacob, and George Wald are one in believing that the only immortality that there is, is in the germ plasm, or as they called it "the loins" (e.g., Gen. 35:11). The only immortality that the earlier strata of the OT knows about is perpetuation through offspring. The OT view is a view of man created of dust who is made a human being by God's energizing power, the "spirit," being blown into the dust. That is also what Ecclesiastes speaks about in that beautiful description of aging (which outdoes T. S. Eliot because that is what he tried to copy) that ends on the note, as you know, "the dust returns to earth, whence it came, and the spirit returns to God who gave it" (12:7). Here the spirit is not the individual's little identity spirit, but the life-giving power of God, the *ruach,* the wind which is withdrawn causing man to disintegrate into dust. Dust to dust, ashes to ashes.

Immortality of the soul is not emphasized. The NT in a very interesting way speaks constantly about resurrection as against immortality. The interesting thing with this is not the discussion that has gone through the whole history of the Christian tradition concerning how resurrection relates to immortality and whether immortality is for the soul and resurrection is the way in which the body is added to that soul, or whatever the relations between them are. That is a later question of theological speculation once the Christian message about the resurrection came up against the Hellenistic and secular preoccupation with immortality. We should rather ask why and for what purpose the NT speaks about resurrection—why that is its proper way of speaking.

Learned scholars have found out—and that is not so hard to do—that the origins of this strange language of the resurrection are to be found in thoughts about martyrdom and that the question to which resurrection is the answer is not the question about what is going to happen to man when he dies. The question is not: What is going to happen to little me? Am I to survive with my identity or not? The question is rather whether God's justice will win out. The martyrs and the righteous are suppressed by the establishment—their own or foreign—the rich are fat-eyed and happy and seem to carry the day while the righteous go down the drain. Resurrection answers the question of theodicy, that is, the question of how God can win, the question of a moral universe. Does crime pay? Will evil win? Where is God's promise and power? Will God ultimately come through? Will the kingdom come somehow so that righteousness flows forth and justice is in the midst of us all? That is the matrix, that is the womb out of which the dream and thought and hope and prayer for the resurrection emerged out of the Jewish community in times of martyrdom and suppression. They spoke about vindication of the righteous and the martyrs. They did not affirm so much the fate of such individuals. They were interested in whether God and justice would have the last word.

You can see this in a strange way, if you are a careful Bible reader. There is a passage in Matthew (27:51–53), where on Good Friday itself, when Jesus dies and there is the earthquake (i.e., the cosmic forces join in the drama), the situation is so jittery, so to speak, so that some of the righteous who had already been suppressed come out of their graves, and the general resurrection that one looked forward to, the ultimate establishment of justice in the world, started to happen.

I am just lecturing you on plain, descriptive biblical studies. It is a simple fact that when Peter said to his friends up in Galilee, "You know, this Jesus whom they crucified and whom we loved so much is risen," the thoughts that went through these people's minds were not, "Oh, that means that there is eternal life for little me." That would be a rather odd way of making such a point. No, to them it meant that there was reason to believe that God's ultimate power of justice, vindicating the oppressed, the suppressed, and the martyred, had manifested itself. Compare Acts 2:22–24, and the way in which Jesus had left his case in the hands of God the just vindicator (1 Pet. 2:23). The kingdom had taken a big step forward as one had been praying, hoping, and dreaming for its coming. So that the issue of the most original Christian way of speaking about the end of life in the sign of the resurrection of Jesus was an issue that did not speak to the question of what is going to happen to my identity, but what is happening in and to the world. Is there reason to believe that justice will win out? It is a concern for where the world is going, not a concern for oneself.

I think about Easter sermons. There is, of course, the type of Easter sermon that capitalizes on the fact that it is spring and nature is coming back to life. It is beautiful, but I guess such preachers should be sent by their mission boards to the Southern Hemisphere for a couple of years. Or perhaps one should be more serious about it and say: no, if Easter means anything in the Christian tradition it means the breaking of the chains of nature, in a certain sense, rather than the affirmation of the cycle of nature. And then, of course, there are those for whom the meaning of Easter is primarily the assurance as to eternal life and the immortality of the soul: the assurance as to the afterlife. I do not know how it is with you or with people you know when the role play between congregations and pastors is broken through, and people say what they really think and are concerned about; but I think it is true to say that an increasing number of men and women are less and less concerned about the immortality of the soul, especially their own. That somehow it is not that obviously attractive and commanding; the glow of the immortality-language has worn off. And why has it, if this is true? It has because that whole way of thinking and speaking, which we, as I said, do not even have in the Bible, is really part and parcel of a whole world view that is basically built on a Platonic view, a Platonic philosophy, and a Platonic understanding of reality—polarity between soul and body. And for centuries and centuries such a Platonic model was not only maintained by the church—and the church never invented it—but it was the lingua franca, the common way of thinking about man and the world. It seemed obvious and self-evident. But now on Easter day the church in many cases has a double duty. On the one hand, it has to convince man that he has that soul so that the message fits because there can be no joy unless he first has the need that the joy is supposed to satisfy. I happen to believe that that whole way of thinking, feeling, and ultimately experiencing oneself in the world is on the way out.

On the other hand, this is not a sign of less human, existential, and ethical seriousness or religious seriousness on the side and part of modern man. What he is concerned about is not so much what is going to happen to him but what is going to happen to this poor world. He is just as concerned with the future of God's plan and creation, the future of justice: Is the kingdom a dream or is it a dream worth believing in, a dream affirmed by God in Christ? That is what the problem is now to many, and as a biblical scholar I must note how that concern is in many ways similar to the concerns of the first Christians as they prayed for the coming of God's kingdom rather than for their own immortality.

In that setting immortality and the concern for immortality appear much *too little,* too selfish, too preoccupied with self or even family, race, and species. The question of prolonged identity somehow does not fit to what is really bothering us as we ask the questions of meaning and we week the rays of hope. And immortality is *too much* since it has a tendency to claim to know more than may be good for us. It is too much because it is too specific, too tied up with a peculiar way of thinking about man, God, and the world. It is too much because it does not ring quite true to many a man's religious experience. Now, it is a funny thing that whenever something suggests itself to a person, even to a theologian, even to a preacher, and it is not quite as it has always been, then he is always accused of being secular or something, of being influenced from somewhere else. But it is in his religious experience and understanding that he finds that somehow this kind of language does not ring true. Against those who know too much, 1 John 3:2 says:

Beloved, we are God's children now; it does not yet appear what we shall be, but we know that when he appears we shall be like him for we shall see him as he is.

The end of life is thus in the mystery of the will of God and in the coming of the kingdom. The issue is not what happens to me but what happens to God's fight for his creation. What it is about is what we pray about in the Lord's Prayer which does not have a single word about little me. That is why it is such a great prayer, and that is why it might even have come straight from Jesus. Have you ever thought about that? When you pray that prayer you really do not pray about yourself, but you just shout: thy kingdom come, thy will be done, and you are just sort of swallowed up in the concern for the victory and coming of the kingdom. And that blows our minds out of preoccupation with ourselves. And it should. It opens up in our time a feeling for the fascination with the billions of years and the galaxies and the possibility of life on other planets. (I have always hoped that there is something like it because it would put us in place, not to be so terribly preoccupied with our own importance.)

The end of life is not in the question of, or the concern for, "my identity." And when I speak about the kingdom and the victory of God and about Jesus then I say to myself: a life like his was a kind of spearheading of the kingdom coming into this world; a life like his was vindicated by God, was resurrected; a life in its weakness, in its death, with a power of weakness, the turning of the other cheek, all these strange things which I like to call the "operation headstart" for the kingdom. I know, the world is just not ready yet for that life style; and we live in a nation that has no respect whatsoever for the power of weakness, or for that whole phenomenon of the coming of the kingdom, of the Christians as the guinea pigs for the kingdom, with what I term the eschatological "itch." You know, it is a very interesting thing that one has always thought about Jesus as teaching people patience and that is partly because of our way of speaking about and thinking about eternal life instead of thinking about the kingdom. Religion has had a tendency of becoming, as Marx rightly said, an opiate for the people, handed out by those in the leading positions: of course, you cannot have it all now, but if you behave you will get it in the yonder somehow. It has given us an image of religion as serving toward patience. But when I read about my Jesus I know nothing less patient—less patient with evil, less patient with sickness, even less patient with death. He went to the attack, he pushed the coming of the kingdom.

Now, what I suggest to you is that the proper image in the center of the Christian life as we look to the end of life is a new one, or rather an older one, one that should come back and engender new theology, new prayer, new faith, new bread and life—the image is the kingdom, the coming of the kingdom. That is what it is about. And that is why the whole concern for individual identity, which is the technical meaning of immortality of the soul, is not to be found in the Good Book because its concern and its focus is elsewhere.

Let me then just observe that in so doing, and especially in using and being inspired by the image of tenderness, love, and weakness in him who came, comes, and will come with the kingdom, we should perhaps also note that one of our problems at this time is not so much our powerlessness, but that we have in a way too much power. We can split the atom, we can manipulate the gene bank, we can make Einsteins galore, we can, we can, we can . . . And we can certainly upset the balance of nature. George Wald has spoken already about the serious ways in which we must be prophets of doom, and I guess both George Wald and I know that a true prophet is one who prays and hopes that he will be proven wrong. I think in a way that applies to Jesus. Jesus expected the end of the world in forty years and the Bible-reading Christians ask, Could Jesus be wrong? But Jesus was a true prophet; he was one of those who prophesied as the Lord had told him and as he saw it but since he was a true prophet, his hottest dream was that his prophecy would not come true. And it did not— but it looks pretty bad now.

Our problem is one of overpower and that is perhaps why we as human beings should take a lower posture. The fighting arrogance of man, even heightened into his projecting his importance into immortality, should perhaps be checked. We have overstepped, and perhaps we should seek to be closer to nature because the kingdom that Jesus speaks about is a funny kingdom. Its prototypes are the children, the lilies, and the birds. And one of the things that is going on right now as you meditate on the kingdom and on Jesus is that we start to understand the importance of seeking ourselves closer to the vibrations of nature. I do not know if you have noticed one of the signs of the generation gap, or whatever you want to call it, but one of them is actually that when my generation spoke about "civilized" the kids speak about "humanized"; and those are two very different things. The kingdom where the child is the ideal is closer to the "humanized" than to the "civilized."

I think that is one of the reasons there is such an attraction, and a sound attraction, toward Eastern religions which have not glorified man by immortality, but rather have seen man finding himself by taking a lower and a lower posture even all the way toward Nirvana. And this had made Eastern religious man sensitive and given him, strangely enough, the tremendous respect for life, for other men's lives, because he did not "up" his own life with a kind of ferocious and arrogant intensity which we might have done. In times of demonic overpower and superpowers and overkill, there is wisdom in the low posture of the East.

So, sisters and brothers, we are very small but we are small in the hands of God. Hence we do not need to increase our importance. George Wald pointed out with striking clarity that man has his immortality in the germ plasm, but man has always liked to have it in his body. And I would add: for a long period of the Christian tradition, he liked to have it in the soul. But perhaps this whole search for identity perpetuation, or immortality, as assurance should be lifted out of the ego and be placed in God. To me it seems that if God is God, I neither care for nor worry about the hereafter; I celebrate the coming of the kingdom by singing hymns and by caressing with words the heaven with angels and saints and the messianic banquet with light and joy and glory. And I know that I paint, but I like to paint and I paint out of love and hope and faith. But when all is said and done I pray that the evil I have put into the world will not cause others to suffer too much, and that my little life will fit somehow into God's plan for the kingdom. The rest I leave. May his kingdom come.

Contributors

1 THOMAS AZAR is a D. Min. Candidate at Emory University. He is a Baptist minister.

2 SYLVIA CRANSTON is the co-author (with Carey Williams) of *Reincarnation: A New Horizon in Science, Religion and Society,* 1984. She has lectured extensively in America and England, including Columbia and Harvard.

3 JAMES R. FLEMING is a Ph.D. Candidate in the History of Science at Princeton University.

4 NICHOLAS F. GIER, Ph.D. (Claremont), is Professor of Philosophy and Coordinator of Religious Studies at the University of Idaho. He is the author of *Wittgenstein and Phenomenology: A Comparative Study of the Later Wittgenstein, Husserl, Heidegger, and Merleau-Ponty,* 1981.

5 ROBERT C. GORDON-McCUTCHAN, Ph.D. (Princeton), is a post-doctoral researcher in Religious Studies at the University of California at Santa Barbara, and Director of Research and Libraries, The Rowny Foundation.

6 LOYDE H. HARTLEY, Ph.D. (Emory), is Professor of Religion and Society at Lancaster Theological Seminary.

7 GERALD E. JONES, Ph.D. (Brigham Young), is Director of the Berkeley Institute of Religion of the Church of Jesus Christ of the Latter-day Saints.

8 MANFRED KERKHOFF, Ph.D. (Munich), has taught since 1964 at the University of Puerto Rico, where he is Professor of Philosophy and currently Chairman of the department. He is the author of many articles and reviews in scholarly journals.

9 **WESLEY A. KORT,** Ph.D. (Chicago), is Professor of Religion at Duke University. He is the author of *Moral Fiber: Character and Belief in Recent American Fiction,* 1982.

10 **GEDDES MacGREGOR,** D.D. (Oxford), D. ès L. (Sorbonne), is Emeritus Distinguished Professor of Philosophy and former Dean of the Graduate School of Religion at the University of Southern California. He is the author of *Reincarnation in Christianity,* 1978, and numerous books, articles, and reviews.

11 **MARY JO MEADOW,** Ph.D. (Minnesota), is Professor of Psychology and Religious Studies at the University of Mankato in Minnesota.

12 **GILBERT E. M. OGUTU,** Ph.D. (Nairobi), is Lecturer in Religious Studies at the University of Nairobi, Kenya.

13 **JOHN C. POLKINGHORNE,** Sc.D. (Cambridge), was Professor of Mathematical Physics at the University of Cambridge from 1968–79, and is now an Anglican priest serving a parish in Blean, Canterbury, England. He is a Fellow of the Royal Society and a Fellow of Trinity College, Cambridge. His works include *Models of High Energy Processes,* 1980, and many articles on elementary particle physics in scientific journals.

14 **DAVID H. C. READ,** D.D.*h.c.* (Edinburgh and Yale), was Chaplain to the University of Edinburgh from 1939–55, and was Chaplain to H. M. the Queen in Scotland from 1952–55. In 1956 he was called to his present pulpit as Minister of Madison Avenue Presbyterian Church, New York City. Famed for his scholarly preaching, he has given missions and broadcasts in several countries and is the author of many books.

15 **ROBERT P. SCHARLEMANN,** Dr. Theol. (Heidelberg), is Commonwealth Professor of Religious Studies at the University of Virginia. He was for some years editor of the *Journal of the American Academy of Religion.* He is the author of *The Being of God,* 1981, and other books.

6 KRISTER STENDAHL, Teol. Dr., Litt. Dr. *h.c.* (Uppsala), Bishop of Stockholm, was for many years Professor and Dean of the Divinity School, Harvard University. He is the author of *Paul Among Jews and Gentiles,* 1976.

7 ANDREW WILSON, Ph.D. (Harvard), is Adjunct Assistant Professor of Biblical Studies at the Unification Theological Seminary.

Index

The numbers in parenthesis refer to notes or footnotes: i.e., 80 (13) refers to note 13 on page 80.